SUPREME COURT

This interdisciplinary review series brings together the perspectives of legal scholars and economists on the work of the United States Supreme Court. Many contributions to the ***SCER*** provide an economic analysis of the situations and events that generate a case or group of cases. Articles often consider the implicit or explicit economic reasoning employed by the Court to reach its decisions, and the economic consequences of the Court's decisions. The ***SCER*** also publishes analyses dealing with the functioning of the Court as an organization.

For its fourth volume, the ***SCER*** has attracted articles from today's most distinguished and respected legal scholars. Past contributors include Armen Alchian, Benjamin Klein, Richard Posner, George L. Priest, Glen O. Robinson, and W. Kip Viscusi. The ***SCER*** is a faculty-edited and peer-reviewed journal.

Volumes 1-3 also available, please see reply card.

Attention Librarians: ***Supreme Court Economic Review*** is edited by Harold Demsetz, Ernest Gellhorn, and Nelson Lund. ***SCER*** is a peer-reviewed annual published by The University of Chicago Press, Journals Division, P.O. Box 37005, Chicago, IL 60637. Volume 4 is priced at $45.00. Standing orders available at a 20% discount. Volumes 1-3 available from the publisher. Please see order form for details. ***Supreme Court Economic Review*** is printed on pH-neutral stock.

CONOMIC REVIEW

Volume 4

Contents include

Daubert's Debut: The Supreme Court and the Economics of Scientific Evidence
Jeffrey S. Parker

The Supreme Court's Predation Odyssey: From Fruit Pies to Cigarettes
Donald J. Boudreaux, Kenneth G. Elzinga, and David E. Mills

The Constitutional Conception of the Corporation
Larry E. Ribstein

Interpreting Health Care Cost Containment Legislation: *Good Samaritan Hospital v. Shalala* and Relative Institutional Competence
Simonetti Samuels

O'Melveny & Meyers v. FDIC: Imputation of Fraud and Optimal Monitoring
A. V. Pritchard

ISBN 0-226-28685-1 216 pages $45.00 Cloth October 1995

Supreme Court Economic Review

PUBLISHER
The University of Chicago Press

SPONSOR
Law & Economics Center of the George Mason University School of Law

Supreme Court Economic Review

VOLUME 4

Supreme Cour

THE UNIVERSITY OF CHICAGO PRESS
Chicago and London

Economic Review

EDITORS

Harold Demsetz, Ernest Gellhorn, and Nelson Lund

Sponsored by the Law and Economic Center at the George Mason University School of Law

INTERNATIONAL STANDARD BOOK NUMBER: 0-226-28685-1
The University of Chicago Press, Chicago 60637
The University of Chicago Press, Ltd., London

Printed in the United States of America

The paper used in this publication meets the minimum requirements of American National Standard for Information Sciences—Permanence of Paper for Printed Library Materials, ANSI Z39.48-1984.

Supreme Court Economic Review

The *Supreme Court Economic Review* is an interdisciplinary journal that seeks to focus scholarship in law and economics, broadly conceived, on the work of the United States Supreme Court. Contributions to the *Review* will typically provide an economic analysis of the situations and events that generated a case or group of cases. They may explore the explicit or implicit economic reasoning underlying the outcome, or the economic consequences of the Court's decisions. Articles and commentaries dealing with the Supreme Court as an organization or with other issues not directly tied to particular judicial decisions are also quite welcome.

Peer review is an important feature of this publication. Accordingly, manuscripts should be accompanied by a cover letter indicating that the submission is being made on an exclusive basis. Inquiries and submissions should be sent to:

Supreme Court Economic Review
George Mason University School of Law
3401 North Fairfax Drive
Arlington, Virginia 22201-4498

Supreme Court Economic Review

Table of Contents

Daubert's Debut: The Supreme Court, the Economics of Scientific Evidence, and the Adversarial System
Jeffrey S. Parker **1**

The Supreme Court's Predation Odyssey: From Fruit Pies to Cigarettes
Donald J. Boudreaux, Kenneth G. Elzinga, and David E. Mills **57**

The Constitutional Conception of the Corporation
Larry E. Ribstein **95**

Interpreting Health Care Cost Containment Legislation: Good Samaritan Hospital v Shalala and Relative Institutional Competence
Simonetti Samuels **141**

O'Melveny & Meyers v. FDIC: Imputation of Fraud and Optimal Monitoring
A. V. Pritchard **179**

Daubert's Debut: The Supreme Court, the Economics of Scientific Evidence, and the Adversarial System

Jeffrey S. Parker[†]

In Daubert v Merrell Dow Pharmaceuticals, Inc., *the Supreme Court replaced the prevailing rule of evidentiary admissibility for scientific testimony with a new standard. Under the older* Frye *rule, admissibility was determined by whether the expert's views enjoyed "general acceptance." Under* Daubert, *the trial judge will simply determine whether the expert's testimony is sufficiently "scientific" to be admitted. This article argues that the* Daubert *approach is economically superior because it reduces the incentives for external interest groups to influence the content of admitted testimony. The article also considers more general proposals to displace adversary party control of evidentiary presentation with more active judicial supervision or with other external constraints. The article concludes that such external constraints are unnecessary and would probably be socially undesirable.*

I. INTRODUCTION

In *Daubert v Merrell Dow Pharmaceuticals, Inc.*,[1] the Supreme Court resolved some two decades of debate over the standard for the admissibility of scientific evidence in federal trials under the 1975 Federal Rules of Evidence.[2] Rejecting the pre-existing

[†] Professor of Law and Associate Dean for Academic Affairs, George Mason University School of Law. Research assistance was provided by William J. Blanton and Barb L. Bettenhausen, and helpful comments were provided by David A. Schum, Nelson Lund, and two anonymous referees.

[1] 113 S Ct 2786 (1993).

[2] As enacted by Pub L No 93-595, 88 Stat 1926 (1975). Although various rules have been added or amended over the years, the expert testimony standards of Rules

 0-226-28685-1/95/0004-0001$02.00

Frye standard of "general acceptance" in the scientific community,[3] the Court established a new standard of admissibility that places less emphasis on acceptance of the testifying scientist's views outside the courtroom. The *Daubert* rule simply requires that proposed scientific expert testimony be "scientific."[4] It remains to be seen whether *Daubert* will still the larger debate over the use of scientific evidence in American trials, a debate that has taken its popular form as a controversy over "junk science" in the courtroom.[5] Even if it does not settle that debate, however, *Daubert* may help turn the discussion in a useful direction.

This article argues that *Daubert* should recast the "junk science" debate by shifting the discussion away from a misguided critique of the law of evidence. Rules of evidentiary admissibility cannot realistically be expected to address all possible misuses of scientific evidence, which stem from more profound causes.[6] *Daubert* sensibly recognizes that fact, and takes a more modest approach to the role of admissibility standards. For that reason, *Daubert* may be as good a decision as we can expect, and it certainly is better than either *Frye* or the other alternatives that have been suggested, such as the creation of a "science court," or the use of court-appointed experts or official expert panels.[7] My thesis is that the Supreme Court got one right in *Daubert,* or as nearly "right" as the decisions of law courts can be in the very messy world of real litigation.

I develop this thesis by applying both transaction-cost and public-choice economics. Transaction-cost economics shows that efficiency is unlikely to be enhanced by legal rules that create diffuse

702 and 703, at issue in *Daubert,* have not been substantively amended since their original enactment.

[3] So named after *Frye v United States,* 293 F 1013 (DC Cir 1923), which ruled that results of a systolic blood pressure test (a precursor to the polygraph test) were inadmissible, on the ground that, in order for "deductions" embodied in expert testimony to be admissible, "the thing from which the deduction is made must be sufficiently established to have gained general acceptance in the particular field in which it belongs." Id at 1014. *Daubert* held that "*Frye* has been superseded" by the Federal Rules of Evidence, and therefore "should not be applied in federal trials." *Daubert,* 113 S Ct at 2794 & n 6.

[4] See id at 2794-98. The new standard, drawn directly from the text of Federal Evidence Rule 702, is "whether the expert is proposing to testify to (1) scientific knowledge that (2) will assist the trier of fact." Id at 2796. Whether *Daubert*'s new standard provides a less or more demanding threshold to admissibility is already a matter of vigorous debate among courts and commentators. See Part V below.

[5] See, for example, Peter W. Huber, *Galileo's Revenge: Junk Science in the Courtroom* (Basic Books, 1991) ("Huber, *Galileo's Revenge*").

[6] See Part IV.D below.

[7] See Part IV.A below.

external effects. Public-choice analysis indicates that granting outsiders a stake in the outcome of a governmental decision will induce them to influence that decision in their own private self-interest, and not in the public interest. Both of these effects were produced by the *Frye* rule. Outside parties—specifically interest groups of expert witnesses—were given a stake in the outcome of private litigation decisions through the "general acceptance" standard. The outsiders' interests, which lay primarily in maximizing their income across a series of cases presenting scientific issues, were unlikely to coincide either with the immediate litigants' interests or with society's interest in resolving the litigants' factual disputes in a neutral fashion. In particular, the outsiders' interests—and especially the need under the *Frye* rule for outsiders to organize themselves into "general acceptance" groups in order to earn income as testifying expert witnesses—likely had a biasing effect on the content of scientific evidence supplied to litigation.

The error of the *Frye* rule was in ignoring its own effect on the supply of scientific information to litigation. I characterize this error as a "free lunch" fallacy because it embodies the assumption that the supply of scientific information to litigation is "free" in the sense that its supply (and its content) are entirely independent of the demand created by litigation and the methods used to determine its admissibility, which in effect set its "price" to the litigants.[8] The assumption of a "free lunch" is unlikely to be valid because the supply of scientific evidence to litigation, like the supply of all other commodities, is likely to be responsive to the opportunity cost of its production and to the nature of the demand for the commodity. If scientific evidence is not "free" in this sense, then *Frye* produced both a suppression of some supply (of "unaccepted" opinions) and a bias in supplied opinions toward what is "accepted."

Unless there is some reason to believe in a high correlation between "general acceptance" and some objectively verifiable standard of accuracy or "truth," then the *Frye* rule did not promote the efficiency or neutrality of fact-finding in litigation. The correlation must be high, not just positive, because admissibility determinations under *Frye* influenced future cases as well as the cases in

[8] According to Robert Hessen's article in *The New Palgrave*, variants of the "free lunch" expression date back to the nineteenth century, but "[a]ll efforts to identify the true originator proved unavailing." Robert Hessen, "Free Lunch," in John Eatwell, Murray Milgate, and Peter Newman, eds, 2 *The New Palgrave: A Dictionary of Economics* 420 (Macmillan, 1987) ("Eatwell, Milgate & Newman, *The New Palgrave*"). As used here, the expression is intended to draw attention to the fact that scientific information, like all other products of human action, is costly. See Part IV below.

which they were made. The correlation between "general acceptance" and "truth," however, does not appear to be very close. In addition, the incentives that *Frye* created for the production of "general acceptance" also appear to be unrelated to "truth" or even to neutrality. Instead, those incentives encouraged adherence to a consistent opinion within relatively small "general acceptance" interest groups of testifying experts, whose income from testifying would have increased if they followed such a strategy.

Seen in this light, *Daubert* is a good decision because it at least partially recognizes that general acceptance cannot provide a "free lunch." Rather than allowing relatively small "general acceptance" groups to dictate admissibility, *Daubert* requires only that proffered expert testimony be "science" in some generic and vaguely defined sense. This is an improvement over *Frye* in two ways.[9] First, if "truth" in fact is more positively correlated with diversity than with commonality of opinion, then *Daubert* may improve results simply by expanding the range of potentially admissible opinion (whether it raises or lowers the average cost of adducing expert opinion). Second, to the extent that *Daubert* dilutes the effect of "general acceptance" on admissibility, it also reduces the incentives for rent-seeking behavior by external interest groups, and thereby reduces the amount of systematic bias on production incentives that is introduced by the evidentiary rules themselves.[10]

With the more internalized threshold standard of admissibility supplied by *Daubert,* incentives to invest in scientific evidence are more closely aligned with the stakes that the parties to litigation have in the particular lawsuit at issue. These stakes, in turn, are driven primarily by the rules of substantive law or, if by the procedural system, by features other than the law of evidence. One might still decry the use of "junk science" in litigation. But that is not a problem that rules of evidentiary admissibility are likely to address effectively.

[9] Arguably, however, *Daubert* does not go far enough because it still adheres to an external standard of "scientific method," and for this reason may be assuming a "free snack."

[10] Part of the analysis here is similar to, and draws upon, recent work by Bruce Kobayashi and Luke Froeb. See Luke M. Froeb and Bruce H. Kobayashi, *Competition in the Production of Costly Information: An Economic Analysis of Adversarial versus Court-Appointed Presentation of Expert Testimony* (GMU School of Law Working Paper, 1994) ("Froeb and Kobayashi, *Competition*"). Their paper shows that adversarial presentation of expert testimony to a "naïve" decisionmaker is not dominated by the alternative of "perfect" court-appointed experts, and that *Frye,* even if modeled favorably as simply narrowing the range of permissible testimony, is at best neutral. This article suggests that, once public-choice considerations are brought in, both *Frye* and court-appointed experts appear to be worse than unrestricted adversarial presentation. See Part IV.B below.

Daubert is a step in the right direction because it is more consistent with the structure of adversarial litigation than any attempt to "regulate" the content of scientific evidence through centralized control, which is fraught with the potential for manipulation by interest groups. The alternatives to the *Daubert* standard all suffer from one or another form of the "free lunch" fallacy. The *Frye* standard of "general acceptance" and its variants embody the fallacy in their assumption of an immutable external standard, whereas in fact any such standard is vulnerable to interest group manipulation. Similarly, replacing the litigants' incentives with governmental organs—as through court-appointed experts or publicly chosen "scientific panels"—creates the same problems in a more familiar form and to a more severe degree. None of these variations of admissibility doctrine seems likely to produce better results, in terms either of disciplining the content of scientific evidence or of minimizing the costs of litigation, than an internalized standard such as *Daubert's*, applied by presumably uninformed trial court judges in a systematically unbiased manner. The problems that remain are not soluble by evidence law doctrine because they are problems of deviations from the standard case of adversarial litigation with symmetrical stakes that are internalized by the immediate parties.

Daubert will produce a pattern of disparate outcomes on similar facts, which may not make a pretty picture for those who equate adjudication with a search for factual consistency. But the adversarial system of adjudication has never produced a neat and tidy picture, and no system of adjudication can pretend to find immutable "truth." As the *Daubert* decision itself notes, even the scientists do not make that claim for their own disciplines,[11] and adjudication operates under a far more severe set of constraints. Let the philosophers seek for "truth." And let the law courts get about the practical business of resolving litigated disputes between the immediate parties to those disputes, on the narrowest possible grounds and with a minimum of external effects.

This argument is developed through the remaining five parts of this article. Part II sets the context by locating the admissibility of scientific evidence within evidence law doctrine and reviewing the competing tests of admissibility involved in the pre-*Daubert* debate. Part III describes the Supreme Court's decision in *Daubert.* Part IV develops the economic analysis of scientific evidence as a form of costly information, showing why the *Daubert* standard is preferable to alternative tests of admissibility.

Part V briefly examines commentators' responses to *Daubert,* and the post-*Daubert* experience in the federal and state courts,

[11] See *Daubert,* 113 S Ct at 2795.

including the federal court of appeals' decision in the *Daubert* case itself on remand from the Supreme Court. Although preliminary indications are ambiguous, there already appears to be some disagreement on the meaning and application of *Daubert*, which may produce inconsistencies in future admissibility outcomes. If that pattern develops, it will be a positive sign for the efficacy of the *Daubert* standard, as it will suggest that the standard is having precisely the unbiased effect that is desirable. Part VI concludes with a discussion of this effect, and of its broader implications for the adversarial system of adjudication.

The Supreme Court's future challenge will be to resist the temptation to tamper with a sensible decision for an imperfect world. As *Daubert* makes its way through the lower federal courts, there is likely to be a dispersion of outcomes on the admissibility of given types of scientific testimony in different cases. So long as the disparities in outcome appear to be relatively random and unbiased, there is no need to intervene. This conclusion will not be intuitively obvious to all observers, many of whom will undoubtedly see the dispersion of outcomes as a sure sign of some underlying pathology. Forgetting, or not realizing, that society has little interest in the factual findings in particular cases, critics may denounce the system's "inconsistency" and call for further "reform." But for the Supreme Court—and for the judiciary's rulemaking committees and the Congress—the better part of wisdom will be to leave well enough alone.

II. EVIDENTIARY DOCTRINE AND THE PRE-*DAUBERT* DEBATE

In evidence law, the special problems of scientific evidence stem from the law's traditional approach to testimonial qualification or, as it is called by some sources, the "competency"[12] or "founda-

[12] Terminology on this topic can be confusing. Modern evidence law doctrine, as exemplified in the Federal Rules of Evidence, tends to use the term "competency" in reference to a witness's mental capacity or legal or institutional qualification to testify at all, see Fed R Evid 601, 605-606, while some sources distinguish between that sense of the competency of witnesses and the "competency" of their testimony in the sense of meeting the threshold requirements to admissibility. See Christopher B. Mueller and Laird C. Kirkpatrick, *Evidence* § 6.1 at 498-99 (Little Brown, 1995). To further compound the confusion, the leading doctrinal authorities insist on drawing a distinction, within the threshold factual requirements to admissibility, between "competency" questions to be decided by the judge and "conditional relevancy" questions that are left to the jury. See John William Strong, ed, 1 *McCormick on Evidence* § 69 (West, 4th ed 1992) ("*McCormick on Evidence*"); 9 *Wigmore on Evidence* § 2550 (Little Brown, Chadbourn rev. 1981); Fed R Evid 104(a) & (b).

tional"[13] requirement of testimonial evidence.[14] As a general rule, testimony is not admissible unless based upon the "first-hand knowledge" gleaned from the witness's personal sense perceptions of relevant events. As "expert" scientific witnesses rarely have such a perception, and because they typically provide their information in the form of inferential "opinion" rather than first-hand "knowledge," their testimony is treated as an exception to this general rule. Much of the debate over the admissibility standards for scientific evidence is fundamentally a debate over an acceptable substitute for the first-hand knowledge requirement. Therefore, it is appropriate first to review the nature and evolution of that requirement, and then to consider its implications for the admissibility of scientific evidence.

A. First-Hand Knowledge as a Principle of Institutional Specialization

The rule of first-hand knowledge determines who will be permitted to testify and what they will be permitted to say. In this respect, the historical background of the rule is instructive. Putting the problem most starkly, two polar opposites logically suggest themselves as starting points: anyone may testify or no one may testify. Strange as it may seem to the modern reader, the early English common law approximated the second pole as its starting point, and has been slowly evolving toward the first over the past millennium.

At early common law, no one could testify—neither parties nor "witnesses" in the modern sense. Instead, common law procedure evolved an elaborate system of responsive pleadings that was designed to reduce a case to issues of law only, or, failing that, to a single, narrowly-defined issue of fact.[15] The institution of the jury

[13] Practicing lawyers and many courts tend to use the term "foundation" in reference to any prerequisite to admissibility, including the requirement of first-hand knowledge under consideration here.

[14] I refer here primarily to "testimonial" evidence as given orally by witnesses in open court because that is the central model of Anglo-American evidence doctrine and the usual context for the presentation of scientific evidence. However, documents or "writings" (as they are traditionally called in evidence doctrine) are no different in principle, as they are conceptualized simply as statements by their authors, and therefore are subject to qualification in the same manner as testimony. In addition, because most writings are prepared outside the courtroom, they are almost invariably subject to several further admissibility hurdles, including the rule against hearsay (which, together with its many exceptions, makes up a large proportion of evidence law doctrine), authentication requirements, and the "best evidence" rule's preference for the "original" writing.

[15] See Fleming James, Jr., Geoffrey C. Hazard, Jr., and John Leubsdorf, *Civil Procedure* § 3.2 (Little Brown, 4th ed 1992) ("James, Hazard & Leubsdorf, *Civil Procedure*").

originally developed as a device for tapping the personal knowledge of the jurors in order to resolve any residual issues.[16] Jurors were selected from the community in which the litigated dispute arose, and for their personal knowledge about the underlying facts and community customs.[17] As the jurors were expected to give their verdict from personal knowledge and their independent investigation of tangible proofs,[18] such as lands and the relatively scarce written records, testimonial evidence was deemed unnecessary and

[16] In the earliest period, issues of fact and law were not nearly so sharply divided as they are today; all of the contested issues would be submitted to the jury. See Frederick Pollock and Frederic William Maitland, 2 *The History of English Law* 629-30 (2d ed 1911) ("Pollock & Maitland, *History of English Law*").

[17] For an overview of the historical development of the jury, see generally Theodore F.T. Plucknett, *A Concise History of the Common Law*, book one, part II, ch 4 (Little Brown, 5th ed 1956). At the time of the Norman conquest, the prevailing modes of Anglo-Saxon trial were by ordeal, by combat, or by "compurgation," also known as "wager of law," whereby the litigants produced a specified number of individuals to swear to the justice of their cause. See F.W. Maitland, *The Forms of Action at Common Law* 14 (A.H. Chaytor & W.J. Whittaker eds., Cambridge U, 1936) ("Maitland, *Forms of Action*"). According to Pollack and Maitland, the jury was introduced to England originally by the Normans, as the royal prerogative of "inquest" in Frankish tradition, and it gradually expanded with the jurisdiction of the royal courts. Pollock & Maitland, 1 *History of English Law* at 138-50; 2 id at 616-59 (cited in note 16).

[18] The qualifications and procedures are stated clearly by Glanvill, a contemporary twelfth-century commentary on English procedure, in describing a realty case in the "Grand Assize," the progenitor of the petit jury:

> When the twelve knights have been elected, they must be summoned to come to court ready to declare on oath which of the parties, that is whether the demandant or tenant, has the greater right in his claim. . . . And meanwhile the twelve shall view the land (or tenement from which services are demanded). . . .
>
> . . . .
>
> When the assize reaches the stage where the recognition is made, then either the true legal position is well known to all the jurors, or else some know and some do not, or else none of them knows. If none of them knows the truth of the matter, and they have stated this on their oath in court, recourse shall be had to others until such as do know the truth of it are found. If, however, some know the truth of the matter and some do not, those who do not shall be rejected and others summoned to court until at least twelve can be found to agree on it. . . . The knowledge required from the jurors is that they shall know about the matter from what they have personally seen and heard, or from statements which their fathers made to them in such circumstances that they are bound to believe them as if they had seen and heard for themselves.

C.D.G. Hall, ed, *The Treatise on the Laws and Customs of the Realm of England Commonly Called Glanvill* 33-35 (English Translation) (Clarendon, 1993).

mostly unwelcome.[19] At this early stage, the jurors *were* the witnesses.[20]

Whatever else might be said of the early common law's adjudicatory methods, they certainly were sensitive to the severe limitations of the fact-finding technology of their era,[21] and they reflected a subtle appreciation for the vicissitudes of human nature.[22] Testimony by litigants was disqualified by their obvious self-interest, and that same rationale was extended to their relatives and other confidants. Originally, even unrelated and apparently disinterested witnesses were placed in that same category: because witnesses were not regularly compelled to give testimony (except by pre-litigation contract) until the sixteenth century,[23] the common law generally reasoned that they must have an interest in the outcome of the litigation, for otherwise they would not come forward.[24] Even when this attitude was relaxed, ascertainably "interested" witnesses were still disqualified from testifying.

[19] See Pollock & Maitland, 2 *History of English Law* at 601 (cited in note 16) ("Besides the oaths of the litigants and their oath-helpers, the law also knew the oaths of witnesses; but apparently in the oldest period it did not have recourse to this mode of proof . . . .").

[20] See Maitland, *Forms of Action* at 15 (cited in note 17) ("[T]rial by jury is far from being what it became in later times; jurors are not 'judges of fact,' they are witnesses . . . .").

[21] Among other things, the relatively high costs of transportation, communication, and information generally made it difficult to verify witnesses' testimony. In these circumstances, it should not be surprising to find a de-emphasis on testimony in the fact-finding process.

[22] See generally Edward J. Imwinkelried, *The Worst Evidence Principle: The Best Hypothesis as to the Logical Structure of Evidence Law,* 46 U Miami L Rev 1069, 1071 (1992) (arguing that "[a] worst evidence principle—a concern about witness perjury—is the best explanatory hypothesis for the logical structure of Evidence law" as developed in the English common law).

[23] The history is traced in detail by Wigmore, see 8 *Wigmore on Evidence* § 2190 (McNaughton rev., Little Brown, 1961) ("*Wigmore on Evidence*"). The earliest stage is summarized by Pollock & Maitland:

> [I]t seems to have been a general rule that no one could be compelled, or even suffered, to testify to a fact, unless when that fact happened he was solemnly "taken to witness." Secondly, when the witness was adduced, he came merely in order that he might swear to a set formula. His was no promissory oath to tell the truth in answer to questions, but an assertory oath.

Pollock & Maitland, 2 *History of English Law* at 601 (cited in note 16).

[24] As Wigmore explains:

> The ordinary witness (such as we now know him) was not only not compelled; he *was not welcomed.* There was a radical and strict discouragement of "maintenance," and the man who comes to labor privately with his neighbors on the jury by generally urging his influence in favor of one of the parties was

As Anglo-American procedure evolved toward its modern form, the old "disqualifications" and "incompetencies" to testimony were transformed into grounds for attack on the credibility of testimony through cross-examination and impeachment by the adverse party,[25] or, in some cases, into evidentiary privileges.[26] In those forms, they remain a part of the law of evidence today. To a very large extent, this transformation reflects not only or even primarily a more permissive attitude toward the reception of evidence, but a growing confidence in the robustness of adversarial testing as an effective check on factual fabrication.[27]

Anglo-American procedure, however, has not traveled all the way to the opposite pole. Although nearly anyone can now testify, not all testimony is "qualified" or "competent." The current qualification standard is analogous to the ancient selection criterion for jurors: to be admissible, a witness's testimony must be based on the witness's own personal knowledge, as distinguished from either second-hand sources or what is called "opinion." In effect, witnesses now have replaced jurors as providers of factual inputs to litigation. The jury now is ideally both an unbiased and an uninformed factfinding body, whose members are chosen primarily for their ignorance of any facts relating to the particular case, or at least are put on their oath to set aside any such knowledge and give their verdict solely on the basis of the evidence presented at trial.

The resulting evidence law doctrine of testimonial qualification generally is known as the "personal knowledge" or "first-hand

> not carefully distinguished from the man who comes merely to tell them what he knows of the facts. He is in either case (they thought) trying to make them decide for one of the parties rather than the other; he is a meddler; that was the law's attitude toward him.

8 *Wigmore on Evidence* § 2190, at 63-64 (cited in note 23).

[25] See 1 *McCormick on Evidence* § 61 (cited in note 12).

[26] For example, the previous disqualification of testimony by the spouse of a litigant generally has now evolved into a "privilege" against testimony exercisable by the litigant or witness spouse, or either of them, and a separate privilege for confidential marital communications. Some jurisdictions have both privileges. See, for example, Cal Evid Code §§ 970-73 (privilege against testimony); §§ 980-87 (confidential marital communications) (West 1966).

[27] By the twentieth century, this development had ripened into Wigmore's famous paean to adversarial testing by cross-examination as

> beyond any doubt the greatest legal engine ever invented for the discovery of truth. . . . If we omit political considerations of broader range, then cross-examination, not trial by jury, is the great and permanent contribution of the Anglo-American system of law to improved methods of trial procedure.

5 *Wigmore on Evidence* § 1367, at 32 (Chadbourn rev, Little Brown, 1974).

knowledge" rule. In essence, the rule requires that a witness's testimony consist of information obtained by the witness from her or his personal sense perception—the familiar instruction that witnesses confine their testimony to "what you saw and heard" (or tasted, smelled, or touched).[28] As the *Daubert* Court pointed out, this rule represents "a 'most pervasive manifestation' of the common law insistence upon 'the most reliable sources of information.' "[29]

The negative correlative to the first-hand knowledge rule is the so-called opinion rule—more accurately characterized as the no-opinion rule—which generally prohibits witnesses from testifying to "opinion" or "conclusion" as distinguished from first-hand "knowledge."[30] As has been pointed out, if this distinction between knowledge and opinion were taken to its epistemological extreme, there would be no such thing as admissible testimony, as virtually any description of sense perceptions is an opinion.[31] Of course, the opinion rule has not been so applied. Instead, both the first-hand knowledge rule and the opinion rule have been applied essentially on the basis of the relative institutional functions of witnesses as compared with jurors (or judges, when acting as fact-finders).

Under modern institutional arrangements, the fact-finder is assigned only part of its original role—what might be called the "inferential" function.[32] The fact-finders, with the assistance of the

[28] The current federal codification of this standard is Rule 602 of the Federal Rules of Evidence, which provides that "[a] witness may not testify to a matter unless evidence is introduced sufficient to support a finding that the witness has personal knowledge of the matter." Fed R Evid 602.

[29] 113 S Ct at 2796, quoting from Advisory Committee's Note on Fed R Evid 602, 56 FRD 183, 263 (1973) quoting from *McCormick on Evidence* § 10, at 19 (West, 1954).

[30] Compare Fed R Evid 602 with id 701 and 702.

[31]
> In a way, all human assertions are opinions. . . . Our whole conscious life is a process of forming working beliefs or opinions from the evidence of our senses, few of them exactly accurate, most of them near enough correct for practical use, some of them seriously erroneous. Every assertion involves the expression of one or more of these opinions. A rule of evidence which called for the exclusion of opinion in this broad sense would therefore make trials quite impossible.

John MacArthur Maguire, *Evidence: Common Sense and Common Law* 24 (Foundation Press, 1947) ("Maguire, *Evidence*").

[32] Despite pioneering work by Wigmore early in this century, culminating in the appearance of the third edition of his work on "proof" as distinguished from admissibility in 1937, the inferential function was largely ignored by legal scholars until relatively recently. See John Henry Wigmore, *The Science of Judicial Proof* (Little Brown, 3d ed 1937). The study of the processes of inference and proof in trials now

adversarial presentations and arguments by the parties, are to take the raw materials provided by the witnesses and draw their own conclusions. From this point of view, the first-hand knowledge and opinion rules—and indeed the majority of evidence law, most of which is concerned with "reliability" standards[33]—operate primarily to protect the institutional function of the fact-finder. They do this by requiring that evidence be "broken down" into a form that exposes the parties' patterns of inferential reasoning to independent evaluation by the fact-finder.[34]

The basic logic here is analogous to the economics of specialization, as applied within the institutional context of litigation.[35] The fact-finders specialize in the inferential function, while the "fact" witnesses specialize in providing observational inputs. This

is undergoing a renaissance, based largely on Wigmore's earlier work. See, for example, Terence Anderson and William Twining, *Analysis of Evidence* (Little Brown, 1991); David A. Schum, *The Evidential Foundations of Probabilistic Reasoning* (John Wiley, 1994).

[33] In terms of admissibility as distinguished from trial procedure or proof, there are only two basic doctrines of evidence law concerned with intrinsic fact-finding: (1) "relevancy," which is a minimal requirement of probative value; and (2) "reliability," which takes in the rules of competency, authentication, hearsay, "best evidence," and the like, designed to provide some assurance that proffered evidence represents a genuine factual input. See *Daubert*, 113 S Ct at 2795-96. The third general topic of admissibility doctrine concerns rules of evidentiary privilege and other rules (such as the rules against evidence of subsequent remedial measures, Fed R Evid 407, or settlement negotiations, Fed R Evid 408) that exclude evidence on the basis of what typically are referred to as "extrinsic" policy considerations.

[34] As articulated by Maguire in his "common sense" terms:

> It is . . . plain good sense to refuse to let a non-expert purport to give evidence about matters he does not understand. He is more likely to mislead than to afford sound guidance. The trier of fact is equally capable of forming its own conclusions. By expanding this last statement we shall get a phrasing of the practice under which courts have tended to exclude testimony consciously cast in terms of opinion and referring to commonplace matters, whenever they believe this testimony can be broken down into its rudiments—that is, normally, into statements of perception from which the relevant opinion or conclusion is to be derived. It is fundamental to our method of litigating factual issues that the trier of fact, whether judge of juror, shall so far as his capacities and the nature of the issues permit draw for himself all the conclusions which build themselves into his determination. Witnesses are to state their perceptions of fact, the triers to appraise credibility, make findings of fundamental fact, and draw the inferences necessary to decision.

Maguire, *Evidence* at 25 (cited in note 31).

[35] In economics, the benefits of specialization have been developed primarily in connection with the gains from trade or exchange in an explicit market. See generally Armen A. Alchian and William R. Allen, *Exchange & Production: Competition, Coordination and Control* ch 7 (Wadsworth, 3d ed 1983). Still, the logic of the spe-

logic is relatively explicit in the legal doctrine, especially in Federal Rule 701's codification of the opinion rule and its exceptions as applied to "lay" (non-expert) witnesses: opinions or inferences by such witnesses are prohibited unless the opinions or inferences are both "rationally based" on the witnesses' sense perception and determined to be "helpful to a clear understanding of the witness' testimony or the determination of a fact in issue."[36] Note that the exceptions follow the same logic as the general rule, in that even "helpful" inferences by fact witnesses still must be based in their observational advantage over fact-finders in terms of personal sense impression.

The same logic applies to expert testimony, which is admissible under the Federal Rule 702 only when there has been a determination that expert testimony (1) actually is "expert" information, in the same sense that it is "specialized" information not possessed by the fact-finders (or too costly for fact-finders to acquire), and (2) "will assist the trier of fact to understand the evidence or to deter-

cialization is analogous in this context, when viewed in the institutional perspective. Identifying the gains from explicit trade simply is one way of recognizing a difference in marginal opportunity costs of production versus trade: in the classical example, the English make cloth and buy wine, because the opportunity cost of the English foregoing cloth production to make wine is higher than the market price of Portuguese wine. Similarly here, the current institutional arrangements imply that the fact-finders make inferences and "buy" observational inputs from the witnesses, which suggests that the opportunity costs of combining both functions in the fact-finders are high. This could be true, for example, if direct observation will actually impair the reliability of the inferences that one later draws within the litigation context.

Something like this logic may account for the historical evolution of specialized roles for jurors and witnesses. Because factual testimony originally could not be compelled, and therefore had to be "bought" in an explicit market, parties may have found it less costly to purchase the testimony from witnesses than to incur the costs of leaving jurors to inform themselves about the underlying facts. Similarly, jurors may have wanted to avoid the opportunity costs of investigating the facts—as they presumably had more productive uses for that increment of their time—and "traded" that right in exchange for specialization in the inferential function. Under this interpretation, both litigants and jurors had positive incentives to acquiesce in the transition to witness testimony. Judges do not appear to have had any strong incentive to resist that transition, especially if it also increased the reliability and therefore acceptability of fact-finding in litigation.

[36] Rule 701 provides:

> If the witness is not testifying as an expert, the witness' testimony in the form of opinions or inferences is limited to those opinions or inferences which are (a) rationally based on the perception of the witness and (b) helpful to a clear understanding of the witness' testimony or the determination of a fact in issue.

Fed R Evid 701.

mine a fact in issue."[37] Thus, the principle justifying the admission of expert testimony appears to be both equivalent to the general doctrine and relatively noncontroversial in concept. The difficulties have arisen not with the principle, but rather with formulating a practical test for admissibility that can be applied by the nonexpert trial judge charged with implementing that principle.

B. The Pre-*Daubert* Debate

The special problems of expert testimony arise from a seeming deficiency in the competence of the trial judge to determine whether proposed expert opinion testimony offers the fact-finder any advantage in drawing conclusions. The trial judge might reasonably be expected to determine whether a lay opinion would be "helpful" to the fact-finder, because the judge, as another "lay" person, presumably is in a position to appreciate the inferential process involved in forming that opinion. But how can the judge make the similar determination that expert opinion will "assist" the fact-finder, when the expert opinion rests on an inferential process that, by definition, is beyond the understanding of lay persons, including the judge? This is the question that has haunted the debates over the admissibility of scientific evidence, from *Frye* through *Daubert*, and the one that has tempted some courts and commentators to the vain hope that there is a free lunch.

The logic of the situation suggests two different points of view, which in fact did emerge as opposing schools of thought in the pre-*Daubert* debate. One point of view is "internal" to the litigation process, while the other is "external." The "internal" point of view manifests a confidence in the ability of the trial judge, with the assistance of adversarial presentation, to distinguish between useful and misleading (or pointless) expert testimony. In contrast, the "external" point of view reflects the belief that the adversarial process is easily fooled, confused, or misled by proffered scientific evidence, making it necessary to judge the admissibility of such evidence by a standard that is external to the litigation process.

The "internal" perspective is associated with what came to be called the "relevancy" or, after its principal exponent, the "McCor-

[37] Rule 702 provides:

> If scientific, technical, or other specialized knowledge will assist the trier of fact to understand the evidence or determine a fact in issue, a witness qualified as an expert by knowledge, skill, experience, training, or education, may testify thereto in the form of an opinion or otherwise.

Fed R Evid 702.

mick" test of admissibility.[38] Under this view, there is no special prerequisite to the admissibility of scientific evidence, which therefore is subject only to ordinary admissibility requirements, primarily relevance. According to McCormick, this was the "traditional" approach to scientific evidence, followed prior to the twentieth century, and the "notion of a special rule for scientific evidence originated in 1923 in *Frye*."[39]

The "external" perspective is represented by the *Frye* (or, more descriptively, the "general acceptance") test for the admissibility of scientific evidence. Under this test, scientific evidence is inadmissible unless it is shown to be based on reasoning that is "sufficiently established to have gained general acceptance in the particular field in which it belongs."[40] In essence, the rationale for this test is that neither courts nor juries—nor any litigation processes—are capable of distinguishing between "good" science and "bad" science by themselves, so that the scientific community must be given the "determinative voice."[41]

The emergence of the *Frye* test opened up a division of authority in the case law, and a spirited debate in the secondary literature, all of which was intensified by the 1975 enactment of the Federal Rules of Evidence.[42] Because the Federal Rules did not mention *Frye*, it was uncertain whether the Rules displaced or incorporated the *Frye* test or its variants. That question created a conflict among the federal courts of appeals, which finally prompted the Supreme Court to grant certiorari in *Daubert*.[43]

III. THE *DAUBERT* DECISION

In June 1993, the Supreme Court resolved the conflict among the federal circuits by ruling in *Daubert* that "the *Frye* test was displaced by the [Federal] Rules of Evidence."[44] Taken alone, this unanimous holding might be viewed merely as a somewhat formalistic exercise in statutory interpretation of the legislatively-en-

[38] See *McCormick on Evidence* § 170, at 362-64 (West, 1st ed 1954).

[39] 1 *McCormick on Evidence* § 203, at 869 (cited in note 13).

[40] *Frye v United States*, 293 F 1013, 1014 (DC Cir 1923).

[41] Paul C. Giannelli and Edward J. Imwinkelried, 1 *Scientific Evidence* § 1-5(A) at 13 & n 76 (Michie, 2d ed 1993) (quoting from *United States v Addison*, 498 F 2d 741, 743-44 (DC Cir 1974)) ("Giannelli and Imwinkelried, *Scientific Evidence*").

[42] The legal literature is vast. For a general survey through 1992, see id at ch. 1. The recent leading sources were cited by the Supreme Court in *Daubert*, 113 S Ct at 2793 nn 4-5.

[43] See *Daubert*, 113 S Ct at 2792.

[44] *Daubert*, 113 S Ct at 2794. Justice Blackmun wrote for the Court, which was unanimous on this point.

acted Federal Rules of Evidence.[45] The Court, however, went on to provide a detailed explanation of its decision, in a portion of the opinion from which two Justices dissented.[46] This explanation displays both an interesting analysis of the evidentiary doctrine surrounding the problems of scientific evidence and at least some appreciation of the policy questions involved.

Daubert itself involved two of the many personal injury cases that had been brought in recent years against Merrell Dow Pharmaceuticals on the allegation that its drug Bendectin, an anti-nausea medication prescribed during pregnancy, caused birth defects in the gestating children. After removal of the two cases from state to federal court in California, Merrell Dow moved for summary judgment. Merrell Dow's most important contention was that the plaintiffs would be unable to present admissible scientific evidence of causation because all of the published epidemiological (human statistical) studies had failed to find a link between Bendectin and birth defects. The plaintiffs conceded the state of the published literature, but joined issue on the admissibility question by proffering expert testimony based upon animal and chemical structure studies, plus unpublished "reanalyses" of the published epidemiological data, all purporting to show evidence of the causative link.

The federal trial court ruled that the experts opinions proffered by the plaintiffs were inadmissible under *Frye,* and therefore gave summary judgment for Merrell Dow.[47] The United States Court of Appeals for the Ninth Circuit affirmed.[48] The animal and chemical structure studies were ruled inadmissible in light of the published epidemiological studies' findings; where substantial human studies are extant, the court concluded, non-human studies are not "generally accepted" as reliable. The "reanalyses" were excluded on the ground that such studies are "generally accepted" only when published and subject to peer review.

The Supreme Court reversed and remanded on the ground that the *Frye* standard did not survive the Federal Rules of Evidence. The Court's basic ruling was predicated on a formal and almost

[45] See id at 2792-94 (Part II-A of the Court's opinion, in which all justices joined).

[46] See id at 2794-99 (Parts II-B, II-C, III, and IV of the Court's opinion, in which seven of the nine justices joined). Chief Justice Rehnquist, joined by Justice Stevens, filed an opinion that dissented from all but Parts I (the factual statement) and II-A (the basic ruling that *Frye* had been displaced by the Federal Rules of Evidence) of the Court's opinion. The dissenters argued that "the Court would be far better advised in this case . . . to leave the further development of this important area of the law to future cases." Id at 2800 (Rehnquist concurring in part and dissenting in part).

[47] *Daubert v Merrell Dow Pharmaceuticals, Inc.,* 727 F Supp 570 (SD Cal 1989).

[48] *Daubert v Merrell Dow Pharmaceuticals, Inc.,* 951 F 2d 1128 (9th Cir 1991).

mechanical legal analysis: finessing the policy implications, the Court simply ruled that the *Frye* standard was not within the purview of the Congress enacting the Federal Rules of Evidence in 1975. The Court read Federal Evidence Rule 402 as a "liberal" standard authorizing the admissibility of any relevant evidence unless there is explicit authority for exclusion.[49] According to the Court's analysis, expert testimony is governed specifically by Rule 702,[50] which did not embody the *Frye* standard and therefore failed to authorize the "general acceptance" standard as a threshold to admissibility.

Up until this point, the Court's *Daubert* opinion could be viewed as an endorsement of the "relevance" test in its most rudimentary form: by simply ruling that the *Frye* test was superseded by the Federal Rules, the Court could have relegated scientific evidence to the same category of presumptive admissibility, subject to the trial court's discretionary authority to exclude for confusion, prejudice, or waste of time, as all other "relevant" evidence. That apparently was the option favored by the two dissenters, as they joined only in this aspect of the ruling. The majority of the Court, however, went on to provide a framework for lower courts to use in addressing the admissibility of scientific evidence.

In place of the *Frye* standard, the *Daubert* majority articulated a concept of "reliability" that is analogous to the "competency" or "foundational" standards associated with non-expert testimony: "[U]nder the [Federal] Rules the trial judge must ensure that any and all scientific testimony or evidence admitted is not only relevant, but reliable."[51] According to the Court, the "primary locus of this obligation is Rule 702,"[52] which was directly analogized by the Court to the foundational requirement of first-hand knowledge. Like that requirement, according to the Court, Rule 702 is designed to assure that "the expert's opinion will have a reliable basis in the knowledge and experience of his discipline."[53]

The Court's opinion resolves the Rule 702 standard into two distinct aspects: (1) whether the proffered evidence is "scientific

[49] Rule 402 provides:

> All relevant evidence is admissible, except as otherwise provided by the Constitution of the United States, by Act of Congress, by these rules, or by other rules prescribed by the Supreme Court pursuant to statutory authority. Evidence which is not relevant is not admissible.

Fed R Evid 402.

[50] Rule 702 is set out in note 37 above.

[51] 113 S Ct at 2795.

[52] Id.

[53] Id at 2796.

knowledge," which means, in essence, that it was arrived at through the scientific method; and (2) whether the evidence "will assist the trier of fact to understand or determine a fact in issue," which means that there is an adequate "fit" or "valid scientific connection" to the factual issues in the litigation.[54] In addition to the Rule 702 standards, the trial court may also apply the balancing test of Rule 403 to exclude scientific evidence when "its probative value is substantially outweighed by the danger of unfair prejudice, confusion of the issues, or misleading the jury, or by considerations of undue delay, waste of time, or needless presentation of cumulative evidence."[55]

There is little doubt that the content of the admissibility standards enunciated by *Daubert* will be the subject of much case law and commentary, as they already have been in the relatively short time since *Daubert* was decided.[56] For purposes of this article, however, the exact contents of the new *Daubert* standards are less important than their general tendencies. First, as noted above, *Daubert* represents an explicit recognition that the threshold standards for the admissibility of scientific evidence are intended to serve the same relatively minimal "reliability" function that is served by the rule of first-hand knowledge for nonexpert evidence. Second, *Daubert* primarily takes the "internal" point of view on scientific evidence, which relies upon the adversarial system itself to police abuses.

This second feature of the *Daubert* ruling was made more explicit in the Court's concluding discussion, where the Court responded briefly to the concerns of both sides in the pre-*Daubert* debate. On the one hand, the Court believed that the "junk science" critique was

> overly pessimistic about the capabilities of the jury, and of the adversary system generally. Vigorous cross-examination, presentation of contrary evidence, and careful instruction on the

[54] Id.

[55] Rule 403 reads in full:

> Although relevant, evidence may be excluded if its probative value is substantially outweighed by the danger of unfair prejudice, confusion of the issues, or misleading the jury, or by considerations of undue delay, waste of time, or needless presentation of cumulative evidence.

Fed R Evid 403.

[56] There have been many individual articles on *Daubert*, and symposia have appeared in 15 *Cardozo Law Review* (nos. 6-7 (combined), April 1994) and 43 *Emory Law Journal* (no. 3, Summer 1994).

> burden of proof are the traditional and appropriate means of attacking shaky but admissible evidence.[57]

On the other hand, the Court believed that fears of overly parsimonious "gatekeeping" by the trial court judges—leading to "a stifling and repressive scientific orthodoxy" also were overdrawn, given the different roles of scientific and judicial fact-finding:

> It is true that open debate is an essential part of both legal and scientific analyses. Yet there are important differences between the quest for truth in the courtroom and the quest for truth in the laboratory. Scientific conclusions are subject to perpetual revision. Law, on the other hand, must resolve disputes finally and quickly. The scientific project is advanced by broad and wide-ranging consideration of a multitude of hypotheses, for those that are incorrect will eventually be shown to be so, and that in itself is an advance. Conjectures that are probably wrong are of little use, however, in the project of reaching a quick, final, and binding legal judgment—often of great consequence—about a particular set of events in the past. We recognize that in practice, a gatekeeping role for the judge, no matter how flexible, inevitably on occasion will prevent the jury from learning of authentic insights and innovations. That, nevertheless, is the balance that is struck by Rules of Evidence designed not for the exhaustive search for cosmic understanding but for the particularized resolution of legal disputes.[58]

With these observations, the Court's *Daubert* opinion displays a refreshing appreciation for both the strengths of the adversary system and the severe limitations of any adjudicative process in discovering immutable "truth." For these reasons, *Daubert* appears generally to be a sound decision. As I will show in the next section, it is an improvement over *Frye,* simply because *Daubert*—unlike *Frye*—at least begins to recognize that the production of scientific information has costs.

IV. THE ECONOMICS OF SCIENTIFIC EVIDENCE

There is no free lunch. Most economists and non-economists alike profess adherence to that axiom. There nonetheless appears to be widespread vulnerability to the fallacy that maybe there is a free

[57] 113 S Ct at 2798.
[58] Id at 2798-99.

lunch—or at least a very cheap lunch—out there somewhere, which we can find if only we are very clever about searching for it, and as long as we do not call it a "lunch." But that quest contradicts the axiom. Perhaps the metaphor in the expression stands as an obstacle to broad understanding and application of its principle. In that case, let us remove the metaphor. Nothing is free. All human action (or inaction) consumes resources, if only in the diversion of human imagination and effort from one opportunity to another.[59] Because all human action consumes resources, all products of human action are costly.

These principles apply to information, just as they do to all other products of human activity.[60] As the economists say, information is costly. And yet, it is precisely in the context of information production—and most especially scientific information—that the "free lunch" fallacy seems to be most seductive.[61] Perhaps that is because there is such a powerful urge to believe that all the secrets of the Universe simply lie waiting to be uncovered, and, once understood,

[59] "Costs are equal to the value attached to the satisfaction which one must forego to attain the end aimed at." Ludwig von Mises, *Human Action: A Treatise on Economics* 97 (Henry Regnery, 3d rev ed 1966). See also James M. Buchanan, *Cost and Choice: An Inquiry in Economic Theory* (U Chicago, 1978). It is especially the failure to consider opportunity costs that can feed the "free lunch" fallacy. See, for example, Steven M. Crafton and Margaret F. Brinig, *Quantitative Methods for Lawyers* 24 (Carolina, 1994).

[60] The economics literature is surveyed in Jack Hirshleifer and John G. Riley, *The Analytics of Uncertainty and Information,* part II, chs 5-7 (Cambridge U, 1992) ("Hirshleifer and Riley, *Analytics*"). In the law-and-economics literature, the fullest generalizations are given by Frank H. Easterbrook, *Insider Trading, Secret Agents, Evidentiary Privileges, and the Production of Information,* 1981 Sup Ct Rev 309 ("Easterbrook, *Insider Trading*"), and in three papers that appeared in a special issue of *The Journal of Legal Studies* in 1980: George J. Stigler, *An Introduction to Privacy in Economics and Politics,* 9 J Legal Stud 623 (1980) ("Stigler, *Introduction to Privacy*"); Edmund W. Kitch, *The Law and Economics of Rights in Valuable Information,* 9 J Legal Stud 683 (1980); and John P. Gould, *Privacy and the Economics of Information,* 9 J Legal Stud 827 (1980).

[61] Stigler summarizes the key problem:

> Economists have come to view the production of knowledge as an expensive, resource-consuming activity, but the dissemination of this knowledge as virtually free. . . . [But] are the production and dissemination of information separable? . . .
>
> The distinction between producing and using information is a hypothesis. It has not been shown to possess a large capacity to generate interesting hypotheses about the working of markets for information. In this undeveloped state it is a poor basis for deducing welfare conclusions.

Stigler, *Introduction to Privacy* at 640-41 (cited in note 60). See also Easterbrook, *Insider Trading* at 313-14, 364-65 (cited in note 60).

will form themselves into a perfect and disciplined whole.[62] Whatever the merits of this belief in immutable "truth," which can be neither created by human understanding nor destroyed by human ignorance, the processes of human understanding and human behavior themselves are quite mutable. Those processes, moreover, do not magically lose their all-too-human qualities simply because they are turned toward a search for immutable truth.

Accordingly, it is a fair question whether any form of information can ever be treated as a "given" for any purpose of law or economics.[63] That general question is beyond the scope of this article, which is concerned with the supply of scientific evidence to litigated matters. As to that species of information, there can be no doubt that production incentives are at work, as the underlying activity is costly.[64] We need only observe that the process of scientific investigation—as opposed to the immutable "truths" for which it seeks—is itself a costly activity that consumes considerable resources and occupies a number of people throughout their lives. Furthermore, when litigation enters the picture, we observe that individuals can earn positive incomes for their scientific "expert" testimony on the matters at issue. Those simple facts are sufficient to frame the economic analysis of scientific evidence, and to show that the *Frye* rule of admissibility—and any variant that purports to regulate the content of scientific evidence by reference to an external standard of "acceptance"—is based on the fallacy that scientific knowledge is somehow just lying around waiting for the courts to make use of it in resolving disputes. This is a fallacy because the quantity and quality of the scientific knowledge that is produced will be affected by the uses to which such knowledge is put by the courts.

Because the provision of scientific expert testimony to litigation is a costly activity, and because the standard of admissibility will affect the incomes of people who provide such testimony, the behavior of individuals engaged in that activity will differ depending on the content of the admissibility standard. In the case of *Frye,* its admissibility standard created incentives for interest groups to form

[62] The basic arguments are traced in Hirschleifer & Riley, *Analytics* § 7.1 (cited in note 60).

[63] The most powerful statement of this general critique is Friedrich A. Hayek, *The Use of Knowledge in Society,* 35 Am Econ Rev 519 (1945).

[64] See Jack Hirshleifer, *The Private and Social Value of Information and the Reward to Inventive Activity,* 61 Am Econ Rev 561 (1971). Although his principal concern is with the question of private over- or under-investment in inventive activity, Hirschleifer's paper shows that, even in a world of perfect and costless exchange, the redistribution of information will affect production incentives.

around the concept of "general acceptance." Those organizational incentives in turn both raised the costs and influenced the content of scientific evidence produced for use in litigation, at least on the margin.

Frye's error was to assume that its admissibility standard would have no effect on scientific "acceptance." At the margin, however, the "general acceptance" standard must affect what scientific research is conducted, what papers are published, and how scientific fields are defined.[65] Those marginal effects, moreover, are likely to be heavily represented in litigated disputes over the admissibility of scientific evidence.[66] It is difficult to say empirically whether *Frye*'s effect on science overall has been large or small, but that does not change the analysis. So long as the effect of *Frye* has not been zero, then it had some effect on the nature of the scientific evidence supplied. But *Frye* could have zero effect only if immutable truths of science both exist (which is widely doubted among scientists) and can be costlessly apprehended. If those conditions were satisfied, however, there would be no need for scientific testimony at all, and the entire question of admissibility standards for scientific evidence would disappear.

From this perspective, *Daubert* is an improvement over *Frye*, though hardly a panacea. *Daubert* may still assume a "free snack" because it recurs to a purportedly external standard of what constitutes "science" for its threshold to admissibil-

[65] The most obvious of many possible examples are suggested by the terms "forensic science" and "forensic medicine." Without the demand created by litigation, these fields of activity would not even exist. Because of that demand, however, these fields, like others, have their professional associations and societies. See Part V below. As the costs of organizing such groups are not zero, their existence—and their necessity under the *Frye* standard—affect the production cost structure.

[66] Virtually by definition, scientific expert testimony is at the "margin" of scientific activity, on both the supply and demand sides. The selection bias in cases that proceed to trial suggests that the closer and more sharply contested cases will provide most of the demand for expert testimony. See George L. Priest and Benjamin Klein, *The Selection of Disputes for Litigation*, 13 J Legal Stud 1 (1984). That condition, in turn, is likely to call forth controversial scientific expert testimony, which will also be the most sharply contested in terms of admissibility.

The usual case of expert testimony may usefully be contrasted with the little-used concept of "judicial notice," which assumes the existence of a "fact . . . not subject to reasonable dispute." Fed R Evid 201(b). In economic terms, this is the "inframarginal" case of scientific information used in courts. Perhaps more importantly for the analysis of this article, it does not utilize expert testimony at all, even if it relates to scientific phenomena. Prospective expert witnesses' incentives essentially are to minimize the application of this concept, which is consistent with its relatively rare appearance in contested matters.

ity.[67] Nonetheless, *Daubert* is a less strictly directive or regulatory standard, and it is vague. In this context, those features have the virtue of discouraging interest groups of litigants, lawyers, and expert witnesses from organizing themselves around the admissibility standard.[68] If the costs of organization and coordination are large enough, then *Daubert* may produce a relatively unbiased supply of scientific evidence to litigation.

The major difference between *Daubert* and *Frye* rests fundamentally in *Daubert*'s more "internal" perspective on fact-finding in litigation. *Frye* and its more recent variants reflect a long period of twentieth-century angst—which continues in several forms to the present—about the efficacy of the Anglo-American system of adversarial adjudication.[69] That angst produces a turn toward "external" guidance. *Daubert* is a reaffirmation of confidence in the adversarial system's internal ability to correct for misleading evidence.[70] The underlying question is whether recourse to some external standard, or a more directive role for public agents such as judges or court-appointed experts, can improve the fact-finding performance of the adversarial system. Certainly in the case of scientific evidence—if not more generally—both transaction-cost and public-choice economics suggest that the answer is "no."

The adversarial system operates essentially by conferring procedural rights on the parties to present whatever evidence they

[67] To the extent that *Daubert* looks to an external standard, it still assumes that this standard is in an important sense "free." This is fallacious because the external standard of what constitutes science, like the *Frye* standard, is potentially manipulable by external interest groups. *Daubert* differs from *Frye* mainly in creating weaker incentives for external interest groups to manipulate the standard because the costs of doing so effectively are higher. See Section B below.

[68] At least one commentator already has observed that "if *Daubert* is taken seriously, then much of forensic science is in serious trouble." Randolph N. Jonakait, *The Meaning of Daubert and What that Means for Forensic Science,* 15 Cardozo L Rev 2103, 2117 (1994). See also Randolph N. Jonakait, *Forensic Science: The Need for Regulation,* 4 Harv J L & Tech 109 (1991).

[69] This theme of "dissatisfaction" with the adversarial system can be traced back at least to the famous 1906 address by Roscoe Pound, then Dean of the Harvard Law School, to the American Bar Association on "The Causes of Popular Dissatisfaction with the Administration of Justice" (reprinted in 29 ABA Reports 395 (1917)). In more recent years, it is exemplified in the criticisms of Marvin E. Frankel, *Partisan Justice* (Hill and Wang, 1980), which expanded on his earlier article, *The Search for Truth: An Umpireal View,* 123 U Penn L Rev 1031 (1975). And see the sources cited at notes 82-87 below.

[70] For defenses of the adversarial system, see Stephan Landsman, *The Adversary System: A Description and Defense* (American Enterprise Institute, 1984); Lon L. Fuller, *The Forms and Limits of Adjudication,* 92 Harv L Rev 353 (1978).

wish, subject only to very loose regulation through the law of evidence and the trial court judge's rulings on procedural points at trial. The parties' incentives to invest in evidentiary presentation are provided by the substantive law of liability and damages. At trial, the basic norm is symmetry of opportunity for each side to present its case, subject to the conventions on burdens of proof. As noted above, fact-finders are chosen for disinterest, neutrality, and ex ante ignorance of the incident in litigation. At least formally, law determination is strictly separated from fact-finding, and fact-finding is subject to very limited appellate review. With some important modern exceptions,[71] the findings of fact are binding only upon the immediate parties. Fact-finding in this system is highly internalized to the immediate litigation and litigants: there is little or no external effect on society, except for the effects following from the determination of the immediate parties' legal rights in the narrow factual context of the litigation.

Within such an inwardly focused system, injecting an external standard of evidentiary qualification is unlikely to improve overall results, given the limited aims and consequences of fact finding in each individual case. On the contrary, recourse to an external standard—particularly one that is manipulable by private or public interest groups—is likely to degrade the performance of the system. Such a standard gives non-parties a stake in the outcome and thereby encourages their interference, which appears to be what occurred under the *Frye* test for scientific evidence.[72] Similarly, increasing the roles of public agents, such as judges or public experts, again would give those agents a stake in the litigation and therefore an incentive to influence the outcome. In neither case would society's interest in the fact-finding function of litigation be advanced materially.

In fact, society has very little interest in the factual—as opposed to the legal—outcome of any one trial, so long as the fact-finding process is tolerably accurate and systematically unbiased.[73] "Accuracy" itself is a difficult concept to define in any precise and prac-

[71] See Parts IV.A and IV.C below.

[72] The situation is therefore analogous to the economics of contract: if the parties fully internalize social costs and benefits, and if transaction costs are low, then bargaining leads to an efficient outcome. R.H. Coase, *The Problem of Social Cost,* 3 J L & Econ 1 (1960). Furthermore, all other things equal, granting non-litigants stakes in the outcome would tend to raise transaction costs and therefore impair efficiency. The number of affected individuals is much larger, and the stakes may no longer be symmetrical.

[73] See Richard A. Posner, *An Economic Approach to Legal Procedure and Judicial Administration,* 2 J Legal Stud 399 (1973). For an extensive recent analysis finding that even the systematic value of accuracy (conceived more broadly to include legal

tical way because the "accuracy" of litigated fact-findings cannot be evaluated on any independent basis. But no one operates under the illusion that perfect "accuracy"—however it might be defined—can or should be the aim of a practical fact-finding process in litigation. As the Court pointed out in its *Daubert* opinion, mistakes will sometimes be made, but that is the inevitable consequence of a fact-finding system "designed not for the exhaustive search for cosmic understanding but for the particularized resolution of legal disputes."[74] The more practical policy question is how the incentives to invest in the fact-finding process should be structured. Given that the social value of the "accuracy"—however defined—of a single factual outcome is by definition small, economics suggests that external social intervention in the parties' investment decisions also should be small.

A. The Functions and Structure of Litigation

In our legal system, litigation has two principal functions: resolving an existing dispute between the immediate parties; and generating rules to govern future conduct.[75] There are important social interests in both functions, but in neither instance does the social interest place a great deal of importance on the precise outcome of the fact-finding process in any one particular case.

The function of generating rules (or declaring law) places little significance on the fact-finding process. Most law declaring in the American adjudicative system is done by appellate courts, in published opinions with factual recitations that often bear only a remote resemblance to the evidentiary facts of record.[76] Appellate review of fact-finding is extremely limited.[77] It is entirely consistent

outcomes) is an enormously complex question, see Louis Kaplow, *The Value of Accuracy in Adjudication: An Economic Analysis*, 23 J Legal Stud 307 (1994). The point here is the much more modest one that the social value of an "accurate" determination in a given marginal case approaches zero, essentially by definition.

[74] See note 58 and accompanying text above.

[75] See generally Richard A. Posner, *Economic Analysis of Law* chs 20-21 (Little Brown, 4th ed 1992).

[76] Perhaps the most famous example of this very common phenomenon is Judge Cardozo's opinion in *Palsgraf v Long Island R. Co.*, 248 NY 339 (1928), which is treated in detail by Richard A. Posner, *Cardozo: A Study in Reputation* ch 3 (U Chicago, 1990).

[77] With few exceptions, American appellate courts follow the federal pattern of highly deferential review of factual findings by the trial court. A trial court judge's findings of fact "shall not be set aside unless clearly erroneous, and due regard shall be given to the opportunity of the trial court to judge the credibility of witnesses," Fed R Civ P 52(a). "Clearly erroneous" is construed to mean that "the reviewing court on the entire evidence is left with the definite and firm conviction that a

with American doctrine that an appellate court would spend a great deal of effort in analyzing the law as applied to a set of facts that the appellate judges do not believe to be true, but are constrained to accept by the narrow scope of appellate review of fact-finding. Aside from the ultimate limitations imposed by doctrines of justiciability such as standing and mootness,[78] appellate courts could overtly make up hypothetical facts on which to declare law.[79] The law-declaring function is defined by the facts as recited by the appellate court, and is largely unaffected by whether those recited facts correspond with the evidence—much less with external reality.

The dispute-resolution function, from society's point of view, places only slightly more emphasis on the fact-finding process.[80] For the most part, factual findings in a particular case have no external effect whatsoever—they are binding only upon the litigants and only for purposes of the immediate litigation. Under this structure of adjudication, the social interest in the outcome of one particular case is negligible. Most members of society are not parties to the case, and will be unaffected by its findings of fact. Society's

mistake has been committed . . . hav[ing] in mind that their function is not to decide factual issues de novo," *Anderson v City of Bessemer City,* 470 US 564, 573 (1985). Appellate review of jury findings is even more constrained. Doctrinally, it does not exist. Functionally, it occurs when an appellate court reviews a trial court's decision whether to grant a directed verdict or a judgment notwithstanding the jury's verdict, under a standard requiring that, when viewing the evidence in the light most favorable to the winning party, no "reasonable" jury could have found the facts as it did. See Fed R Civ P 50(a)(1); *Galloway v United States,* 319 US 372 (1943).

[78] These doctrines are designed to limit judicial authority to concrete and particularized disputes between identifiable named parties and, in the case of standing, to concentrate the right to sue in one or a few parties. As such, they serve to reinforce the internalization effects of the adversarial system.

[79] In fact, appellate courts often do declare law on admittedly hypothetical facts by including dicta in their opinions, which are sometimes not distinguished from holdings by subsequent courts.

[80] The discussion in this section is directed primarily to private civil cases, which form the principal model of litigation in our system. It may be true that the social interest in fact-finding differs in criminal cases or in public civil cases, where a particular factual determination arguably has a broader significance. Our legal system's traditional response to this situation has been to provide for publicly financed enforcement, which focuses the social interest through the representative public party rather than by modifying the usual rules of evidentiary admissibility to take in the interests of non-parties, and therefore does not deviate from the basic pattern of internalization through the parties' incentives. In some instances of public enforcement, such as criminal prosecution, the rules of procedure and burdens of proof—the prime example being proof of guilt beyond a reasonable doubt—appear to have been modified to counteract agency-cost problems that arise in the system of publicly financed enforcement, which itself tends to disrupt the symmetry of stakes that is characteristic of the standard model. See Part IV.C below.

interest is limited to assuring that the fact-finding system is tolerably accurate and unbiased. If adjudicative fact-finding is wildly inaccurate or systematically biased, then litigants will no longer look to the courts for dispute resolution, and the entire rationale for publicly financed courts will be defeated.[81] However, once one crosses the threshold of tolerable accuracy and neutrality, fact-finding in litigation has a rapidly diminishing marginal product from society's point of view.

Of course, the immediate parties to the litigation take a very different view of things. From the parties' perspective—assuming

[81] The basic bargain made by private litigants with the public is to exchange their adversarially contested case of facts and law, as an input to the law-declaring function, for a peaceful and neutral resolution of their particular dispute. Thus, the public interest in particular cases is slight, but so is the public subsidy to private litigation.

Taking the federal courts as an example (and using figures from the 1990 Annual Report of the Director of the Administrative Office of the United States Courts ("*AO Report*")), the total budget for the entire federal judiciary, excluding the Supreme Court, was approximately $1.6 billion in 1990. *AO Report,* at 39 (Table 26). Total civil cases filed in the federal courts that year were approximately 218,000. Id at 8 (Table 6). In addition, there were about 50,000 criminal cases filed, id at 10 (Table 8), and another 725,000 bankruptcy petitions (of which 55,000 led to adversarial proceedings), id at 240, 242 (Tables F-2 and F-8), plus some 450,000 minor matters (mostly relating to petty offense prosecutions and other criminal proceedings) handled by U.S. Magistrate Judges. Id at 25 (Table 15). Even if we ignore the Magistrate Judges' work, exclude nonadversarial bankruptcy matters, and weight civil and criminal cases equally (notwithstanding that criminal cases typically consume a good deal more judicial resources), the average per-case public subsidy is only $5,000. At that level, in all but the very simplest of federal civil cases, the average total public expenditure would fall well short of a modest fee that could be charged by a lawyer for preparing the plaintiff's initial complaint, which is only the first of many tasks required of the lawyers for each litigant. Clearly, public expenditure is dwarfed by private litigation costs, and, in exchange for the modest public expenditures, the courts receive all of the raw material for the entire edifice of federal case law.

Using the average per-case figure of $5,000, and excluding all criminal cases, and the approximately 67,000 civil cases in which the United States Government was a party, see id at 8 (Table 6), but including all adversarial bankruptcy matters, the total federal expenditure on private civil litigation was approximately $1 billion, which represents something less than *one one-thousandth* of total federal outlays. By way of comparison, in 1990 the Congress spent about $2.2 billion on itself, $5.1 billion to run the Environmental Protection Agency, $9.76 billion on agricultural subsidies, $24 billion on food stamps, and $38.75 billion on education, not to mention some of the larger programs. See US Bureau of the Census, *Statistical Abstract of the United States 1993* at 332-33 (Table No. 514).

On a broader basis, all public expenditures by all levels of government federal, state, and local on all aspects of law enforcement, criminal and civil, public and private, and including all police, sheriffs, prosecutors, public defenders, prisons, and courts, accounted for only about 4% of public spending in this country. See US Dep't of Justice, *Sourcebook of Criminal Justice Statistics-1993* at 2 (Table 1.1); 1993 *Economic Report of the President* 439 (Table B-77).

that they are not repeat litigants—the fact-finding process in a particular case may be the dominant feature of the adjudicative system. The American legal system's response to this divergence between social and private interest has been the tradition of party control and party presentation of evidence and argument, with the fact-finder playing essentially a passive role. In recent times, however, the tradition of adversary party control has come under increasing attack, through such mechanisms as "managerial" judging,[82] expanded disclosure requirements imposed upon litigants,[83] "public interest" duties imposed upon lawyers,[84] and unfavorable comparisons of the adversarial system with the "inquisitorial" system that prevails in civil law countries.[85] The *Frye* test and other mechanisms seeking to impose an "external" control on scientific

[82] See Judith A. Resnik, *Managerial Judges,* 96 Harv L Rev 374 (1982). In 1983, Rule 16 of the Federal Rules of Civil Procedure was amended extensively to promote such a "case management" role for the trial judge, which deviates substantially from the traditional pattern of judicial deference to party initiatives. See generally Arthur R. Miller, *The Adversary System: Dinosaur or Phoenix,* 69 Minn L Rev 1 (1984) (discussing the impact of reform proposals as modifying the traditionally passive role of the trial judge).

[83] In recent years, the adversarial character of the "discovery" process in federal civil cases has been subject to intense criticism. See, for example, Wayne Brazil, *The Adversary Character of Civil Discovery: A Critique and Proposals for Change,* 31 Vand L Rev 1295 (1978); William W. Schwarzer, *The Federal Rules, the Adversary Process, and Discovery Reform,* 50 U Pitt L Rev 703 (1989); William W. Schwarzer, *Slaying the Monsters of Cost and Delay: Would Disclosure Be More Effective Than Discovery?,* 74 Judicature 178 (1991). In 1993, Rule 26 of the Federal Rules of Civil Procedure was amended to add a new "disclosure" phase, in which litigants were required spontaneously to produce, inter alia, a copy or description of all documents "relevant to disputed facts alleged with particularity in the pleadings," and the names and addresses of all individuals "likely" to have information about such facts, in both instances without waiting for any request from the adversary. This amendment, however, was subject to a local "opt-out" power, and, within a year after its adoption, a majority of federal districts had "opted out" of the new rule. See Bruce H. Kobayashi, Jeffrey S. Parker, and Larry E. Ribstein, *The Process of Procedural Reform: Centralized Uniformity versus Local Experimentation* (GMU School of Law Working Paper, 1994).

[84] Rule 11 of the Federal Rules of Civil Procedure, which imposes sanctions—primarily on lawyers—for "frivolous" pleading, was amended in both 1983 and 1993, in both cases to expand the scope of its application, essentially on the rationale that lawyers have a duty to the courts and the public to screen their own clients' factual and legal contentions for objective "reasonableness." See Bruce H. Kobayashi and Jeffrey S. Parker, *No Armistice at 11: A Commentary on the Supreme Court's 1993 Amendment to Rule 11 of the Federal Rules of Civil Procedure,* 3 S Ct Econ Rev 93 (1994).

[85] See John H. Langbein, *The German Advantage in Civil Procedure,* 52 U Chi L Rev 823 (1985) ("Langbein, *German Advantage*"); Gordon Tullock, *Trials on Trial: The Pure Theory of Legal Procedure* (Columbia, 1980). And see the sources cited in note 69 above.

evidence—such as court-appointed experts[86] or official expert panels[87]—simply are variations on this same theme, which suggests that the adversary system needs protection from itself. Economics suggests that this entire critique is based upon a series of fallacies, all revolving around the central fallacy of the "free lunch."

Exploding the Fallacies. Scientific evidence provides a useful context for exploring whether the adversary system needs protection from itself, and if so, whether such protection is worth its costs.

Unlike the case of ordinary fact evidence, scientific "expert" evidence does not even arguably present a situation where an existing asset can be used by the adjudicative system for "free," without affecting its supply. For example, the paradigm of a fact witness is the disinterested bystander who accidentally observes the event in litigation. In that case, the witness is compelled to testify without remuneration on a "public duty" rationale.[88] The conventional wisdom wants to assume either that there has been no effect on behavior or on the production of information[89] or that an alternative

[86] See Tahirih V. Lee, *Court-Appointed Experts and Judicial Reluctance: A Proposal to Amend Rule 706 of the Federal Rules of Evidence,* 6 Yale L & Policy Rev 480 (1988). See also E. Donald Elliott, *Toward Incentive-Based Procedure: Three Approached for Regulating Scientific Evidence,* 69 BU L Rev 487 (1989); Langbein, *German Advantage* (cited in note 85).

[87] This type of proposal has been made for some years, in varying forms. One is a "science court"—essentially, a separate governmental agency to "screen" scientific developments for courtroom use. See Arthur Kantrowitz, *Controlling Technology Democratically,* 63 Am Sci 505 (1975); James A. Martin, *The Proposed "Science Court,"* 75 Mich L Rev 1058 (1977). More recently, essentially the same proposal has resurfaced in suggestions for the use of "expert consensus groups," to be staffed or assembled by governmental entities such as the National Academy of Sciences or the National Institutes of Health. See Kenneth R. Foster, David E. Bernstein, and Peter W. Huber, eds, *Phantom Risk: Scientific Inference and the Law* 438-40 (MIT, 1993) ("Foster, Bernstein & Huber, *Phantom Risk*").

[88] As noted above (see notes 23-24 and accompanying text), early common law imposed no compulsion to testify, even after the use of witnesses was permitted. However, beginning in the sixteenth century, the "rule of compulsion" appeared—primarily through legislation designed to close an important gap in powers between the competing systems of "law" and "equity" courts and the "public duty" rationale was developed as a justification for the change. See 8 *Wigmore on Evidence* §§ 2190, 2192 (cited in note 23).

[89] In economics, this form of the "free lunch" fallacy often operates under the terminology of "economic rent" and "quasi-rent." For the conventional economic definitions, see Armen A. Alchian, "Rent," in Eatwell, Milgate & Newman, 4 *The New Palgrave* at 141 (cited in note 8). The basic notion is that a rent or quasi-rent is earned when the supply of a resource is insensitive to the price paid. Thus, "fact" testimony is conceived as representing information that would have been acquired regardless of the needs of litigation, and therefore any payment for its use would be a "rent." The concept degenerates into the "free lunch" fallacy when it is used as a

system of compensation for fact witnesses would cause difficult hold-out problems or reduce the reliability of factual inputs to litigation. Although each of those points is debatable even in the fact-witness context, they are certainly not applicable to scientific expert evidence. By definition, an expert witness lacks first-hand knowledge of the facts in litigation, is qualified to testify only by specialized training or experience, and may not be compelled to testify without remuneration.[90]

Therefore, even if the expert's testimony is drawn entirely from her or his off-the-cuff reactions, without further analysis or investigation, it may not be confiscated and therefore will be sold for an explicit price. Given that the expert's information is a valuable asset—often accumulated through a lifetime of study and experience—then we should not be surprised to find that the content of the expert's opinions will be affected by their value in the litigation "market." This is really all that is meant by the popular critique of "junk science" in the courtroom.

To be sure, there are many other influences on the content of experts' opinions, including the inherent discipline of the expert's field, the effects of peer review and professional reputation, other opportunities for teaching and research income, and the like. As is discussed below, not all of these are entirely neutral for litigation purposes, but the immediate point is that, all other things equal, the marketability of the expert's opinions is influenced by the needs of litigation and by admissibility standards. To take a current example, consider whether there is any doubt whatsoever that the incomes of DNA identification experts would be lower if such tests were universally inadmissible into evidence.

Now consider the effect of an admissibility test like the *Frye* standard of "general acceptance." Under this rule the income potential of the expert's opinions in litigation becomes partially a function of their "acceptability" to the expert's peers. In that situation, the expert has two choices. The expert can adopt "acceptable" opinions. Or, that expert can join with other experts in a mutually self-supporting network of "acceptability," optimally of

justification for governmental confiscation of the resource, on the ground that any payment would be a "social loss" because the resource will exist ex ante regardless of the ex post confiscation. That is unlikely to be true in general, or as to factual testimony in particular. In the case of expert testimony, even the conventional view does not assume it to be a "rent" because obviously there would be fewer (or less expert) experts if the "expertise" were subject to confiscation by the courts.

[90] Thus, under current Rule 706 of the Federal Rules of Evidence, even court-appointed experts are entitled to compensation, and may not be appointed "unless the witness consents to act." Fed R Evid 706.

limited size in order to reduce organizational and coordination costs. This amounts to the same thing unless the expert happens to locate a support network that spontaneously comes to the same view costlessly. In either case, the content of the marketed opinions is likely to have been influenced by the admissibility standard.

Because the expert's options under *Frye* increase the cost of marketing expert opinion, the likely effect of *Frye* was to reduce both the volume and the diversity of the expert opinions reaching adjudicative fact-finders. Although some commentators appear to argue otherwise,[91] this result seems at best ambiguous from the perspective of social policy. Even if we assume that there is some "truth" out there to be discovered, both science and economics would suggest that, all other things being equal, the *Frye* standard would *reduce* the likelihood of that "truth" reaching the courtroom, by reducing the volume and diversity of opinions expressed in the market for expert testimony. Certainly, the history of scientific thought provides no indication that the type of group-think promoted by *Frye* optimizes the potential for discovering "truth."[92]

Instead, the *Frye* test seems to be predicated on the "free lunch" fallacy, combined with doubts about the ability of the adversary system to protect itself. The "free lunch" apparently was supposed to have been supplied by the scientific community at large, which was expected to police "unacceptable" opinion by rebutting the testifying experts' views. The problem with this mechanism is that the scientific community had no marginal incentive to do so. To the contrary, the incentives provided by *Frye* were for the scientific community to segment itself into testifying and non-testifying specialists, and, within testifying specialists, into ever-smaller "general acceptance" groups. For the non-testifying scientist, there was little or no payoff to debunking "unacceptable" opinions expressed in the courtroom, and the entire ethic of open scientific inquiry worked against that outcome. And once a scientist became a testifier, even in the "debunking" mode, he or she inevitably became subject to the *Frye* influences on marginal income. Ultimately, the *Frye* test relied for its discipline on altruism, in that it required the consistent performance of "public service" to the litigation system without private reward and possibly at considerable cost. Expecting this actually to happen is yet another manifestation of the "free lunch" fallacy.

[91] See Huber, *Galileo's Revenge* at 204 (cited in note 5).

[92] See generally, for example, Thomas S. Kuhn, *The Structure of Scientific Revolutions* (U Chicago, 2d ed 1970); F.A. Hayek, *The Counter-Revolution of Science: Studies on the Abuse of Reason* (Liberty Press, 2d ed 1979); Robert Scott Root-Bernstein, *Discovering* (Harvard, 1989).

Why was there ever any need for an "external" standard of any kind? The argument for an external standard was apparently based on the view that fact-finders are easily misled by expert opinion.[93] But what has never been clear in this critique is why the adversary system is inadequate to cope with that danger.

Property Rights in the Adversarial System. The fear that fact-finders are easily misled by expert opinion seems to overlook the role of the adverse party in the adjudicative system. The adversary may counter expert testimony through a variety of means—cross-examination and impeachment of the expert, argument, rebuttal evidence that undermines the factual basis for the expert's assumptions, and, most obviously, by hiring its own expert to give rebuttal expert testimony. Aside from *Frye*-like constraints on admissible opinion, the law of evidence generally places very few limitations on the rebuttal mechanisms available to the adversary. Here as elsewhere, the law of evidence is more enabling than prohibitive in nature: so long as the minimal standard of relevance is satisfied, and the evidence is cast in acceptable form, the adversary's options are very broad. Moreover, the basic norm observed in trials is to afford the adversary at least as much of the fact-finder's time and attention as the proponent of expert testimony is afforded.

In its traditional and still predominant form, the adversarial system also provides a symmetry of incentives to invest in presentation, through a symmetry in the stakes of the litigation, secured by a system of private "property rights" in litigation.[94] The paradigm of litigation is a private civil action for damages, in which the stake is simply a transfer payment from the defendant to the plaintiff, contingent upon the outcome of the litigation. Because the stakes are the same from each side's point of view, both sides—at least under the American rule that litigants bear their own costs—have equivalent private incentives to invest in their presentations of evidence and argument. If the plaintiff wins, then the plaintiff has a private property right to collect the judgment from the defendant, and only the defendant. If the defendant prevails, then the defendant has a private property right to protection from further litigation of the same claim by the same plaintiff, and only by the same

[93] See, for example, *United States v Baller*, 519 F 2d 463, 466 (4th Cir 1975) ("[N]ot every ostensibly scientific technique should be recognized as the basis for expert testimony. Because of its apparent objectivity, an opinion that claims a scientific basis is apt to carry undue weight with the trier of fact.").

[94] I use the term "property right" here in the conventional law-and-economics sense of an entitlement exercisable solely at the option of its owner, which has the characteristic of fully internalizing to its owner the consequences of its exercise.

plaintiff. In this way, the private costs and benefits of the litigation are fully internalized to the immediate parties. No one else can gain or lose by the factual outcome of the case.

In this basic model of litigation, there is no reason to doubt the efficacy of the adversarial system for dealing with any problems of "misleading" expert testimony. If one side chooses to retain an expert and bear that cost, then presumably it does so because it believes, on the basis of its private self-interest, that doing so will improve its chances of success on the merits. Similarly, if the adverse party chooses not to rebut even "misleading" expert testimony, presumably that decision reflects its decision that its private expenditures on litigation are better directed elsewhere.[95]

From a social point of view, we have no reason to second-guess the parties' decisions in this regard. Under the existing rules of procedure, parties are permitted, and generally are encouraged, to stipulate to a resolution—perhaps even a "misleading" one—of a factual issue that otherwise would be the subject of expert testimony. Indeed they could stipulate away the entire case by settlement, or stipulate to all of the facts and present the legal issues alone, because there is little social interest in the factual outcome of a particular case. To be sure, these decisions are likely to be affected by the applicable rules of substantive law and evidentiary standards. But within those constraints, the parties' decisions will reflect their private costs and benefits, including the costs and benefits of "misleading" expert testimony. In the absence of any other social interest in the particular outcome, the parties' decisions also would be efficient from a social point of view.

Given these conditions, it is difficult to understand quite what is meant by the criticism that expert testimony is sometimes "mis-

[95] Setting aside irrational behaviors or unusual risk preferences, this analysis is unaffected by the relative wealth of the parties. In the absence of external effects, even a "rich" party would be foolish indeed to invest beyond the stakes in the litigation. Any "rich" party that did so would find itself a regular target of litigation, which eventually would solve its "richness" problem. The "poor" party, if it is the plaintiff, simply faces the need to finance litigation costs in order to realize on its asset. The market has provided a ready mechanism to accomplish this function—and to minimize the effect of risk aversion—through the contingent fee, which regularly finances large volumes of litigation. If the "poor" litigant is the defendant, then that problem also is self-correcting: if the defendant is "poor" enough, then its insolvency ultimately will deter the action or defeat the result by preventing collection of the judgment, while if the defendant is not that "poor," then its incentives to invest are the same as if it were "rich." It is only in this last case of the marginally solvent defendant that risk aversion may have some effect, which is why people buy liability insurance that not only indemnifies them but also imposes a duty to defend upon the insurer.

leading" to fact finders. If it is "misleading" because fact-finders will place undue weight on expert testimony because of the expert's qualifications, then that advantage to the proponent is offset by the cost of purchasing the expert's testimony in the marketplace. And the marketplace will also provide the opponent with the opportunity to purchase rebuttal expert testimony. If expert testimony is somehow inherently "misleading," then we must ask whether that factor introduces systematic bias into the fact-finding system. If all expert testimony is "misleading," then the effect is simply to degrade the accuracy of the fact-finding system symmetrically, which will most affect the immediate parties. If not systematically biased, then both sides of the litigation will be spending more and getting less, which, with the internalization of costs and benefits, eventually will reduce the demand for expert testimony.

What is clear, however, is that a standard like *Frye* does not mitigate this type of problem, and instead is likely to make the problem worse, by disrupting the assignment of property rights to the parties in litigation and thereby introducing systematic bias. The idea of *Frye* was to limit expert testimony to "generally accepted" opinions. As noted above, the increased costs of arranging general acceptance raised the overall cost of expert testimony. However, that cost could be amortized over multiple litigations, and therefore the litigant relying on generally accepted opinion was likely to face an incremental cost advantage. But what about the litigant whose case turned on a point of expert opinion for which there was not yet a "general acceptance" group? That litigant faced a marginally higher cost of obtaining expert testimony, as it now had to organize (or join with other litigants to organize) its own "general acceptance" group. By interposing the external standard of "general acceptance," the *Frye* test externalized some of the costs and benefits of evidentiary presentation beyond the immediate parties to the litigation.

In law and economics, we often speak of legal rules as "internalizing externalities." *Frye* does exactly the opposite—it "externalized" what previously was an "internality." Furthermore, *Frye*'s externalization introduced a systematic bias against unconventional expert opinion testimony, by imposing higher costs on litigants who sought to rely upon such testimony. In some sense, this was the very purpose of the *Frye* test—to make unorthodox expert testimony more costly, if not altogether impossible.[96]

[96] Froeb and Kobayashi show that adversarial reporting of expert opinion does not dominate a neutral and "perfect" court-appointed expert, even when the fact-finder is "naïve" (modeled as "splitting the difference" between the adversarial experts) where the underlying distribution of opinion and the parties' costs of taking "draws" (selecting expert opinions) are symmetric. Froeb & Kobayashi, *Competition* (cited in

While the motivation—and possibly the effect—of *Frye* may have been to reduce litigants' aggregate expenditures on expert testimony, its principal consequence was to re-shape the incentives of both parties and experts toward the objective of organizing for "general acceptance." Instead of merely contracting with a single expert whose opinions supported a litigant's position in a particular case, parties now had to take account of a secondary market in "general acceptability" that ranged far beyond the needs of the particular litigation. With *Frye,* litigants (and expert witnesses) now had to solve a collective action problem in addition to the problems of their own case.

Simply in terms of transaction-cost economics, *Frye* would be inefficient even if it had no biasing effect. By replacing a straightforward system of internalized costs and benefits with a collective action problem, *Frye* raises the transaction costs of obtaining expert testimony without any apparent benefit, as the social interest in the factual outcome of the litigation is unchanged. Thus, *Frye* appears to be no better than a dissipated excise tax on expert testimony, and it could be worse. In terms of the relatively minimal social interest in factual accuracy on the margin, *Frye* is not beneficial unless orthodoxy has a strong positive correlation with accuracy *and* accuracy otherwise threatens to fall below an acceptable range from the social perspective. *Frye* is detrimental to the extent that useful expert opinion has been priced out of litigation by the costs of organizing to obtain "general acceptance" for useful opinions.[97]

But the more profound effects of *Frye* follow from its external biasing effect. From this perspective, *Frye* is more like a progressive tax on "unaccepted" expert testimony, and, worse yet, the tax is at least partially recoverable by the purveyors of "accepted" expert

note 10). They model *Frye* as truncating the tails of the sampling distribution symmetrically, and then show it has no advantage over unrestricted adversarial presentation. Id at 22-24. They refer only in passing to the public agency cost problem, and they suppress public choice considerations. Id at 22 n 34.

The argument here suggests that *Frye* is likely to be somewhat worse than the Froeb-Kobayashi results. In terms of the Froeb-Kobayashi model, my argument suggests that *Frye*'s external effect: (1) raises both sides' costs of taking "draws" from a base case without either the *Frye* or *Daubert* rules; and (2) introduces an asymmetry in the cost of taking draws, or, what amounts to the same thing, an asymmetrical truncation of the sampling distribution, that works against the litigant with a demand for the non-"consensus" opinion. In addition, the following Section B considers the public choice and public agency problems more explicitly.

[97] Thus, *Frye* operated somewhat like a legal rule that imposes a minimum firm size as a requirement for a "license" to engage in a particular line of business. While there will still be competition among the "licensed" firms, there is an efficiency loss to the extent that the minimum "legal" firm size excludes smaller firms who could participate at lower costs.

testimony. The incentives created by this structure lead to rent-seeking behaviors very similar to those observed in lobbying for legislation or other governmental action.

B. Public Choice and Public Agency Cost

By imposing an external standard of acceptability as the threshold to the admissibility of scientific evidence, *Frye* and similar concepts create a scenario familiar in public-choice economics, which is concerned with the influence of private interests on governmental action, classically legislation and more recently administrative actions such as licensing.[98] In essence, *Frye* created an opportunity for rent-seeking behavior by non-party interest groups in litigation that is analogous to the opportunities presented by legislation or licensing.[99] Moreover, several of the suggested alternatives to *Frye* and *Daubert*—such as court-appointed experts or a government-sponsored expert "science court"—would make that same problem worse, by adding the self-interest of government officials to the private interests involved. All of these devices share the common theme of granting external or public agents more control over the litigants' factual presentation, thereby diluting the system of private property rights in litigative fact-finding. Given the minimal social interest in the particular factual outcome of the litigants' case, this is likely to have a detrimental effect from a social perspective.

Traditionally, adjudication has been the most insulated of governmental actions from the influences of private interest groups. The mechanisms for insulating adjudication have included unelected judges, limits on adjudicative jurisdiction, and the system of private property rights in litigation discussed above.[100] Ideally, the

[98] For a general (and somewhat critical) introduction to public choice, see Daniel A. Farber and Philip P. Frickey, *Law and Public Choice* (U Chicago, 1991). A more technical survey of the public choice literature is Dennis C. Mueller, *Public Choice II* (Cambridge U, 1989) ("Mueller, *Public Choice II*").

[99] "Rent seeking" refers to activity that aims to secure a monopoly rent (a supracompetitive return) through favorable government action, such as a tariff against competing goods. See, for example, Gordon Tullock, *The Welfare Cost of Tariffs, Monopolies, and Theft,* 5 Western Econ J 224 (1967). Tullock's paper was the first general discussion of the activity in the modern era, although the term "rent seeking" was not used until Anne O. Krueger, *The Political Economy of the Rent-Seeking Society,* 64 Am Econ Rev 291 (June 1974). The literature through the late 1980s is summarized in Chapter 13 of Mueller, *Public Choice II* at 229-46 (cited in note 98).

[100] Of course, law declaring was a traditional exception to this structure, on the rationale that outside persons or groups—or society at large—may be affected by the legal rule declared in a particular case, and therefore legitimately could be heard as amici curiae or the like, subject to the limitations on ex parte contacts and the

full internalization of the costs and benefits of fact-finding in litigation to the immediate parties minimizes the influence of outside interest groups by eliminating any prospect of gain or loss to those groups from the outcome. By deviating from that model of full internalization, the *Frye* test inevitably creates incentives for non-parties to influence the factual presentation in their own self-interest, which is unlikely to be perfectly correlated with either the immediate parties' interests or society's interest in resolving the parties' dispute on a neutral and unbiased basis.

Let us explore the implications by taking a hypothetical example based in the surroundings of the *Daubert* decision. As litigated in the lower courts under the *Frye* rule, the case had focused on such things as whether animal studies or "reanalyses" of epidemiological data were "generally accepted" and therefore would be admissible. This was critical in the case because this disputed evidence was apparently the only evidence supporting the plaintiffs' claims that Merrell Dow's drug Bendectin caused birth defects in their children. Quite aside from the resources devoted by the immediate parties to these preliminary questions, notice how a number of non-parties may now have some stake in the outcome.

By definition, "general acceptance" involves some multiplicity of actors: some group of scientists or experts has to "accept" the concept involved, say "reanalysis."[101] Now we have the possibility of an "American Reanalysis Association" entering the picture. Its members may have a variety of motivations: they may wish to publish without doing original research, which requires more knowledge, creativity, and resources; they may be more focused on a particular subject, such as drug-induced birth defects, and they may believe that "reanalysis" is the key to holding the pharmaceutical companies to account; more simply, they may dislike pharmaceutical companies; or they may be interested in future work as a "reanalysis" expert, in litigation or otherwise, and obviously the "acceptability" of reanalysis affects their prospective income. Only some of these interests are in any way related to whether Bendectin caused the birth defects in the *Daubert* plaintiffs' children; some of them are entirely unrelated. And yet, they all give these various actors at least some interest in joining the

safeguard of searching appellate review on the law. Even so, the traditional doctrine of precedent limited the external effects of case law decisions, by permitting future litigants and courts to distinguish prior cases on their facts.

[101] "Reanalysis," also known as "meta-analysis," involves the re-grouping of data from multiple prior empirical studies. It has been the subject of much debate in the scientific and popular literature. See *Research News: Meta-Analysis in the Breach,* 249 Science 476 (1990).

"American Reanalysis Association," thereby giving "acceptability" to the opinions of the experts on which the *Daubert* plaintiffs sought to rely, and in that way externally assisting the plaintiffs' case.

More broadly, consider the plaintiffs' bar, which has some interest in reducing its costs of achieving plaintiffs' verdicts generally. If "reanalysis" helps to reduce that cost, the plaintiffs' bar as a group now has an incentive in invest in its promotion, perhaps by making charitable contributions to the non-profit "American Reanalysis Association" in order to subsidize its organizational costs.[102] That investment can be recovered over a wide range of future cases utilizing "reanalysis," whether or not those cases have anything to do with Bendectin or any drug-induced injury. As the plaintiffs' bar in the aggregate represents millions of potential plaintiffs, the effects could be quite profound.

All of the same incentives also exist on the defense side of the case. As a repeat litigant, a firm like Merrell Dow already has incentives that range beyond the *Daubert* case itself. To the extent that the acceptability of "reanalysis" increases its prospects of losing any type of case—not necessarily the *Daubert* case or any case involving Bendectin—then Merrell Dow has an incentive to invest in assuring that the technique is not "generally accepted."[103] That incentive is to some extent shared by other pharmaceutical firms, and perhaps more broadly by all manufacturers subject to product liability exposure, or by all business firms beset by the plaintiffs' bar. Consequently, the defense side may make generous contributions to a competing "American Original Research Association," populated by scientists who wish to preserve the brand name value of their product against the "reanalysts." They may value their product for its use in producing litigation or research income, or because they are scientific purists, or because they like drug companies, or for any number of other

[102] Lawyers' self-interest is the principal argument raised by Huber in *Galileo's Revenge* (cited in note 5), although Huber unaccountably fails to consider the interest-group potential of the *Frye* standard. In a post-*Daubert* article, Lester Brickman suggests that *Daubert* may not be adequate "to counter the inherent incentive structure underlying the expert witness industry," considering the interests of both lawyers and expert witnesses. Lester Brickman, *On the Relevance of the Admissibility of Scientific Evidence: Tort System Outcomes Are Principally Determined by Lawyers' Rates of Return,* 15 Cardozo L Rev 1755 (1994) ("Brickman, *On the Relevance*").

[103] This would be true even without an external preclusive effect. It is all the more true when considering the modern law of "offensive" collateral estoppel, under which Merrell Dow faces the very real prospect of being precluded, by one loss, from defending in many future cases. See Part IV.C below.

reasons.[104] Here again, very few of these motivations bear any relation to the particular matter at issue in *Daubert.* But they will influence the costs of presenting expert testimony in that case, whether intended to do so or not.

This example is not meant to suggest that there is anything sinister—or necessarily inefficient—in all of the interest group activity.[105] People have interests, and they have every right to join together voluntarily to promote those interests. Nor is there a fundamental economic objection to private organization of this type. To the contrary, private organization to advance common interests can be economically beneficial, so long as it is driven by market forces. Much of the same sort of interest group activity would exist with or without *Frye,* and we should not expect it to disappear with *Frye*'s demise.

What makes the marginal effect of *Frye* pernicious, as in the case of legislation or licensing, is the addition of governmental sanction to the private organization. In effect, *Frye* gives quasi-official status to the private interest groups, by allowing them—rather than the litigation process—to determine the admissibility of scientific evidence. Although the effect is not as powerful as the government-sanctioned monopoly conferred by licensing, it still requires the litigant to buy a "ticket" for the admissibility of its evidence, on pain of exclusion by governmental action for non-compliance. Furthermore, the ticket-purchasing process is less visible and less subject to public scrutiny and debate than overt governmental licensing, simply because it is private. As a result, and given the incentives of the interest groups that are likely to be in play, the price of admission may well be reflected in the content of the opinions expressed. Thus, the marginal consequences of the *Frye* standard are not merely to raise the cost and reduce the supply of expert testimony, but also to bias its content toward what is "popular" with the various interest groups that influence "general accep-

[104] Of course, the defense bar also has group interests, but they appear to be somewhat more complex than the plaintiffs' bar, as the defense bar is not simply interested in minimizing their clients' overall liability costs.

[105] Nor is there anything hypothetical about the effect, though my example uses hypothetical interest group names. When *Daubert* reached the Supreme Court, some two dozen amici briefs were filed. A partial listing of the amici includes: Association of Trial Lawyers of America; American Society of Law, Medicine and Ethics (an "organization of scientists, lawyers, and others with expertise on the use of scientific information in legal proceedings"); American College of Legal Medicine; Defense Research Institute; New England Journal of Medicine; American Medical Association (with 16 related groups); and the National Association of Manufacturers.

tance."[106] This will not necessarily bear any relation to anyone's idea of "truth,"[107] and will almost certainly be influenced by a far broader agenda than the particular issue in litigation.

Nor does substituting governmental licensors for private interest groups solve the problem. In some ways, it makes the situation worse. This is the more conventional public-choice problem: it eliminates the prospect of competition among private ticket-sellers, in exchange for presumably enhanced public scrutiny of the governmental monopoly licensing board. Particularly in the case of expert and scientific opinion—which by definition is not well-understood by the public at large—that tradeoff is unlikely to be favorable. The interest groups will still have the most influence, and now the governmental officials' personal interests also would come into play. The most likely form that such a proposal would take would be something like "expert panels" or a "science court" funded by the federal government, with members appointed for fixed terms, so as to avoid "political" influences. The individuals making up these panels are still people, with the same needs, hopes, and faults as the rest of us. They would need to earn a living, either during their service, or afterward, or both. Presumably, they would have to be established experts in their fields, which is very likely to mean that they already had an intellectual and perhaps a financial commitment to a certain point of view. "Political" influences

[106] This effect of the *Frye* standard did not go unnoticed by the courts and commentators. In *United States v Williams,* 583 F2d 1194, 1198 (2d Cir 1978), the court observed that "whatever the scientific 'voting' pattern may be, the courts cannot in any event surrender to scientists the responsibility for determining the reliability of that evidence." See also David L. Faigman, Elise Porter, and Michael J. Saks, *Check Your Crystal Ball at the Courthouse Door, Please: Exploring the Past, Understanding the Present, and Worrying about the Future of Scientific Evidence,* 15 Cardozo L Rev 1799, 1805-09 (1994).

[107] Some of the criticism of the *Frye* standard and its variants has been placed explicitly on the interest-group basis:

> [D]owsers, who use divining rods to locate water or minerals underground, have a professional organization, the American Society of Dowsers, which has 68 chapters and holds an annual conference that, in 1989, lasted five days. A credentialed dowser proffered as an expert witness could therefore probably produce peer support for his opinions from his professional "community."

Brian Stuart Koukoutchos, *Solomon Meets Galileo (and Isn't Quite Sure What to Do with Him),* 15 Cardozo L Rev 2237, 2242 n 33 (1994). Much of the critique of "junk science" by Huber in *Galileo's Revenge* (cited in note 5) is predicated on the view of lawyers as a rent-seeking interest group. But both that work and Foster, Bernstein, & Huber's *Phantom Risk* (cited in note 87) inexplicably suggest a return to *Frye* and reliance on "professional standards" promulgated by (non-hypothetical) groups such as the National Academy of Forensic Engineers and the American Academy of Forensic Scientists. See id at 438.

would enter if they had aspirations for future appointments. And, of course, the government as an institution has its own interests that are not necessarily aligned with a broader concept of social welfare.

If all of this sounds familiar, that is because it is: this structure essentially is the model of the "expert" and "independent" administrative agency that has become a fixture of modern government over the past several decades. Our accumulated experience with that mechanism could hardly be characterized as positive in general,[108] and it seems particularly inappropriate to the governance of expert scientific testimony in courts. As applied in the federal courts, it would further undermine the independence of the judiciary, and create very difficult problems of cross-review between the courts and the "expert" panels, making it even less likely that the panels would be responsive to public control. In the end, we might even end up with the Congress—certainly no authority on science, and hardly a model of probity on any topic—voting on the "validity" of scientific opinions.[109] If also applied by the federal government to the states, it would have some of the same effects at the state level, and further erode the balance of federal and state power. And as applied in the many cases where the government is a party, such as criminal prosecutions, the absurd result is that the government decides on the admissibility of its own expert evidence. That problem is severe enough under our current system. It would bid fair to become intolerable with an "independent" expert-testimony agency.

Although governmental expert panels are likely to be somewhat worse than *Frye,* they share the same basic error of injecting external stakes into litigation that are out of proportion to the social interest, if any, in the fact-finding outcome of a particular case, while at the same time introducing the more serious problem of systematic bias in fact-finding. To return to the example based on *Daubert,* society at large has only a minimal interest in whether the facts in that particular case are found correctly, but it has a

[108] See, for example, Mueller, *Public Choice II* ch 14, at 247-73 (cited in note 98); Richard A. Posner, *The Behavior of Administrative Agencies,* 1 J Legal Stud 305 (1972).

[109] The closest analogy in the existing edifice of federal agencies may be the United States Sentencing Commission, which by law is "an independent commission in the judicial branch." 28 USC § 991(a) (1988). Although it is "in" the judicial branch, its actions—primarily the promulgation of sentencing guidelines governing the federal courts—are not subject to direct review by the courts. See 28 USC § 994(x) (1988) (applying the notice-and-comment procedures of the Administrative Procedure Act, but not the judicial review provisions). But the Commission's actions can be overruled by Act of Congress. See 28 USC §§ 994(p) (1988).

much more important interest in assuring that errors are unbiased. Suppose that "reanalysis" does in fact lead to more accurate determinations of medical causation on some objective basis. But then also suppose—as apparently was the case in the lower courts in *Daubert*—that the coordination costs imposed by the *Frye* standard were prohibitive of all plaintiffs' ability to meet the "general acceptance" criterion. Now the effect of *Frye* is to introduce systematic bias into the fact-finding process because no plaintiff can reach the jury with "reanalysis" evidence. This applies not only in *Daubert* itself but in all cases of ambiguous medical causation.

From the public-choice perspective, *Daubert* is an improvement over *Frye* because *Daubert* mutes the incentives for private organization around the admissibility standard by reducing the returns to successful organization. Although the *Daubert* majority substituted a test of something like "scientific method," that test is less subject to public-choice style manipulation simply because it reduces the admission "price" and increases competition among ticket-sellers, who now potentially include virtually any scientist in any field. Groups such as the hypothetical American Reanalysis Association and the American Original Research Association might still be organized to market their products, in litigation and otherwise, but the governmentally sanctioned rents that they can earn are now smaller. It still might be possible to organize an American Scientific Method Association—or adapt an existing association to that end—but the cost of doing so would be very high because, in order to earn substantial returns, it would be necessary to organize a much larger proportion of the scientific community into a single cartel.[110] From this point of view, the somewhat vague and diffuse nature of *Daubert*'s admissibility test—criticized on that basis by some legal commentators[111]—is a policy virtue, as it further raises the cost of successful cartelization.

Of course, *Daubert* does still leave the trial court judge in the somewhat vaguely defined "gatekeeping" role, and judges are people too. However, here the judge's lack of "expert" knowledge seems to be a virtue rather than a vice because it makes it less likely that enough judges will know enough about various scientific

[110] Of course, the cost may not be prohibitively high if the federal government steps in and appoints, say, the National Academy of Sciences, as the ultimate arbiter of "scientific method."

[111] See, for example, Bert Black, Francisco J. Ayala and Carol Saffran-Brinks, *Science and the Law in the Wake of Daubert: A New Search for Scientific Knowledge,* 72 Tex L Rev 715, 801 (1994); Margaret G. Farrell, *Daubert v. Merrell Dow Pharmaceuticals, Inc.: Epistemology and Legal Process,* 15 Cardozo L Rev 2183 (1994).

fields to be biased in a systematic way.[112] Moreover, outside of criminal prosecutions, it seems unlikely that the judiciary as a whole will be systematically biased for or against any particular scientific theories or opinions. Normal human curiosity, as well as trial judges' aversion to reversal, may suggest a bias toward admissibility in all cases, but if there is to be any bias, that one probably is the least objectionable. In any case, the admissibility decisions of the trial court judges—unlike the interest groups and probably unlike the "expert panels"—are subject to appellate review, and do not present fundamentally different concerns from the myriad other rulings made at trial.

C. Stakes, Symmetry, and External Effects

So far, the analysis has focused on the basic model of private litigation involving symmetrical stakes and no external effects of the fact-finding outcome. What about variations from that model?

The important variations are two: (1) litigation to which the government is a party; and (2) external preclusive effects through nonmutual collateral estoppel. Both cases involve asymmetrical stakes. In the government case, this is caused by the detachment of governmental agents' incentives from the stakes of a particular case. In the preclusion case, it is caused by the "capitalization" effect of the abandonment in many jurisdictions of the traditional rule of "mutuality" of collateral estoppel, which was one of the legal mechanisms assuring the internalization of litigation fact-finding results.[113]

[112] Interest groups will remain active, however, and judges should be vigilant against more subtle forms of interest group influence. The appearance of the Federal Judicial Center's *Reference Manual on Scientific Evidence* in late 1994 is a somewhat troubling signal. This document includes "Reference Guides" on each of several scientific fields, written with private support to the authors and reviewers. Id at vii. The lists of authors and reviewers includes a number of individuals who are not disinterested observers, and the *Manual* provocatively discloses that "[t]he names of several reviewers have been omitted from the list at their request." Id at 623. The danger is that this *Manual* will become a sort of "official" orthodoxy about scientific matters—far more rigid and monolithic than anything *Frye* could have produced—and that its contents could be influenced by private interests. In any event, it gives us a taste of what a federal "science court" might involve.

[113] Under the traditional rule of mutuality, a prior judgment could not be utilized for factually preclusive effects unless the party seeking to use the judgment in its favor would have been bound by an adverse determination in the prior action. This usually meant that the party seeking to use the judgment was a party or in "privity" with a party (a transactional successor to that party's property right) to the litigation leading to the prior judgment. See *Bigelow v Old Dominion Copper Mining & Smelting Co.*, 225 US 111 (1912). This doctrine therefore was a very explicit manifestation

In these and other cases of asymmetry in stakes, one side has the incentive to "outspend" the other, on expert evidence as well as other litigation expenditures, because one side has (or acts as if it has) more to gain or lose than the other. To the extent that litigation expenditures influence the factual outcome, asymmetry can bias fact-finding. The shift from *Frye* to *Daubert* as a standard for the admissibility of scientific evidence does not redress these asymmetries. However, here again *Daubert* is something of an improvement over *Frye,* because the *Frye* test has a tendency to exacerbate the biasing effect of asymmetrical stakes.

The non-mutual estoppel case illustrates the effect most clearly. Returning to the example of the *Daubert* facts, Merrell Dow is in the position of the repeat litigant with more to lose (from non-mutual collateral estoppel) than the plaintiffs have to gain. Under the rules of collateral estoppel now prevailing in most jurisdictions, Merrell Dow faces the prospect of being precluded from offering a defense on at least some issues in future cases brought by similarly-situated plaintiffs by a loss in the first case. In contrast, future plaintiffs' cases would be unaffected by a Merrell Dow victory in the first case—they would be free to relitigate all issues.[114] For a repeat litigant like Merrell Dow, the simple summary of the law is "if you win one, you win one; while if you lose one, you lose them all" (at least as to certain issues that are likely to be the same among the cases, such as basic negligence or product liability determinations). Thus, the modern rules of non-mutual collateral estoppel create an asymmetry of stakes through external preclusive effects on one side only.

Given these incentives, Merrell Dow is likely to invest more in defending each case than any one plaintiff invests in prosecuting it,

of the policy of internalizing the costs *and* benefits of adjudicative fact-finding to the immediate parties. Given that the vastly predominant form of stake was a cash transfer payment, which was embedded in remedial law's reluctance to grant relief other than in the form of monetary damages, the mutuality rule also promoted symmetry of stakes. Under the mutuality rule, the only "capitalization" effect of present fact-finding on future litigation was also between the immediate parties, and generally also symmetrical.

[114] For a general summary of current collateral estoppel rules, see James, Hazard, & Leubsdorf, *Civil Procedure* ch 11 (cited in note 15). Non-mutual estoppel can create asymmetric stakes for repeat litigants who are either plaintiffs, which is referred to as "defensive" use, or defendants, which is referred to as "offensive" use. See *Blonder-Tongue Laboratories v University of Illinois Foundation,* 402 US 313 (1971) ("defensive" use against a patent holder-plaintiff who had lost a prior case on patent validity); *Parklane Hosiery Co. v Shore,* 439 US 322 (1979) ("offensive" use against a defendant who had lost a prior securities fraud case against the government, applied in favor of a private plaintiff).

at least in the early cases.[115] Of course, potential plaintiffs as a group could counter that effect by joining together to pool resources, but, in order to do so, plaintiffs would have to solve a collective action problem. Not only do the potential plaintiffs face positive costs of locating each other and organizing themselves, but also each plaintiff has the incentive to wait for another plaintiff to sue and then "free ride" on a judgment against Merrell Dow. Furthermore, and similarly to the interest-group situation generally, not all plaintiffs will have exactly identical interests.

Now add the *Frye* standard to this scenario. As discussed above, *Frye* itself creates a collective-action problem. But it is a somewhat different problem, involving a wider range of interests and actors, than would be presented by considering only the common interests of potential plaintiffs against Merrell Dow in Bendectin cases. Thus, on the plaintiffs' side of multiple litigation with collateral estoppel potential, *Frye* makes an existing collective-action problem even more complex. It also will be more costly unless there are positive economies of combination, which does not seem probable, though perhaps it is possible. On the defense side, *Frye* increases the return to investing on the basis of external effects, as it creates another line of defense for Merrell Dow against all potential plaintiffs. But the marginal costs of defense investment in organizing around the *Frye* standard may be relatively smaller than for the plaintiffs, especially if Merrell Dow by itself faces enough litigation to justify unilateral action to organize its own "general acceptance" group.

On both sides of multiple litigation with collateral estoppel potential—as in the general case—*Frye* has the effect of raising the external "stake" in the litigation, and thus moving the litigation even farther away from the model of fully internalized costs and benefits. Although *Frye* also creates an additional issue of common interest among successive parties with the relatively lower stake (plaintiffs in the example), it does not seem likely that this effect will redress the asymmetry, and it may well increase the distortion of the fact-finding process by introducing the interests of non-litigants, such as the expert witnesses themselves. To the extent that *Daubert* mutes the incentives for "general acceptance" organization extrinsic to the litigation, it will reduce this distorting effect. Furthermore, to the extent that *Daubert* shifts the admissibility of scientific evidence from a "general" issue to one that is decided on

[115] Fully characterizing defense expenditures in this sequential-defense scenario is somewhat complex. However, as a first approximation, it is likely that a party in Merrell Dow's position would view its expenditures on previous cases as "sunk" costs, and therefore re-evaluate defense expenditures at each successive phase on the basis of its remaining capitalized exposure under non-mutual collateral estoppel.

the basis of the facts of each particular case, it actually may reduce the effects of asymmetry, by eliminating an issue that is considered common to a series of otherwise similar cases.

The effects in a case involving the government are similar, though the mechanism differs somewhat. To some extent, the government tends to "capitalize" all of its cases simply because it is the government (an entity that does not strongly internalize any of the costs and benefits of its litigation activity). As government agents are almost never called to account for their litigation expenditures in the same manner as private agents, the government tends to spend out of proportion to the stakes, and to be influenced in its expenditures by all sorts of extrinsic factors—publicity, pride, symbolism, the "public interest," the career ambitions of the government lawyers or executives handling the case, and the like.[116] The only constraint on any of this is the political process, which is far too diffuse to place any sort of meaningful control on expenditures in a particular case.

As in the case of non-mutual estoppel, adding *Frye* to the government case exacerbates the tendency to invest out of proportion to individual case stakes. On issues of scientific evidence that the government litigates frequently, the biasing effect can be profound. For example, consider the "science" of fingerprint identification, which is virtually a governmental monopoly. In that field, the only "generally accepted" principles are those accepted by at least some of the government's fingerprint identification experts. In this instance, we have an overt case of "scientific" principles in a particular field being dictated by a governmental bureaucracy.[117] Although the advent of *Daubert* is hardly likely to break the government's hold on fingerprinting expertise or other aspects of "forensic science" used predominantly in criminal prosecutions, at least it would theoretically permit a private expert to offer some evidence that is not based on principles already accepted by the government. In contexts where the government's dominance is less

[116] The clearest example is criminal prosecutions. Only in rare cases is it even known publicly how much taxpayers' money is spent on a particular prosecution. While prosecutors' offices generally have budgets and finite resources, those limitations primarily affect the selection of cases to pursue. As a practical matter, there is no budget for a particular criminal prosecution, and any proposal to create such limits on prosecution expenditures would be met with objections to putting a "price tag" on such non-pecuniary interests as public safety or victims' suffering.

[117] Giannelli & Imwinkelried further report that the FBI Laboratory's services, which extend to a variety of "criminal forensics," are made available without charge to state and local governments, and "include both the examination of evidence and the court appearance of the expert." Giannelli & Imwinkelried, 1 *Scientific Evidence* at 110 (cited in note 41).

complete, the shift from *Frye* to *Daubert* is likely to be more meaningful, and, like the case of non-mutual estoppel, may tend slightly to mitigate the effects of asymmetry.

In neither of these variations are the effects of asymmetry of stakes vitiated by something like the *Frye* test. Indeed, they may be aggravated. Although the shift to *Daubert* may be ameliorative to some extent, it does not operate on the underlying asymmetries of incentive to invest in litigation, which are driven by external effects. This exposes the more general point that problems such as asymmetrical stakes and external effects are not fundamentally problems of evidence or fact-finding at all, and they are not problems that evidence law is likely to be able to address effectively.

D. The Domain of Admissibility Doctrine

Asymmetries of stakes created by external effects are not the only cause of "junk science" in the courtroom, nor the most important one. Far more important are the magnitudes and variance in the stakes of litigation, which are functions of the substantive law of liability and damages. The ever expanding scope of legal liability, together with the ever increasing likelihood of large damage awards, punitive and otherwise, are the principal reasons for the growth in the use and importance of expert testimony in litigation. In simple economic terms, there is a strong demand for expert testimony (along with all other forms of litigation expenditure) derived from the increasing returns to litigation as a means of wealth transfer. As the explicit pricing of "fact" evidence is suppressed by the formal system of unremunerative compulsion, the explicitly priced supply of expert and scientific evidence makes it an easy target of criticism.

The returns to litigation activity are raised still higher by certain features of the modern procedural system, such as liberal pleading rules and broad discovery and, most recently, "disclosure" obligations. The emergence of "mass tort" and other forms of multiple litigation, together with non-mutual collateral estoppel, raises the stakes in litigation further, and provides incentives for interest groups to organize for coordination across multiple cases. With or without facilitative legal rules, interest groups have formed to litigate "public interest" cases that seek to establish broad principles or policies rather than overtly to secure a transfer payment from a particular defendant to a particular plaintiff. And, of course, with the growth of statute and regulatory law, government at all levels has increasingly become involved in litigating broad issues of social policy.

As against all of these powerful forces tending toward increased investment in litigation expenditure, the evidentiary standard for the admissibility of scientific evidence can have only a limited marginal effect.[118] The problem with the *Frye* standard and its suggested variants is that its marginal effect is in the wrong direction—toward reinforcing rather than dampening all of the other influences that tend both to raise and to externalize the stakes of litigation. But no standard of evidentiary admissibility could stem that tide.

More fundamentally, no test of evidentiary admissibility that looks to an "external" guidepost seems likely to improve the performance of litigation fact-finding because all such standards will partake to some extent in the "free lunch" fallacy. It is a tempting fantasy to believe that somewhere out there is the polestar that can guide the imperfect course of adjudication at law. Tempting as it is, it is a fantasy nonetheless. Questing for the Polaris of "true" scientific evidence—assuming that it exists at all—cannot be done with the naked eye. It requires a telescope. Someone, who wants to get paid, has to make the telescope. Not all telescopes are equal, and the "consensus" telescope may very well be distorted. In terms of the fact-finding needs of a particular case, it is likely to be distorted by the broader interests of the consensus-makers.

Daubert does not entirely eliminate this problem. On one level, it seems to replace the "consensus" telescope with a scenario of looking through competing telescopes, or perhaps alternative navigational aids, so long as they all qualify under some generic standard as "scientific" methods. At a more profound level, *Daubert* also could be read as questioning whether Polaris exists at all or, even if it does, whether its location is important or even useful to the adjudicatory enterprise.

Ultimately, *Daubert*'s rhetoric in this respect may be more important than whatever "test" eventually emerges in the lower courts. The majority's opinion in *Daubert* is a welcome recognition that fact-finding in litigation is not a search for "cosmic understand-

[118] This is the essential thesis of Brickman in *On the Relevance* (cited in note 102), although his analysis focuses narrowly (too narrowly, in my view) on lawyers' incentives. If lawyering is a competitive business, lawyers' rates of return are unlikely to be much different from anyone else's. The effect is more fundamentally in *litigants'* rates of return, which are determined by the stakes in litigation as set by the substantive law of liability and damages. Whether contingent legal fees consume a large or small proportion of recoveries is beside the point: the typical contingent-fee plaintiff's return is astronomical by any measure because these plaintiffs essentially risk nothing and invest only a small amount of their own time and energy in the litigation. In effect, they have bought a lottery ticket by purchasing an option in litigation at a very low premium. See Bradford Cornell, *The Incentive to Sue: An Option-Pricing Approach*, 19 J Legal Stud 173 (1990).

ing." Many of the influences that are operating to increase the stakes (and expenditures) in litigation appear to be based on the opposite view that the factual findings in a single litigation are a matter of broad social import. To the extent that *Daubert* helps provide an antidote to that thinking, it will make a positive contribution to the law and economics of litigation.

In operational terms, *Daubert* reorients admissibility doctrine more closely to what one might reasonably expect of evidence law. As was discussed in Part II above, the entire problem of admissibility of scientific evidence is simply a matter of finding an acceptable analog in expert testimony to the foundational requirement of "first-hand knowledge" in ordinary testimony. *Daubert* makes that analogy explicit, and therefore provides a basis for extending the underlying logic of foundational requirements to scientific evidence. For ordinary testimony, the requirement of first-hand knowledge is a minimal standard designed to ensure that the witness has an observational advantage over the fact-finders. It does not require or imply that the witness is the definitive source, or that the witness is correct in his or her perceptions.

There does not appear to be any reason why a similar approach should not guide the application of the *Daubert* standard. As with opinion testimony by ordinary witnesses, if the expert's testimony is "rationally based" (not in personal sense impression but rather in the specialized "scientific" knowledge of the expert's field) and, as the Court stated in *Daubert,* "pertinent" to the factual issues of the case, then the testimony presumptively is admissible, subject to the ordinary counterweights.

Asking more of the standard of admissibility is asking too much of evidence law. If problems remain with "junk science" in the courtroom, they are far more powerfully related to the incentives of substantive law and other features of the procedural system, and they can be addressed far more effectively by attending to those causative factors rather than overstressing or distorting the law of evidence. As illustrated by *Frye,* seeking to address those problems through inappropriate admissibility doctrine can make them worse.

V. POST-*DAUBERT* EXPERIENCE

In a paper concerning scientific evidence, one would hope to formulate a falsifiable hypothesis. The analysis presented above does lead to testable predictions regarding the expected consequences of *Daubert.* Unfortunately, however, *Daubert* is still too new—even at this writing, some eighteen months after the decision was announced—to have generated systematically observable effects. Even when, and if, it does, the methodological problems of isolating *Daubert*'s effects will be formidable. The observable experience to date, which is only suggestive and mostly episodic, does provide some support for the argument of this article. However, the preliminary signals are mixed.

The basic prediction of the analysis presented here is that decisions on the admissibility of scientific evidence under *Daubert* will be subject to less influence from the external interest groups necessary to achieve "general acceptance" than were comparable decisions under *Frye*. Even under the best of circumstances, isolating this effect will be difficult. Aside from the general condition that social and particularly legal observations often can defy experimental design, the effect may be subtle. *Daubert* preserves "general acceptance" as one of several factors that trial judges may consider in applying its broader standard.[119] Furthermore, even in the pre-*Daubert* era, the *Frye* test was neither universally accepted nor uniformly applied where it was accepted.

Two general approaches suggest themselves. First, one could examine the "internal" effect of *Daubert* on admissibility decisions in the reported case law, ideally by comparing otherwise similar decisions between courts applying *Frye* and *Daubert*, either longitudinally or cross-sectionally. The prediction is that, if all else is held constant, admissibility decisions under *Daubert* will exhibit less consistency—more dispersion in admissibility outcomes for a given type of expert testimony—than decisions under *Frye*. This would be a direct indication that interest groups have less to gain under *Daubert*. Second, one could look to the "external" effect on the funding, size, and distribution of the "general acceptance" interest groups. From this perspective, the prediction would be that—all else equal—at least the more narrowly-based interest groups will tend to decline in size and funding. Broader interest groups, which might have some plausible claim to representing the "scientific method" more generally, may gain members. But overall, to the extent that these groups are predicated on litigation rent-seeking, their total membership, total financing, or both, should decline, if *Daubert* has reduced realizable rents.

However, it appears that *Daubert* is still too new to have generated unambiguous effects from either perspective. Reported case law (and commentary), and available summary data on organizations' membership, show mixed results.

An examination of the post-*Daubert* case law in the federal and state courts has not identified instances where applications of

[119] See *Daubert*, 113 S Ct at 2797.

Daubert show detectably greater dispersion in admissibility outcomes than applications of *Frye.*[120] However, to the extent that differing doctrinal interpretations may presage ultimate differences in outcomes, there already are at least two distinct interpretations of the *Daubert* standard. One group of courts focuses on the "liberal admissibility" aspect of *Daubert* to view the new standard as establishing a lower threshold to admissibility.[121] Another group of courts takes *Daubert*'s emphasis on scientific validity and the "gatekeeping" role of the trial court judge as tight-

[120] Research for this article encompassed all reported federal and state cases citing *Daubert* through August 1994, and more selective research in prior and subsequent cases.

As prior law presaged *Daubert* in some instances, such as the Third Circuit's decision in *United States v Downing,* 753 F 2d 1224, 1232-37 (3d Cir 1985) (Judge Becker) (rejecting *Frye* and adopting a test of "reliability" and "fit" similar to *Daubert,* see 113 S Ct at 2795-96), it may be possible to perform cross-sectional analysis in the prior law, although I have not undertaken to do so for this article. However, some of the possibilities are suggested by the experience with the type of expert testimony involved in *Downing,* which was opinion on the reliability (or lack thereof) of eyewitness "fact" testimony. Courts following the *Frye* test consistently excluded this type of scientific evidence. See, as the leading authorities, *United States v Rincon,* 984 F 2d 1003 (9th Cir 1992); *United States v Larkin,* 978 F 2d 964 (7th Cir 1992); *United States v Serna,* 799 F 2d 842 (2d Cir 1986); *United States v Fosher,* 590 F 2d 381 (1st Cir 1979); *United States v Amaral,* 488 F 2d 1148 (9th Cir 1973).

In *Downing* itself, the Third Circuit reversed and remanded the exclusion of such testimony for reconsideration in light of its rejection of *Frye.* On remand, the district court adhered to the original outcome of exclusion, and the Third Circuit affirmed. *United States v Downing,* 609 F Supp 784 (ED Pa 1985), aff'd without opinion, 780 F 2d 1017 (3d Cir 1985). Much the same result ensued from the Ninth Circuit's decision in *Rincon* (cited earlier in this footnote), excluding that same type of testimony under *Frye,* which was vacated and remanded by the Supreme Court, 114 S Ct 41 (1993), for further consideration in light of *Daubert.* On remand, the Ninth Circuit adhered to the original outcome under the *Daubert* test, and the Supreme Court denied certiorari. *United States v Rincon,* 28 F3d 921 (9th Cir 1994), *cert denied,* 115 S Ct 605 (1994).

In the meantime, however, another Third Circuit opinion by Judge Becker (the author of *Downing*) had reversed a district court decision excluding expert testimony on eyewitness reliability—the same outcome ultimately affirmed in *Downing*—in *United States v Stevens,* 935 F 2d 1380, 1397-1402 (3d Cir 1991). See also *United States v Garcia,* 40 M J 533 (USAF Ct Mil Rev 1994) (post-*Daubert* decision reaching the *Stevens* result).

While this evidence is purely anecdotal, it does suggest that the *Daubert* standard is less directive of particular outcomes than *Frye.* Under the analysis of this article, that is the predicted effect.

[121] Among the federal circuits, see *United States v Chischilly,* 30 F3d 1144, 1152 (9th Cir 1994) (*Frye* described as "more arduous" than *Daubert*); *United States v Bonds,* 12 F3d 540, 566 n 21 (6th Cir 1993) (*Daubert* "more liberal" towards admissibility); *United States v Bynum,* 3 F3d 769, 773 (4th Cir 1993), *cert denied,* 114 S Ct 1105 (1994). The Eight Circuit seems to be on the fence: in *Sorensen v Shaklee*

ening the standard for admissibility.[122] Both strands of case law, as well as most of the commentary on *Daubert,* seem to acknowledge that *Daubert* did shift admissibility doctrine away from deference to external acceptance of the content of proffered scientific evidence and toward an evaluation of the method for arriving at the scientific opinion that is more internalized to the judicial process.[123]

Perhaps the best current indicator of this shift in doctrinal emphasis, and its likely effect of decreasing the predictability of admissibility outcomes, is the Ninth Circuit's treatment of the *Daubert* case itself on remand from the Supreme Court. In June 1993, the Supreme Court vacated the Ninth Circuit's original decision excluding the plaintiffs' proffered expert testimony, and remanded the case for reconsideration in light of the newly announced *Daubert* standard. In January 1995, the Ninth Circuit issued its opinion on remand, which adhered to the original result of exclusion upon application of the new standard.[124] Judge Kozinski's opinion for the Ninth Circuit describes the analysis required by *Daubert* as "a far more complex and daunting task" than Frye demanded,[125] and one that "puts federal judges in an uncomfortable position":

> [T]hough we are largely untrained in science and certainly no match for any of the witnesses whose testimony we are re-

Corp., 31 F3d 638 (8th Cir 1994), the court described *Frye* as "more restrictive" than the new *Daubert* standard, id at 646 n 13, but seemed to apply the opposite view in substance. See also *United States v Martinez,* 3 F3d 1191 (8th Cir 1993), *cert denied,* 114 S Ct 734 (1994). On the state level, see *State v Alberico,* 116 NM 156, 861 P2d 192 (1993); *Hart-Albin Co v McLees Corp.,* 264 Mont 1, 870 P2d 51 (1994); *State v Cephas,* 637 A2d 20 (Del 1994).

[122] Federal cases suggesting a more demanding interpretation of *Daubert* include, in addition to the *Daubert* case itself on remand (discussed below), *In re Paoli RR Yard PCB Litigation,* 35 F3d 717, 741-50 (3d Cir 1994) (extensive discussion of *Daubert* and *Downing* by Judge Becker, the author of *Downing*), *Robinson v Missouri Pacific R Co.,* 16 F3d 1083, 1088-89 (10th Cir 1994) (emphasizing the trial judge's "gatekeeping" role), and *Porter v Whitehall Laboratories, Inc.,* 9 F3d 607 (7th Cir 1993). At the state level, see *State v Foret,* 628 S2d 1116 (La 1993).

[123] An example of a shift away from external interest group influence is *Bradley v Brown,* 852 F Supp 690 (ND Ind 1994), which involved proffered testimony by "clinical ecologists" on "Multiple Chemical Sensitivities" syndrome. The clinical ecologists were well-organized, with peer-reviewed literature and, within their self-defined field, "general acceptance" of their views. Nonetheless, the evidence was excluded by the district court under *Daubert* on the rationale that the field involved insufficient scientific testing. See id at 698-700.

[124] *Daubert v Merrell Dow Pharmaceuticals, Inc.,* 43 F3d 1311 (9th Cir 1995).

[125] Id at 1315.

viewing, it is our responsibility to determine whether those experts' proposed testimony amounts to "scientific knowledge," constitutes "good science," and was "derived by the scientific method."

The task before us is more daunting still when the dispute concerns matters at the very cutting edge of scientific research, where fact meets theory and certainty dissolves into probability. As the record in this case illustrates, scientists often have vigorous and sincere disagreements . . . . Our responsibility, then, unless we badly misread the Supreme Court's opinion, is to resolve disputes among respected, well-credentialed scientists about matters squarely within their expertise, in areas where there is no scientific consensus as to what is and what is not "good science," and occasionally to reject such expert testimony because it was not "derived by the scientific method." Mindful of our position in the hierarchy of the federal judiciary, we take a deep breath and proceed with this heady task.[126]

Notwithstanding Judge Kozinski's reticence, the Ninth Circuit in fact did proceed to reject qualified experts' testimony, and Merrell Dow ultimately won its case.

Of course, any new legal standard announced by the Supreme Court is bound to create uncertainties and disagreements in its initial applications. But Judge Kozinski's remarks on remand in *Daubert* appear to represent something more durable: in essence, they are a restatement of the perennial question in scientific evidence—whether judges are competent to evaluate scientific opinion testimony.[127] The Supreme Court's opinion in *Daubert* gives an answer: rely on the adversarial system, in full recognition that such a system sometimes errs. If Judge Kozinski's concerns are well-founded, then "unqualified" judges are likely to make differing and sometimes inconsistent decisions on similar types of scientific testimony. A deferential standard of appellate review of such decisions—if applied under *Daubert*—all but ensures that such inconsistencies will enter the reported case law. If so, the resulting body of decisions may have an untidy appearance to some observers, but it will be positive for social welfare if the disparities in outcome are relatively random and unbiased: that will indicate that *Daubert* has decreased the influence of external interest groups.

[126] Id at 1316.
[127] See Part II above.

If that development proceeds, then we should expect to see such interest groups undergo a relative decline in size and funding.[128] However, it appears to be too soon to conduct a controlled empirical study, at least with generally available data. A preliminary review of the available summary statistics from the *Encyclopedia of Associations* as of mid-1994 indicates that self-identified "forensic" associations[129] are growing at a slightly smaller average rate than a random sample[130] of all associations.[131] However, there is no indication that this difference is significant,[132] or that it suggests any general trend at all. Furthermore, these samples are very small, the data appear very rough, and this comparison does not control for other factors—such as the total volume or value of litigation—that may affect litigation-related organizations differentially.

[128] Of course, there are many possible influences on associations' membership and funding, but the prediction is that, holding all else constant, "scientific evidence" associations should decline in relative importance.

[129] Based upon the 1991 and 1995 editions of the *Encyclopedia of Associations* and *International Encyclopedia of Associations* (Gale, 1990 & 1994), there were 21 U.S.-based nationwide or international associations classified in the "forensic sciences" and "forensic medicine" categories and reporting membership in both 1990 and 1994. Of those, only one reported a drop in membership: the International Society of Stress Analysts, which dropped from 250 to 50 members. Eleven others reported the same membership: American Academy of Forensic Psychology (120 members); American Association of Police Polygraphists (700 members); American Polygraph Association (2500 members); Evidence Photographers International council (500 members); Independent Association of Questioned Document Examiners (175 members); American Board of Forensic Anthropology (39 members); International Reference Organization in Forensic Medicine and Sciences (1200 members); Milton Helpern Institute of Forensic Medicine (405 members); National Bureau of Document Examiners (50 members); National Forensic Center (5000 members); World Association of Document Examiners (500 members). The remaining nine reported increases: American Academy of Forensic Sciences (from 3300 to 3750 members); American Society of Crime Laboratory Directors (from 250 to 300 members); American Society of Questioned Document Examiners (from 50 to 110 members); Association of Forensic Document Examiners (from 25 to 30 members); National Association of Forensic Economists (from 325 to 520 members); American Board of Forensic Psychiatry (from 220 to 227 members); International Association for Identification (from 2500 to 3600 members); National Association of Document Examiners (from 65 to 130 members); and Society of Forensic Toxicologists (from 300 to 425 members).

[130] Random selection on the basis of association number as used in the directory produced 25 observations, of which 2 were excluded as not reporting membership for both 1990 and 1994.

[131] The average percentage growth of the "forensic" group was +17.7% (with a standard deviation of 54.1%), while the random group's average percentage growth was +19.7% (with a standard deviation of 38.8%).

[132] Given the large standard deviations (see the preceding note), there is no confidence that there is any statistical difference between these two rates.

In time, it may be possible to construct a controlled empirical study using a similar data source that would show whether a subset of organizations or associations identified as having an interest in expert testimony had experienced a relative decline that could be attributable to *Daubert*.[133]

VI. CONCLUSION

Assessing the ultimate effect of *Daubert* on the admission of scientific evidence is likely to require several more years of judicial experience followed by rigorous empirical study. Certainly, the amount of attention lavished on *Daubert* to date by the commentators, and the emerging disagreements among the federal and state courts on its meaning, suggest that its doctrine will matter. But at this point, there is little agreement on how it will matter. Respectable opinion predicts both less and more stringent attitudes towards the admissibility of scientific evidence, and some predict little or no effect on outcomes at all.

This article has argued that the disagreements over *Daubert*'s meaning may themselves be indicators of yet another effect of *Daubert* that ultimately may be more profound. Whether *Daubert* increases or decreases the cost of presenting scientific evidence generally, it is likely to reduce the influence of external interest groups on the content and costs of scientific evidence proffered under its standard. If that prediction is correct, the results certainly will do no harm to science, and will be favorable for the adjudicatory system, as it will remove or at least reduce one source of external bias on the supply of scientific evidence to litigation.

In a broader view, *Daubert* focuses our attention on the virtues and vices of the adversarial system as it operates on fact-finding at trial. Whatever its vices, adversarial presentation of evidence has the signal virtue of internalizing the costs and benefits of fact-finding to the immediate parties, much as substantive property rights do in the contracting process. While litigation, given its coercive aspect, is not entirely analogous to contracting, it comes closest in the context of fact-finding in a particular case, where the social interest in the particular outcome approaches zero. Much of the criticism of the adversarial system in recent years seems to ignore this point. The Supreme Court's decision in *Daubert* reminds us

[133] If the absence of measurable effects at present is mainly the result of the fact that *Daubert* is a new decision, that problem should cure itself. There are, of course, other possibilities. The interest groups, for example, may (now or later) shift their activities to other interests of the members, which will create measurement problems of a different kind.

that fact-finding in particular cases is not an "exhaustive search for cosmic understanding." Accordingly, *Daubert* instructs trial judges to apply the ordinary tools of the adversarial system to determine when to receive scientific evidence, even when that task casts judges in what the Ninth Circuit on remand believed was the "uncomfortable position" of resolving disputes among respected, well-credentialed scientists.

Unfortunately, there is no better alternative to the judges' discomfort. The judicial system cannot have a free lunch any more than others can. Judges will make mistakes. Under *Daubert,* those mistakes can and should be confined in their effect to the particular legal dispute in which they are made. Under *Frye,* judicial error could be induced and then multiplied to other cases under the influence of external interest groups with a stake in "general acceptance." To assume that judicial determinations can be improved or assisted by reference to a manipulable external standard is to assume that there is a free lunch. Thus, the answer to the perennial question of how we can expect "inexpert" judges to evaluate expert testimony is simply that their doing the best they can is better than the next best alternative.

To avoid the free lunch fallacy, courts and law reformers need only attend to the proper limitations on the social consequences of fact-finding in particular litigated matters. Litigation will never be a neat and tidy business, and perhaps it should not be. Some degree of uncertainty in litigated outcomes probably is desirable, as it provides incentives for parties to avoid litigation ex ante. When trials cannot be avoided, the imperfections of the fact-finding process should be confined to the immediate parties, and not exported into other cases. Whatever the imperfections of the adversarial process in fact-finding, they are highly unlikely to be cured by creating diffuse external effects.

The Supreme Court's Predation Odyssey: From Fruit Pies to Cigarettes

Donald J. Boudreaux,[†] *Kenneth G. Elzinga,*[††]
and David E. Mills[†††]

Brooke Group, Ltd. v Brown & Williamson Tobacco Corp.—*the Supreme Court's first predatory pricing decision under the Robinson-Patman Act since* Utah Pie in 1967—*makes clear the Court's heightened skepticism toward claims of predatory pricing. Under* Brooke, *plaintiffs must show not only that a defendant had a genuine possibility of bankrupting or disciplining its prey, but also that the defendant had a strong prospect of recouping its predatory losses. While applauding the Court's decision, the authors question the Court's refusal to accept a rule of* per se *legality to govern price cutting by members of noncollusive oligopolies. For reasons the Court itself spelled out, price cutting by members of noncollusive oligopolies is so unlikely a means of successful monopolization that such pricing behavior ought to be governed by a rule of* per se *legality.*

I. INTRODUCTION

Brooke Group, Ltd. v Brown & Williamson Tobacco Corp.[1] is the first Supreme Court decision on predatory pricing under the Robinson-Patman Act since the 1967 *Utah Pie* case.[2] The outcome and

[†] Associate Professor of Legal Studies, Clemson University.
[††] Professor of Economics, University of Virginia.
[†††] Professor of Economics, University of Virginia.
Elzinga and Mills served as consultants to Brown & Williamson during the *Brooke* litigation. The authors thank Karol Ceplo, Don Dewey, Adam Pritchard, Bruce Yandle, and two anonymous referees for helpful discussion and comments.

[1] 113 S Ct 2578 (1993). At oral argument, the Supreme Court witnessed a battle of two antitrust titans: Philip Areeda (for appellant Brooke Group) and Robert Bork (for appellee Brown & Williamson).

[2] *Utah Pie Co. v Continental Baking Co.*, 386 US 685 (1967).

 0-226-28685-1/95/0004-0002$02.00

reasoning of *Brooke* could not have been more different from this earlier ruling. In *Utah Pie,* the Court held that predatory intent could be inferred from nothing more than bellicose language in defendants' internal memoranda or from declining price structures caused by defendants' pricing practices. This legal standard paid no attention to the likelihood that an accused predator could actually succeed in monopolizing the market. Under *Utah Pie,* courts did not ask whether the alleged predatory pricing scheme allowed the predator a respectable chance of recouping its predatory losses. This standard for assessing competitive injury, it has been strongly argued, obstructs vigorous price competition.[3]

In contrast to *Utah Pie, Brooke* is the opinion of a Court highly skeptical of plaintiffs' cries of predation. Although the Court did not openly admit to undoing *Utah Pie,* undo *Utah Pie* it did.[4] A finding of predation now requires not only a showing that the defendant enjoyed a real possibility of running its prey from the industry or disciplining its prey into coy obedience via below-cost pricing, but also a showing that the defendant possessed a decent chance of recouping its predatory losses: "If market circumstances or deficiencies of proof would bar a reasonable jury from finding that the scheme alleged would likely result in sustained supracompetitive pricing, the plaintiff's case has failed."[5]

The *Brooke* decision completes a sea-change from an earlier view (represented well by *Utah Pie*) in which competition is so fragile and delicate that any significant price reductions by larger firms threaten competition and consumer welfare.[6] The Court is now more sophisticated. The *Brooke* Court understood that below-cost pricing is not a sufficient condition for monopolization. And, im-

[3] See Kenneth G. Elzinga and Thomas F. Hogarty, Utah Pie *and the Consequences of Robinson-Patman,* 21 J L & Econ 427 (1978); Ward S. Bowman, *Restraint of Trade by the Supreme Court: The* Utah Pie *Case,* 77 Yale L J 70 (1967).

[4] "The *Brooke* holding effectively overrules the Court's earlier *Utah Pie* decision." Phillip Areeda and Herbert Hovenkamp, *Antitrust Law* 1262 (Little Brown, Supp 1993).

[5] *Brooke,* 113 S Ct at 2589.

[6] This change began with *Matsushita Electric Industrial Co. v Zenith Radio Corp.,* 475 US 574 (1986). Effectively rejecting a predation claim by Zenith against several Japanese electronics manufacturers, the Court in *Matsushita* held that summary judgment for a defendant in a predatory pricing case is appropriate if the plaintiff fails to offer an economically plausible theory of how the alleged predation could pay off for the defendant. The Court recognized explicitly that allegations of predation make no sense if recoupment of predatory losses is unlikely. The Court also understood that because predatory pricing schemes are rare, legal standards that are generous to plaintiffs threaten vigorous and healthy price competition.

Matsushita was decided under Section 2 of the Sherman Act, while *Brooke* was decided under Section 2(a) of the Clayton Act (as modified by the Robinson-Patman Act).

portantly, it also understood that adjudicatory attempts to police markets against predatory pricing risk extinguishing price competition.

II. FACTS OF *BROOKE*

A. The Cigarette Industry and Generics

Six firms compose the U.S. cigarette industry. Despite its concentration and the absence of new entrants, market shares within this industry have been unstable (see Table 1). For example, today's industry leader—Philip Morris—now enjoys a market share of more than 40%; in 1965, Philip Morris was the fourth largest cigarette manufacturer with a market share of just over 10%. The industry leader in 1965, R.J. Reynolds, is now in second place with a market share in 1993 of about 31%. The two litigants in *Brooke* (Brown & Williamson and Liggett) also underwent market-share changes. The market share of Brown & Williamson rose from 13% to nearly 17% between 1965 and 1970, and then fell to 11% in 1993. During the same period, the market share of Liggett—which during the litigation was acquired by Brooke Group, Ltd.—fell from 9% to 6.5% to 2.4%.[7]

Table 1. U.S. Cigarette Market: Share of Domestic Unit Sales

	1965	*1970*	*1975*	*1980*	*1985*	*1990*	*1993*
Philip Morris	10.3	16.7	23.9	30.9	35.9	42.2	42.2
RJR	32.9	31.8	32.6	32.6	31.6	29.6	30.6
B&W	13.2	16.7	17.2	13.7	11.9	10.3	11.0
Lorillard	9.1	8.5	8.0	9.7	8.1	7.7	7.1
American	25.2	19.6	13.9	10.8	7.5	6.8	6.7
Liggett	9.0	6.5	4.3	2.3	5.0	3.4	2.4

Source: Maxwell Reports, various issues. This source provides numerical data on cigarette sales and product introductions used elsewhere in the paper.

[7] Liggett's market share during the past 25 years has been particularly volatile. From 6.5% in 1970, Liggett's share fell to 2.3% in 1980. In 1984 its market share had risen to 5.7% because of its introduction of generic cigarettes. See William B. Burnett, *Predation by a Nondominant Firm: The* Liggett *Case (1993)*, in John E. Kwoka, Jr. & Lawrence J. White, eds, *The Antitrust Revolution* 260, 263 (Scott Foresman, 2d ed 1994) ("Burnett, *Predation*"); Kenneth G. Elzinga and David E. Mills, *Trumping the Areeda-Turner Test: The Recoupment Standard in* Brooke Group, 62 Antitrust L J 559, 565, 581-82 (1994) ("Elzinga & Mills, *Trumping Areeda-Turner*").

Before 1980, cigarette manufacturers competed mainly on non-price bases, with list prices to customers—tobacco wholesalers and retail chains—often identical across brands. Advertising and promotions, packaging, and product innovation were the primary methods of rivalry. Slightly higher prices were charged for longer (100mm) cigarettes, and slotting payments sometimes were paid in return for stocking new brands or securing desirable shelf space. Otherwise, prices were uniform across all cigarette manufacturers.

During the early 1980s, however, this price uniformity began unraveling. As smoking became less popular, excess capacity emerged in the cigarette industry, whose capital is durable and not readily redeployed to other activities.[8] Price-cutting pressures intensified.

One early manifestation of this demand-supply imbalance came in the early 1980s when Topco, a wholesale buying organization of retail grocers, asked Liggett to produce a generic (or "black and white") cigarette. Although initially skeptical that smokers would purchase unbranded cigarettes, Liggett agreed to produce them for Topco at a price below that charged for branded (or "full revenue") cigarettes. Liggett was pleasantly surprised, for generic cigarettes proved hugely successful.

Building upon its success with Topco, Liggett expanded its production of generic cigarettes, offering its own line of generics to other customers. These cigarettes were priced about 30% below full revenue brands. Liggett also offered rebates on generics to selected customers in an attempt to promote adoption and volume purchases of its generic line. Liggett's efforts paid off. By early 1984, Liggett's generic cigarettes accounted for an impressive 4% of total cigarette sales.

In 1983, R.J. Reynolds reacted to Liggett's generics by introducing its Century brand. For the same price as other brands containing 20 cigarettes per pack, each pack of Century contained 25 cigarettes. In 1984, Reynolds repositioned Doral, formerly a full revenue brand, as a discount cigarette product. Doral's wholesale list price was lowered to generic levels and rebates were offered on volume purchases.

Brown & Williamson followed Reynolds in reacting to Liggett's success in the discount cigarette segment. After launching its own "value-25" brand (like Reynolds' Century), Brown & Williamson introduced black and white generic cigarettes in July 1984. Mimicking Liggett and Reynolds, Brown & Williamson promoted sales of its discount cigarettes by offering volume rebates.

[8] Cigarette sales in the U.S. peaked in 1981 when 627 billion "sticks" were sold. Since then, domestic cigarette sales have declined steadily. See Burnett, *Predation* at 263 (cited in note 7).

Reynolds' entry into the discount segment prompted Liggett to increase its rebates. When Brown & Williamson announced in June 1984 its plans to introduce its own line of generic cigarettes, Liggett expanded its rebate program, which further prompted Brown & Williamson to increase its rebates to prospective customers. In the brief period between Brown & Williamson's entry announcement and its first shipment of generics in July 1984, Liggett and Brown & Williamson engaged in five rounds of rebate increases—rebates that, when deducted from list prices, caused the prices these manufacturers received for their discount cigarettes to fall further and further.

These low prices prevailed for more than a year. In mid-1985, Liggett raised its list prices without diminishing its rebates. Brown & Williamson followed suit a few months later. Both firms then reduced their rebates, and the rebate war ended.

B. Liggett's Charge Against Brown & Williamson

In June 1984, Liggett filed a federal lawsuit, charging that Brown & Williamson's generic cigarette packaging violated Liggett's trademarks. Subsequently, Liggett amended its complaint to include a Robinson-Patman charge.[9] Liggett's Robinson-Patman claim, which was made possible by the discriminatory nature of Brown & Williamson's volume rebates, posited an elaborate predatory scheme that Liggett inferred from selected Brown & Williamson internal memoranda.

According to Liggett, Brown & Williamson feared that the expanding demand for generic cigarettes threatened its ability to charge supracompetitive prices on its full revenue brands. To nip this threat in the bud, Brown & Williamson began its own line of generics. Brown & Williamson entered generics, Liggett argued, only to smother the competition that generics posed to full revenue brands. Under this theory, Brown & Williamson tried to discipline Liggett into keeping the price of generics high enough so that sales of discount cigarettes would not undermine the supracompetitive profits earned on full revenue brands.

After 115 days of trial, a jury awarded Liggett $49.6 million in damages, which the trial court trebled to $148.8 million. The court, however, awarded Brown & Williamson a judgment notwithstanding the verdict on the ground that Liggett's case failed as a matter

[9] The trademark claim was rejected by the trial court and Liggett did not appeal the ruling. The appeals process focused upon the Robinson-Patman charge exclusively.

of law. The judge concluded that Liggett did not show injury to competition.[10] This ruling was affirmed by the United States Court of Appeals for the Fourth Circuit.[11] By a 6-3 vote, the Supreme Court affirmed the Fourth Circuit's ruling.[12]

Some analysts contend that this was no ordinary case of predation because "Liggett had unusually strong evidence on its side" that Brown & Williamson had employed a credible predation strategy—one more likely to succeed than run-of-the-mill predatory pricing.[13] Brown & Williamson's alleged game plan included two distinguishing components.

First, full revenue cigarette brands are said to have sold at supracompetitive prices even before the alleged predation began because of tacit oligopolistic coordination among the nation's six major cigarette manufacturers. This pricing enabled cigarette producers to earn higher than normal profits year after year.[14] These returns rendered Brown & Williamson's predation less speculative because Brown & Williamson already knew it could earn supracompetitive profits if only the up-start generics segment could be squelched. That is, recoupment is alleged to have been easier for Brown & Williamson because Brown & Williamson sought only to restore pricing discipline in the U.S. cigarette market rather than monopolize a market *de novo.*

Second, recoupment was said to be simultaneous with predation.[15] Liggett claimed that Brown & Williamson contrived a way to inflict losses on Liggett without boosting the demand for generic cigarette sales (as would occur under conventional predatory pricing). This scheme allowed recoupment to begin as soon as Brown & Williamson began to prey on Liggett because it *retarded,* rather than accelerated, the growth of generic sales during the period of low prices. If Brown & Williamson had reduced the list prices of its

[10] *Liggett Group, Inc. v Brown & Williamson Tobacco Corp.,* 748 F Supp 344 (MD NC 1990).

[11] *Liggett Group, Inc. v Brown & Williamson Tobacco Corp.,* 964 F2d 335 (1992).

[12] *Brooke Group, Ltd. v Brown & Williamson Tobacco Corp.,* 113 S Ct 2578 (1993). Justice Kennedy wrote the majority opinion. Justice Stevens filed a dissent, which was joined by Justices White and Blackmun.

[13] Kenneth L. Glazer, *Life After* Brooke Group: *Predatory Pricing and Beyond,* 62 Antitrust L J 605, 606 (1994) (Glazer, "*Life After*"). See also Justice Stevens' dissenting opinion in *Brooke.*

[14] These rates of return are reported to be approximately 50% higher than the average earned by firms in the broader food and consumer-products industry. See Glazer, *Life After* at 608 (cited in note 13).

[15] Id at 609; Burnett, *Predation* at 273 (cited in note 7); Petition for Writ of Certiorari in *Liggett Group Inc. v Brown & Williamson Tobacco Corp.* (Sept 15, 1992), at 15 (submitted by Phillip Areeda on behalf of petitioner Liggett).

generics sold to wholesalers and distributors, this would have led to lower retail prices for generics and greater generic-cigarette sales. Brown & Williamson prevented this outcome, Liggett argued, by increasing the rebates Brown & Williamson paid to its generic-cigarette customers instead of cutting list prices. The higher rebates would be captured entirely by Brown & Williamson's wholesale customers and would not be transmitted downstream to consumers in the form of lower prices. Further, Brown & Williamson's higher rebates forced Liggett to raise its own rebates and prevented it from using its financial resources to lower list prices or to finance retail promotions, either of which would have increased generic sales.

III. EVIDENTIARY ISSUES IN *BROOKE*

A theme we shall embroider throughout this paper is the difficulty confronting courts and administrators seeking to fine-tune market arrangements by means of antitrust laws. The informational and institutional limitations of courts and administrators make successful fine-tuning problematic. To avoid unnecessary stifling of competition, as well as to discourage rent-seekers from using antitrust to pursue their narrow self-interests,[16] antitrust law should proscribe only flagrantly anticompetitive behaviors, confident that the law of property, contract, and tort, on the one hand, and the forces of profit-seeking, on the other, will generally protect consumers from severe long-term harm.[17]

In *Brooke,* the Court endorsed this point of view in one respect, but failed to endorse it in another. By emphasizing the importance

[16] See, for example, Fred S. McChesney and William F. Shughart II, *The Causes and Consequences of Antitrust: The Public-Choice Perspective* (U Chicago, 1995); William J. Baumol and Janusz A. Ordover, *Use of Antitrust to Subvert Competition,* 28 J L & Econ 247 (1985); Roger L. Faith, Donald R. Leavens, and Robert D. Tollison, *Antitrust Pork Barrel,* 25 J L & Econ 329 (1982); William Breit and Kenneth G. Elzinga, *Antitrust Enforcement and Economic Efficiency: The Uneasy Case for Treble Damages,* 17 J L & Econ 329 (1974).

[17] See Harold Demsetz, *The Trust Behind Antitrust,* in Eleanor M. Fox & James T. Halverson, eds, *Industrial Concentration and the Market System* 45 (ABA, 1979) ("Demsetz, *Trust Behind Antitrust*") (arguing that American antitrust laws are built upon the assumption that market processes are generally superior to governmental processes at the task of allocating resources); Joseph A. Schumpeter, *Capitalism, Socialism and Democracy* 83 (Harper, 1942). Schumpeter argued that deviations of actual market outputs and prices from perfectly competitive outputs and prices are seldom long lasting or substantial in light of what he called the "process of creative destruction." Id. This process "incessantly revolutionizes the economic structure *from within,* incessantly destroying the old one, incessantly creating a new one. This process of creative destruction is the essential fact about capitalism." Id (emphasis in original).

of recoupment for assessing predatory pricing claims, *Brooke* compels plaintiffs to posit internally consistent economic theories of defendants' actions. These actions must be plausible in light of known facts, and other elements of evidence presented in support of a claim cannot overcome the lack of a plausible economic theory. As we argue below, however, the *Brooke* Court bypassed an opportunity to curtail fine-tuning by refusing to adopt a rule of *per se* legality to govern price cutting by members of noncollusive oligopolies.

A. The Areeda-Turner Test in *Brooke*

In the period before Areeda and Turner's landmark article on predation,[18] courts often focused excessively on internal memoranda for evidence purporting to reveal defendants' subjective intent. These documents, often rife with military metaphors and aggressive language, are not well suited for determining whether defendants' conduct will actually affect competition adversely. One great benefit of Areeda and Turner's article was that it drew attention away from this kind of evidence and refocused attention on objective economic data.[19]

Areeda and Turner proposed that a firm cannot be a predator unless its prices are so low as to be unremunerative in the short run. The specific test they proposed compares an alleged predator's prices with its average variable costs (AVC), with AVC serving as a proxy for the firm's marginal costs. Evidence of prices below AVC is deemed necessary for proving a predatory pricing claim.

Although appealing in its simplicity, the Areeda-Turner test is not beyond controversy. F.M. Scherer, among others, disagrees with the AVC standard, arguing instead that prices below a firm's average total cost (ATC) should be regarded as potentially predatory if such

[18] Phillip Areeda and Donald F. Turner, *Predatory Pricing and Related Practices Under Section 2 of the Sherman Act*, 88 Harv L Rev 697 (1975) ("Areeda & Turner, *Predatory Pricing*").

[19] As two of the present authors remark elsewhere:

> In the long term, the most notable impact of Phillip Areeda and Donald Turner's collaboration may not be their price-cost test, but rather their rejection of subjective intent language, dismissing it as "empty formulae." It is testimony to the influence of the 1975 Areeda-Turner contribution that planning documents, speeches by management, and intracompany memoranda currently play such a minor role in the judicial decision calculus.

Elzinga & Mills, *Trumping Areeda-Turner* at 581 n 66 (cited in note 7).

prices make it more difficult for a would-be rival to enter the industry.[20] Of course, regardless of which measure of cost is chosen for a cost-based predation test, attempts to determine costs in any particular factual circumstances are laden with difficulty. This was evident in the *Brooke* litigation.

In pre-trial preparation, both parties in *Brooke* devoted enormous attention to the question of whether Brown & Williamson had priced its generic cigarettes "below cost." Under a conventional Areeda-Turner inquiry, the question whether Brown & Williamson's generic cigarette price-cost differential was positive or negative would be critical to the outcome. More specifically, the question was whether or not Brown & Williamson covered its "reasonably anticipated average variable cost."[21] An assembly of attorneys, economists, and accountants on both sides of the case addressed that question in mind-numbing detail.

Liggett contended that Brown & Williamson, as a consequence of its extensive rebates, had priced its generic cigarettes below the variable costs incurred in producing them during the 18 months of the alleged predation.[22] Liggett's testifying expert estimated that Brown & Williamson's generic cigarette revenues were $11.4 mil-

> 20 The most fundamental problem [with the Areeda-Turner test] is that the rationale for setting price equal to marginal cost presupposes myopic short-run welfare maximization criteria, but pricing that alters the structure of an industry is a long-run phenomenon. It is easily demonstrated that if pricing at marginal cost but below average total cost (for example, when there is excess capacity) drives out (or keeps out) competitors, so that prices are raised above marginal costs in some other market, or over some later period in time, overall long-run welfare . . . can be reduced.

F.M. Scherer and David Ross, *Industrial Market Structure and Economic Performance* 472 (Houghton Mifflin, 3d ed 1990) (footnote omitted) ("Scherer & Ross, *Industrial Market Structure*"). See also F.M. Scherer, *Predatory Pricing and the Sherman Act: A Comment,* 89 Harv L Rev 869 (1976); George A. Hay, *A Confused Lawyers' Guide to the Predatory Pricing Literature,* in Steven C. Salop, ed, *Strategy, Predation, and Antitrust Analysis* 155, 161-66 (FTC, 1981).

21 "A price below reasonably anticipated average variable cost should be conclusively presumed unlawful." Areeda & Turner, *Predatory Pricing* at 733 (cited in note 18).

22 Although the definition of price (unlike the definition of cost) was undisputed in *Brooke,* price is not always an easily measured variable. When manufacturers offer trade deals to downstream vendors—for example, price discounts that involve vendor performance (such as building an aisle display at the vendor's expense)—the "price" for Areeda-Turner purposes is not merely the list price less the trade deal. That would represent the "price" if no downstream services were involved in the transaction. The price variable also can be muddied if a potential predator offered favored customers "low prices" in the form of in-kind services, such as overweight shipments, liberal credit, quality upgrades, or the forbearance of shipping and pallet charges.

lion to $16.0 million below their variable costs for the 18 month period July 1984 through December 1985.[23]

Brown & Williamson's cost expert initially estimated that Brown & Williamson lost $8.1 million (pre-tax) during this period. This estimate embraced "costs" that Liggett's expert did not include, such as manufacturing-cost variances and machine-speed-adjustment costs.[24] But Brown & Williamson's expert concluded that Brown & Williamson was better off by about $3.6 million (at the end of the 18-month period) after considering the particular tax benefits that resulted from Brown & Williamson's entry into generics.[25] Moreover, Brown & Williamson argued that it had not been the firm's expectation to incur losses on generic cigarettes during this period.

The principal difference on the cost side between the litigants centered around three expenditures Brown & Williamson incurred to produce and sell generic cigarettes. These differences added up to about 73 cents per 1000 cigarettes produced. From the revenue side, the differences centered on the role that anticipated tax savings should play in assessing a pricing strategy alleged to be predatory. These tax savings equaled about 77 cents per 1000 cigarettes.

Average Variable Cost Estimates. There were numerous disagreements about Brown & Williamson's variable costs. Disputed items included Brown & Williamson's manufacturing overhead, its retail promotion program, and its Direct Account Incentive Program (DAIP). Brown & Williamson's expert accountant estimated the cost of the manufacturing overhead attributed to Brown & Williamson's generics during the 18-month period to be in the range of 22 to 25 cents per 1000 cigarettes ($2.4 million). Liggett contended that Brown & Williamson's manufacturing overhead for its generic cigarettes was 50 cents per 1000. Both figures were anchored in Brown

[23] See Affidavit of William B. Burnett, *Liggett v Brown & Williamson* (MD NC), Jan 30, 1987, at 21-32.

[24] There were approximately $2 million in variable costs that Brown & Williamson attributed to its generic output that Liggett did not. For example, Brown & Williamson's cost expert added over $500,000 to variable costs as "Authorized Variances" because generic cigarette production costs exceeded standard manufacturing costs by this amount. In addition, because generics were produced on Brown & Williamson's machines of medium efficiency, this production may have pushed branded-cigarette production onto less efficient machines. This cost increase on these cigarettes was attributed to Brown & Williamson's generic entry during the 18-month period and represented an upward adjustment of over $1 million. See Affidavit of Roman L. Weil, *Liggett v Brown & Williamson* (MD NC) Dec 29, 1986, at 18.

[25] Id at 11.

& Williamson documents that were not prepared in conjunction with the litigation.

Another major disagreement concerned the proper cost allocation for Brown & Williamson's retail promotion program. During the last two months of 1984, customers could receive cents-off stickering on two cartons of Brown & Williamson's full revenue cigarettes for every carton of generic cigarettes purchased under the program. The stickers, of course, made the full revenue cigarettes more attractive to consumers (at no cost to retailers). The stickers were not applied to cartons of Brown & Williamson's generics. Because three cartons of cigarettes were involved in each application of this promotion—two full revenue cartons (usually Kools) and one generic—Liggett's expert attributed one-third of the expenditure to generics, or 15 cents per 1000 cigarettes.

Brown & Williamson's cost expert allocated none of the cost of this program to Brown & Williamson's generics. Because the stickers were applied exclusively on full revenue product, and not on generic cigarettes, he concluded that the primary benefit was to full revenue sales; consequently, he argued that it would be inappropriate to charge this cost against generics (unless one added the benefits—the incremental net revenues on branded products—to the generic segment as well).

The third major cost-allocation disagreement pertained to Brown & Williamson's Direct Account Incentive Program. This program gave participating customers an end-of-the-year rebate based on *total* cigarettes purchased from Brown & Williamson throughout the year. Stocking all (or, for some customers, a particular subset) of Brown & Williamson's product line—including generics—was a qualification for DAIP.

Liggett's expert construed DAIP as leveraging Brown & Williamson's generics into accounts that normally stocked only Brown & Williamson's full revenue product. These accounts, eager to secure the percentage rebate based on their annual purchases of Brown & Williamson's branded cigarettes, would succumb to ordering Brown & Williamson's generic line. For this reason, Liggett argued that the cost of DAIP associated with generics was greater than the dollar value of the rebate based on generic purchases alone. Liggett claimed that the cost ranged up to the full value of DAIP payments on all Brown & Williamson cigarettes during the 18-month period. This would have attributed 50 cents per 1000 cigarettes to the variable cost of Brown & Williamson's generic cigarettes.

Brown & Williamson's cost expert claimed there was no leveraging to generics from Brown & Williamson's branded products on account of DAIP payments by Brown & Williamson. DAIP was similar to rebate programs already offered by Brown & Williamson's rivals and was conceived independently of Brown & Williamson's decision to enter the generic segment. Because Brown & Williamson would have been making DAIP payments anyway, Brown & Williamson's cost expert added to the variable cost of Brown & Williamson's generics only those DAIP payments made for generic purposes.[26]

Disputed Tax Savings. Cigarette manufacturing requires that tobacco be aged before it is used. As a consequence, manufacturers maintain large tobacco inventories. Cost-accounting conventions for tobacco kept in inventory affect manufacturer profits and tax obligations. In an era when cigarette sales are growing, or at least not declining, and when tobacco prices are rising, LIFO (last in, first out) is advantageous because it reduces a firm's taxable income. Brown & Williamson calculated the cost of tobacco consumed in cigarette manufacturing using the LIFO convention. Using LIFO instead of FIFO (first in, first out) reduced taxable income and the company's tax bill because it allowed Brown & Williamson to cost the tobacco used in making today's cigarettes at recent, high tobacco prices. As long as the absolute size of Brown & Williamson's tobacco inventory did not decrease, the "inexpensive" tobacco acquired years ago need never be consumed (for cost-accounting purposes).

During the mid-1980s, when Brown & Williamson introduced its generic cigarettes, the company's sales of branded cigarettes were contracting. Thus, Brown & Williamson faced the prospect of curtailing tobacco purchases and being forced to consume some of the "inexpensive" tobacco in its inventory. Had this happened, Brown & Williamson's income taxes would have increased. The company expected to avoid this turn of events by entering the generic segment and expanding sales in order to avoid an inventory reduction. That is, one financial consequence of the new generic product line

[26] The parties also disagreed over the proper inventory-carrying costs for generic cigarettes. At one point, Brown & Williamson estimated a slightly higher carrying cost than Liggett, then revised that figure to one that was below Liggett's estimate. This revision was due in part to the fact that a portion of the tobacco used in generics was produced and dried overseas (therefore not imposing inventory costs upon Brown & Williamson). The parties also disputed whether the proper interest rate to be applied against inventory was 10%, 12%, or the prime rate plus .25 percent; and whether all of Brown & Williamson's leaf costs for generic cigarettes are variable (Liggett's contention) or in part fixed. Brown & Williamson's cost expert argued that $505,000 of Brown & Williamson's leaf costs were appropriately categorized as fixed costs; Liggett disagreed. There was close agreement on the allocation of display (or fixture) costs associated with Brown & Williamson's generic entry: 33 cents per 1000 (Liggett's view) versus 35 cents per 1000 (Brown & Williamson's view).

was to capture tax savings. The expected value of these tax savings was substantial, about $8 million or 77 cents per 1000 cigarettes.

At trial, the parties disputed whether these tax savings ought to have any bearing on the Areeda-Turner analysis. Liggett contended that tax savings are irrelevant in the Areeda-Turner test, arguing that Brown & Williamson should not be allowed to pass the test because of the government's tax treatment of its tobacco inventories. Brown & Williamson contended otherwise, reasoning that if the Areeda-Turner test is to be applied to detect whether or not its pricing was remunerative in the short-run, ignoring tax consequences would be an error. Excluding tax consequences amounts to pretending that Brown & Williamson makes business decisions on a pre-tax basis—that $8 million in expected tax savings had no role in determining the firm's actions.

If the tax savings anticipated by Brown & Williamson were apportioned to diminish the costs incurred producing and selling its generic cigarettes, Brown & Williamson argued that its price in the discount segment would have exceeded its anticipated AVC in that segment. Or equivalently, when favorable tax consequences are added to Brown & Williamson's sales revenues from its generic cigarettes during the 18-month period, the sum exceeds the company's variable costs of producing generic cigarettes.

Brown & Williamson's contention—that its tax savings from LIFO decrement avoidance is relevant in an Areeda-Turner test—rested on the standard definition of the short run: the resulting tax savings were variable in relationship to output and were under management control for a time-frame shorter than the long run.

Liggett insisted that Brown & Williamson's revenues from LIFO decrement avoidance should be ignored because they were not permanent savings. That is, the benefit was not tax saving, but tax postponement. If, at a later date, Brown & Williamson's sales of cigarettes were to decline rapidly, or if the price of green-leaf tobacco were to fall, and the company had to retreat into earlier low-cost layers of its tobacco inventory, the company's tax exposure would increase at that date. On this issue, Liggett's arithmetic is sound, but the premise on which its position rested is faulty.

The decisive factor is Brown & Williamson's expectation about its future tobacco inventory at the time it entered the discount segment. Brown & Williamson argued that it believed its generic sales would enable the company to postpone *indefinitely* having to use the earlier-purchased tobacco. Deferring an expense forever—even a tax expense—is economically the same as avoiding it altogether. In fact, at a reasonable discount rate, postponement even for a decade or two is virtually the same as avoidance.

Comparing only pre-tax prices and costs, as Liggett wanted to do, may neglect a class of nontrivial tax benefits that should not be overlooked if the Areeda-Turner test is to avoid sustaining false accusations of predation. With most applications of this test, the tax issue would never surface. *Brooke* is an exception. In this case, a mechanical comparison of pre-tax prices and costs drawn from accounting data do not provide the kind of guidance intended, namely, detecting whether Brown & Williamson's prices are inconsistent with short-run profit maximization. In assessing whether or not a course of action is profitable in the short run, tax considerations merit attention. The economic theory of the firm, which is the foundation of the Areeda-Turner test, is not built on the supposition that firms disregard taxes.

Costs and Expectations. Liggett also purported to show, *sans* a detailed assessment of costs, that the Areeda-Turner test had been violated by Brown & Williamson.[27] This approach centered on Brown & Williamson's internal documents about the company's entry into generics. For example, one Brown & Williamson report read: "Brown & Williamson is prepared to spend [i.e., pay rebates] up to net variable margin as a first step response to competitive counteroffers; if required, we are also prepared to go up to, but not beyond, full variable margin to gain entry into the generic market."[28] In Brown & Williamson's financial parlance, full variable margin included items such as manufacturing overhead that are included in its AVC. Consequently, Liggett interpreted this statement to mean that Brown & Williamson was prepared to pay rebates so high that its prices would be below AVC.

Liggett's focus on the document indicating Brown & Williamson's willingness, if necessary, to "spend down to full margin" was selective. Other Brown & Williamson documents predicted that rebates of this magnitude would not be necessary. For example, Brown & Williamson's 1985 budget projected promotional spending on generic cigarettes of almost $6 million *less* than the company ultimately spent. But when the competitive fray in the discount segment began in earnest, Brown & Williamson found it essential

[27] See Affidavit of Thomas F. Keller, *Liggett v Brown & Williamson* (MD NC), Jan 29, 1987, at 3-10.

[28] See "BROWN & WILLIAMSON GENERIC PROPOSAL," which is found in Hogeland Affidavit, Exhibit 4, at 086993, and referenced in the Keller Affidavit at 5 (cited in note 27). Another Brown & Williamson source cited in Keller's affidavit reads: "B&W will be prepared to spend full margin in order to displace Liggett & Myers as the trade source of generic and private labels, although not contributing to trading profit, it will give us short term volume and share enhancement." Id at 6.

to offer greater discounts than it had expected in order to induce customers to switch to Brown & Williamson's generic product.

Brown & Williamson's cost expert also emphasized that the Areeda-Turner focus on historical cost and revenue data does not account for the capital (or "going concern") value that Brown & Williamson expected to enjoy from having established itself in the discount segment. None of the costs incurred by Brown & Williamson during the 18-month period was charged against future periods (1986 or beyond) in either analyst's Areeda-Turner computations. Brown & Williamson's cost expert argued that excluding "going concern" considerations was extremely conservative given that Brown & Williamson was an entrant into the generic segment, with expectations of a long-term presence.

Alfred Marshall, who is often credited with inventing the time-period analysis from which the short-run/long-run distinction flows, understood the distinction between fixed costs and variable costs to be an abstraction. He wrote that the occasions on which one might "divide one case sharply from the other" would be "neither frequent nor important."[29] Marshall did not anticipate the Areeda-Turner test, and the important demands it places upon his time-period framework for analysis. That a firm might 'pass' or 'flunk' the Areeda-Turner test based upon the accounting classification of its Direct Account Incentive Program, or its adoption of LIFO accounting, suggests an infirmity in the Areeda-Turner test's emphasis on assigning costs.

But any assessment of the economic issues in *Brooke* would be incomplete without giving an account of the Areeda-Turner dispute. Initially, Areeda-Turner occupied enormous attention in the litigation. One would not be aware of the attention devoted to the Areeda-Turner test in *Brooke* merely by reading the appellate opinions.[30] The pitfalls and deep ambiguities of this test provoked Brown & Williamson to alter its economic theory of the case in a manner that ultimately led the appellate courts to focus on recoupment.

Liggett continued throughout the litigation to stress its claim that Brown & Williamson's generic prices were below AVC. Brown

[29] Alfred Marshall, 1 *Principles of Economics* 378 (MacMillan, 9th ed 1961).

[30] The difficulty of defining price and AVC has been encountered in prior predation cases as well. In fact, conducting an Areeda-Turner cost-based inquiry in *Brooke* was *less* complex than the norm: the production process for cigarettes was well developed, and the amounts of money spent on marketing generic cigarettes was relatively small. The fact that an Areeda-Turner test in *Brooke* remained difficult further underscores the value of using recoupment as an analytical filter or screen before resort to the task of estimating a firm's price and average variable cost.

& Williamson, however, largely abandoned the issue because, as its economic expert testified, Brown & Williamson had not charged prices below AVC (or even ATC) in the (stipulated) relevant market of all cigarettes. Consequently, even if Brown & Williamson's *generic* prices had been below their AVC, this would not enable Brown & Williamson to prey successfully in the discount cigarette segment.

B. Recoupment as a Practical 'Screen' for Predation Claims

In light of the obstacles to determining a defendant's costs—as the experience in *Brooke* indicates—a more functional screen for predation cases would be valuable. The Court's explicit endorsement of the recoupment standard is promising in this regard. A reliable assessment of the prospects for recoupment may require less detailed, and less ambiguous, information about a defendant's implicit logic than divining corporate memoranda or debating the nuances of costs.[31] The information requirements confronting courts that first ask "Is recoupment feasible under the plaintiff's theory of predation?" are fewer than those burdening courts whose first question is "Did the defendant price below an appropriate measure of cost in the relevant market?"

Recoupment analysis focuses on questions regarding the likelihood of exit by target firms, and the likelihood of new entry (or reentry of former rivals) once the predator tries to recoup. If exit of rivals is implausible or can be accomplished only after a long delay, or if entry into the industry is easy, then the plaintiff's predation claim is discredited. In a case in which recoupment is sufficiently unlikely, the plaintiff's claim should be dismissed even before an elaborate price-cost comparison is undertaken.

A positive answer to any of the following questions justifies dismissal of a plaintiff's predation claim because prospects for recouping predatory losses are too remote to justify further court attention.

[31] Although we do not deny that measures of cost can be constructed from real-world data, and that such measures are often quite useful for some regulatory and adjudicatory purposes, it is also imperative to keep in mind that economic costs are subjective. Monetary measures of costs ultimately are proxies for the foregone utilities that are the true costs confronting decision makers. See James M. Buchanan, *Cost and Choice* (Markham, 1969). Because costs are foregone utilities—the satisfaction that the decisionmaker expects she *would have* received had she chosen option B rather than option A—costs are inescapably bound to the expectations of decisionmakers. And reasonable people may have different expectations regarding future states of the world.

- Does the alleged predator currently confront substantial competition from noncollusive rivals (other than its intended victims) within the relevant market?[32]
- Is entry into the relevant market devoid of high entry barriers?[33]
- Do customers in the alleged market have credible counter-strategies that are likely to defeat a predatory scheme?[34]
- Is the industry in rapid decline?[35]

Only if the previous questions are answered in the negative would a court be justified in allowing the parties to undertake the expensive and complicated task of gathering and presenting data on price-cost comparisons.

Although negative answers to all of these questions do not prove that predation is occurring, the possibility of predation could not be dismissed. Hence, a price-cost comparison á la Areeda-Turner is a possible next step. A positive answer, however, to any of these questions should suffice to dismiss an allegation of predation. The complexities of price-cost comparisons would thus be avoided in many instances.

In *Brooke,* each court answered one of these questions affirmatively: Brown & Williamson did indeed confront substantial com-

[32] For example, in *American Drugs, Inc. v Wal-Mart Stores, Inc.,* E-92-1158 (Chancery Ct. of Faulkner County, Ark, Oct 1993), Wal-Mart was accused of preying on smaller rivals in the market for pharmaceuticals and health and beauty aids in Faulkner County, Arkansas. Although Wal-Mart lost at trial (under Arkansas's 1937 Unfair Practices Act), the trial court ignored the fact that within the relevant market Wal-Mart faced competition from other national retailers such as Kroger's and Fred's. Even if Wal-Mart priced below cost for the purpose of driving 'mom & pop' drug stores out of Faulkner County, such predatory expenditures by Wal-Mart would have been to no avail because Kroger and other national chains operating in Faulkner County would have remained. Wal-Mart would not have been able to charge the monopoly prices necessary to recoup its predatory expenses.

Wal-Mart appealed to the Arkansas Supreme Court. As of this writing, Arkansas's high court has yet to hand down its decision in the case.

[33] Although entry barriers do not guarantee recoupment, the *absence* of entry barriers surely does guarantee that recoupment will not occur.

[34] Buyers, of course, are harmed by monopolies. If the customers are relatively few in number, they can be expected to protect themselves from attempts to monopolize their supply sources. Entering into long-term supply contracts at competitive prices is one way for customers to protect themselves from future monopoly prices while simultaneously protecting efficient suppliers from predation. See Frank H. Easterbrook, *Predatory Strategies and Counterstrategies,* 48 U Chi L Rev 263, 269 (1981) ("Easterbrook, *Predatory Strategies*").

[35] An industry in which consumer demand is in dramatic secular decline (for example, the U.S. typewriter industry in the 1980s) is not an industry conducive to recoupment. Market demand in the future is likely to be lower than demand today, making recovery of predatory expenses a dubious outcome.

petition from rivals within the relevant market. This scotched Brown & Williamson's chances for recoupment under Liggett's predation hypothesis. Brown & Williamson stood to gain only a fraction of whatever benefits would have flowed to the oligopoly from disciplining Liggett successfully. Philip Morris, the industry leader (with 36% market share), and R.J. Reynolds (with 32%) each had a larger share of the cigarette market than did third-place Brown & Williamson (with 12%).[36] Other firms—such as Lorillard and American Tobacco Co.—also would have gained from Brown & Williamson's diminishing the threat posed by generic cigarettes. Whatever industry benefits were promised from successful predation by Brown & Williamson would have been shared among Brown & Williamson's rivals even though the full cost of the predation would be borne by Brown & Williamson alone.

Of course, it is imaginable that members of a noncollusive oligopoly could tacitly orchestrate a predation campaign in which one member of the oligopoly acts as 'hit man.' But predation under such circumstances is little more than imaginable. Tacitly orchestrated predation by a noncollusive oligopoly is too implausible to take seriously, given plausible alternative explanations, because of difficulties confronting individual oligopolists who must coordinate their actions during the predatory period as well as during the recoupment period. The *Brooke* Court correctly recognized—and eloquently explained—these difficulties.

> However unlikely predatory pricing by multiple firms may be when they conspire, it is even less likely when, as here, there is no express coordination. Firms that seek to recoup predatory losses through the conscious parallelism of oligopoly must rely on uncertain and ambiguous signals to achieve concerted action. The signals are subject to misinterpretation and are a blunt and imprecise means of ensuring smooth cooperation, especially in the context of changing or unprecedented market circumstances. This anticompetitive minuet is most difficult to compose and to perform, even for a disciplined oligopoly.
>
> . . . [O]n the whole, tacit cooperation among oligopolists must be considered the least likely means of recouping predatory losses. In addition to the difficulty of achieving effective tacit coordination and the high likelihood that any attempt to discipline will produce an outbreak of competition, the predator's present losses in a case like this fall on it alone, while the later supracompetitive profits must be shared with every

[36] *Brooke*, 113 S Ct at 2590.

> other oligopolist in proportion to its market share, including the intended victim.[37]

The implausibility of such tacit coordination among Brown & Williamson and other cigarette producers was decisive for the Court, which was properly skeptical of a predation claim requiring such detailed and delicate coordination among firms who are not wrapped up in an explicit collusive arrangement.

C. Noncollusive Oligopolistic Predation and the *Per se* Rule

The Court refused to take what would have been an appropriate next step, namely, to create a rule of *per se* legality to govern price cutting by members of noncollusive oligopolies.[38] The Court declined to take this step because, "[h]owever unlikely that possibility [of noncollusive oligopoly predation] may be as a general matter, when the realities of the market and the record facts indicate that it has occurred and was likely to have succeeded, theory will not stand in the way of liability."[39] This refusal to create a rule of *per se* legality is puzzling in light of the Court's oft-repeated justification for *per se* rules.

Justice Marshall adeptly explained the rationale for *per se* rules:

> *Per se* rules always contain a degree of arbitrariness. They are justified on the assumption that the gains from imposition of the rule will far outweigh the losses and that significant administrative advantages will result. In other words, the potential competitive harm plus the administrative costs of determining in what particular situations the practice may be

[37] Id (citations omitted). The Court went on to note:

> In this case, for example, Brown & Williamson, with its 11-12% share of the cigarette market, would have had to generate around $9 in supracompetitive profits for each $1 invested in predation; the remaining $8 would belong to its competitors, who had taken no risk.

Id.

[38] As the Court put it: "We decline to create a per se rule of nonliability for predatory price discrimination when recoupment is alleged to take place through supracompetitive oligopoly pricing." Id at 2591. Such a *per se* rule of legality was adopted by the Fourth Circuit, and the Supreme Court's refusal to endorse it is one instance in which the Court, in its recent antitrust rulings, did not opt for greater objectivity and certainty. This refusal is an exception to Calkins' observation that "[w]hen faced with a choice between achieving individualized justice and adhering to relatively clear, generalized rules, [the Rehnquist Court] has usually chosen the latter." Steven Calkins, *The October 1992 Supreme Court Term and Antitrust: More Objectivity than Ever*, 62 Antitrust L J 327, 327 (1994) ("Calkins, *More Objectivity*").

[39] *Brooke*, 113 S Ct at 2591.

> harmful must far outweigh the benefits that may result. If the potential benefits *in the aggregate* are outweighed to this degree, then they are simply not worth identifying in individual cases.[40]

This rationale was echoed by Justice Stevens in his majority opinion in *Arizona v Maricopa County Medical Society*:

> The costs of judging business practices under the rule of reason . . . have been reduced by the recognition of *per se* rules. Once experience with a particular kind of restraint enables the Court to predict with confidence that the rule of reason will condemn it, it has applied a conclusive presumption that the restraint is unreasonable.[41]

Just so. But what works in one direction for rules of *per se* illegality also works in the opposite direction for rules of *per se* legality. If a particular business arrangement or practice is highly unlikely to harm the competitive process, the Court should declare such a practice or institutional structure to be *per se* legal. This is true even if it were possible that under a rare concatenation of circumstances the arrangement or practice in question may generate more harm than good. To paraphrase Justice Stevens, "once experience with a particular kind of complaint by a plaintiff enables the court to predict with confidence that the trial courts will find, using the rule of reason, that the complaint is implausible, the Court should apply a conclusive presumption that the complaint is untenable or that the complained-of practice or institutional structure is *per se* legal."[42]

[40] *United States v Container Corp. of America*, 393 US 333, 341 (1969) (Marshall dissenting) (emphasis added). See also Justice Black's justification for a rule of *per se* illegality for price fixing:

> This principle of *per se* unreasonableness not only makes the type of restraints which are proscribed by the Sherman Act more certain to the benefit of everyone concerned, but it also avoids the necessity for an incredibly complicated and prolonged economic investigation into the entire history of the industry involved, as well as related industries, in an effort to determine at large whether a particular restraint has been unreasonable—an inquiry so often wholly fruitless when undertaken.

Northern Pacific Railroad Co. v United States, 356 US 1, 5 (1958).

[41] 457 US 332, 343-44 (1982) (footnotes omitted).

[42] Because well-chosen *per se* rules help to avoid wasteful litigation, the antitrust establishment may be the only long-term beneficiary of refusals to implement a *per se* rule of legality when such rules are justified.

> If the full-blown rule of reason approach required to implement the policy were itself costless, it should be adopted. But it is not costless. There are

Per se rules would be unjustified if adjudication were costless and if a court could always determine accurately, after a lengthy-enough trial and examination of the record, whether a particular business practice was harmful or beneficial. Even horizontal price fixing might then be governed under a rule of reason because it has been shown that, in certain circumstances, such price fixing redounds to the long-run benefit of society.[43] But adjudication is costly and courts are fallible. Therefore, courts are justified—given their belief that price fixing almost always harms society—to proscribe it with a *per se* rule of illegality.[44] The same reasons justify using a rule of *per se* legality when the likelihood

> definite costs in the form of added uncertainty, more complex adjudication, and an enhanced probability of erroneous and irrational choices.
>
> . . . .
>
> Much more impressive would be the costs of adjudicating and enforcing the policy, for each case would become, in the jargon of the antitrust law firms and economic consultants who would be the significant financial beneficiaries, "the big case." . . . A thorough investigation [of the kind that occur when no *per se* rule governs] conducted under traditional antitrust procedures would be so costly in terms of money and, more important, high-level talent that the enforcement agencies would find the number of cases they could undertake sharply limited.

Scherer & Ross, *Industrial Market Structure* at 336 (cited in note 20).

[43] See William Sjostrom, *Collusion in Ocean Shipping: A Test of Monopoly and Empty Core Models,* 97 J Pol Econ 1160 (1989); George Bittlingmayer, *Decreasing Average Cost and Competition: A New Look at the Addyston Pipe Case,* 25 J L & Econ 201 (1982); Donald Dewey, *Information, Entry, and Welfare: The Case for Collusion,* 69 Am Econ Rev 587 (1979); Scherer & Ross, *Industrial Market Structure* at 335 (cited in note 20) ("Given the complexity of the links between market structure, conduct, and performance, it seems almost certain that there are at least some conditions under which agreements to fix 'reasonable' prices will permit better economic performance than unfettered competition.").

[44] Scherer & Ross, *Industrial Market Structure* at 336-37 (cited in note 20), identify three costs of a rule-of-reason approach to price-fixing cases:

> For one, the rules of evidence applied in antitrust cases are cumbersome in the extreme. . . . Second, jurists are seldom trained in economics, and many lack the knowledge to separate sense from nonsense in the contending parties' briefs or to get a firm analytic handle on the conduct and performance variables at issue. . . . Third, the whole adversary process on which the courts operate is best suited for reaching either-or decisions: Is the defendant guilty, or not? . . . Indeed, the facts and arguments are often so complex that they swamp the judge's ability to comprehend and integrate them logically. He or she may then arrive at a decision on the basis of raw instinct.

Thus, using *per se* rules when the activities or institutional structures in question are strongly believed to be either harmful an overwhelming number of times, or benign an overwhelming number of times, avoids these costs at little sacrifice.

is small that a particular practice or institutional structure is detrimental.[45]

Given the *Brooke* Court's crisp articulation of the extreme coordination difficulties facing members of a noncollusive oligopoly, such a situation is the kind that suggests a rule of *per se* legality. It should be of little consequence that successful noncollusive-oligopoly predation is imaginable or possible.[46] What is of consequence is the expected social cost of such predation compared with the costs of adjudicating accusations of such predation every time they are raised. The expected social cost is vanishingly small because, for reasons the *Brooke* Court itself illuminated, such predation seldom will be feasible. Thus, nothing is gained by avoiding a rule of *per se* legality to govern plaintiffs' claims of predation by noncollusive oligopolists.[47] The Court erred in not promulgating such a rule in *Brooke*.

[45] There is no logic for supporting *per se* rules of illegality when these are appropriate, while refusing to support *per se* rules of legality. Judge Easterbrook suggests that the "never fallacy" underlies the refusal of courts and commentators to see the benefits of rules of *per se* legality. Adherents of the "never fallacy" insist that unless a practice or institutional arrangement *never* harms consumers it is proper for the courts to determine in each specific case whether or not the practice or institutional arrangement should be proscribed. Judge Easterbrook calls for jettisoning this fallacy. Endorsing symmetry between the use of rules of *per se* illegality and rules of *per se* legality, he adds that "[s]ociety can't endure an antitrust law in which heads-the-plaintiff-wins-tails-its-a-jury-question." Frank H. Easterbrook, *Ignorance and Antitrust* in Thomas M. Jorde & David J. Teece, eds, *Antitrust, Innovation, and Competitiveness* 119, 129-30 (Oxford U, 1992). See also Richard A. Posner, *The Next Step in the Antitrust Treatment of Restricted Distribution: Per Se Legality,* 48 U Chi L Rev 6, 23 (1981) ("Posner, *Next Step*") ("The same considerations of judicial economy and legal certainty that justify use of per se rules of illegality in some cases justify the use of rules of per se legality in others.").

[46] For an explanation of how tacitly colluding oligopolists might discipline a price-cutting rival, see Robert H. Porter, *A Study of Cartel Stability: The Joint Executive Committee, 1880-1886,* 14 Bell J Econ 301 (1983). Note that in Porter's model, *all* members of the noncollusive predatory oligopoly lower, and then increase, their prices simultaneously. In *Brooke,* Brown & Williamson was the only firm accused of preying on Liggett.

[47] Rules of *per se* illegality are believed to be more common in antitrust law than are rules of *per se* legality. According to Judge Posner, American antitrust law "rarely use[s]" rules of *per se* legality. See Posner, *Next Step* at 23 (cited in note 45). This is to miss the obvious. There are rules of *per se* legality that the law applies with such frequency that regulators, courts, and scholars are unconscious of their existence. In fact, a far greater number of business practices are *per se* legal than not. For example, it is *per se* legal for a manufacturer that owns its retail outlets to require managers of these outlets to charge some minimum price, just as it is *per se* legal for this minimum price to be the same in all manufacturer-owned outlets. It is *per se* legal for a firm, say, not to open for business on Sundays. In addition, antitrust enforcement practices have created areas of *per se* legality. The Merger Guidelines' "safe

IV. FURTHER IMPLAUSIBILITY OF THE CASE AGAINST BROWN & WILLIAMSON

The Court's focus on the implausibility of predation in an oligopoly was appropriate and sufficient to justify its rejection of Liggett's predation claim. There were, though, other notable economic issues raised in the course of the *Brooke* litigation. In this section we explore some of these, particularly the specific arguments offered by Liggett in support of its predation hypothesis. For even if Brown & Williamson had been Liggett's only rival—or if Brown & Williamson were the dominant cigarette producer—Liggett's predation hypothesis would remain unsalvageable.

A. Predation in a Segment of the Market

An important issue in many antitrust cases is the delineation of the relevant market. This litigation was no exception. While both parties stipulated at trial that generics are in the same market with full revenue brands, much of the trial litigation was conducted as though this stipulation was forgotten. Generic cigarettes often were treated as though they constituted a different market from that of full revenue brands.[48]

harbor" rule, for example, under which the federal enforcement agencies decline to challenge horizontal mergers whenever the newly structured industry will have a post-merger HHI below 1000, constitutes a domain of *per se* legality. See *DOJ and FTC Horizontal Merger Guidelines,* 62 BNA Antitrust and Trade Regulation Reporter, Special Supp., § 1.51, 2 April 1992, at S-8.

The reason no one argues that firms should be prohibited from unilaterally choosing to close on Sundays is that no one suspects that such decisions can have anticompetitive consequences. But if the possibility of anticompetitiveness were raised, and a court responded—as it should—by ruling that the likelihood of anticompetitive effects is too remote to justify judicial attention to this matter, the court would have explicitly created a rule of *per se* legality. We argue here that price cutting by members of noncollusive oligopolies is similar to unilateral decisions by firms to close on Sundays insofar as the probabilities of anticompetitive consequences from such activities are too slight to justify any rule other than one of *per se* legality.

[48] Although both parties stipulated that the relevant product market was all cigarettes, the Court in fact "analyzed economy cigarette pricing separately from regular pricing." Calkins, *More Objectivity* at 389 (cited in note 38). See also Jonathan B. Baker, *Predatory Pricing After* Brooke Group: *An Economic Perspective,* 62 Antitrust L J 585, 595-96 (1994) ("Baker, *Predatory Pricing*") ("As the Court described the facts the cigarette market has two relevant segments: a low-priced generic segment and a high-priced branded segment. . . . Liggett argued that Brown & Williamson predated in generics but expected to recoup the costs of predation primarily in brandeds, a much larger segment of the market. . . . Here, predation occurs in one market segment—generics—while recoupment occurs primarily in another segment—brandeds.") (footnotes omitted).

Settling the question of whether or not products are in the same market can be problematic because in reality products may exist on a continuum of substitutability for each other. However, unlike some antitrust litigation in which the delineation of the relevant market is pivotal, settling the question of whether generics and full revenue brands are in the same or separate markets was not essential to determine the plausibility of Liggett's predation claim.

If the trial stipulation is correct—namely, all cigarettes constitute the relevant market—then the Court was justified in ruling in favor of Brown & Williamson on Areeda-Turner grounds.[49] If the relevant market is all cigarettes, then the appropriate price-cost comparison is the relationship between Brown & Williamson's prices and AVC across *all* of its domestic cigarette sales. No one disputed that Brown & Williamson's *total* revenue exceeded its total costs and, *a fortiori,* its variable costs. The relationship of its prices to AVC in a segment of the relevant market—the discount segment—is immaterial.

Pricing its output below AVC in one segment while making up the deficit elsewhere in the market would be a futile predation strategy for Brown & Williamson, or any would-be predator.[50] The hapless predator's losses in one segment would prove ineffectual in injuring its rivals because the rivals can take refuge from the siege of low prices elsewhere in the market. Liggett's concessions—that (1) generics are in the same market as full revenue brands; and (2) Brown & Williamson never lost money on its cigarette sales in total—are fatal to Liggett's case against Brown & Williamson. This conclusion holds even if Brown & Williamson priced its generic cigarettes below their AVC.

Liggett's predation charge is not salvaged by treating generics and full revenue brands as if they are sold in two distinct markets. Liggett moved into generics even though (by its own assumption) it could have sold all of its cigarettes at supracompetitive prices as

[49] See Calkins, *More Objectivity* at 379 n 282 (cited in note 38) ("The [trial] court found that . . . antitrust injury was missing because there was no below-cost pricing in the cigarette market as a whole.").

[50] See Michael L. Denger & John A. Herfort, *Predatory Pricing Claims after* Brooke Group, 62 Antitrust L J 541, 551-52 (1994) (footnotes omitted):

> Most courts have reasoned that predatory pricing on only a fraction of a product line cannot exclude or drive competitors out of a competitively meaningful market—or impair competition—consisting of the entire product line. The existence of non-predatory pricing in the remaining, competitive part of the market means that competitors in the market are neither threatened with elimination from the market nor likely to be intimidated into supracompetitive pricing in the future, as required by the recoupment standard.

full revenue brands. Thus, Liggett perceived its potential profits in generics to be higher than in full revenue lines. The fact that Brown & Williamson (again, by Liggett's own assumption) had no intention of permanently exploiting the profit potential of generics[51] suggests that Liggett had a comparative advantage, relative to Brown & Williamson, in producing and marketing generics. Under such circumstances, Liggett's theory of predation is really one in which a less efficient firm (Brown & Williamson) preys on a more-efficient incumbent (Liggett). Liggett's incentive to slug it out with Brown & Williamson under such circumstances would have been too great to make predation by Brown & Williamson a rational strategy.

Additional weaknesses mar Liggett's allegation of predation. Even assuming that generics and full revenue brands differ from each other on the demand side, they are very close substitutes on the supply side.[52] Cigarette producers readily can (and do) shift output from generics to full revenue brands on the same production lines. Supply-side substitutability undercuts Liggett's theory of price predation.

If Liggett knew that Brown & Williamson was preying in generics in order to protect supracompetitive prices on full revenue lines, then Liggett had an incentive to switch its cigarette output more heavily into full revenue lines (where, after all, Liggett insisted supracompetitive profits were being made). Liggett either could have lowered prices on its full revenue brands below the alleged cartel price, or sold its brands at this price.

The particular strategy chosen would have depended on Liggett's assessment of the reactions of other cigarette producers to Liggett's lower prices on full revenue brands. Either way, Liggett's survival was not threatened by Brown & Williamson's alleged predation, for Liggett could always turn to branded product as a profitable source of sales and switch back to generics once Brown & Williamson stopped predating.[53]

[51] Liggett argued that Brown & Williamson intended to thwart the market for generics. See Calkins, *More Objectivity* at 378 (cited in note 38) ("Liggett alleged that [Brown & Williamson] sought to achieve a sufficient share of the generics business to be in a position to limit and then reduce the spread between generic and regular cigarette prices, thus limiting the growth of generics . . . .").

[52] Liggett's generic cigarettes were physically identical to cigarettes sold in its branded packages.

[53] We assume here that Liggett is as efficient at cigarette production as is Brown & Williamson. Thus, if Brown & Williamson stood to earn supracompetitive profits in the full-revenue market, Liggett likewise stood to earn such profits.

B. Counterstrategies to Predation

Liggett argued, though, that Brown & Williamson would have been content to discipline rather than eliminate Liggett. Because Brown & Williamson's predation losses would have been higher than the losses it imposed on Liggett, this claim raises the question of why Liggett would capitulate to Brown & Williamson's predatory actions.[54] Unless Brown & Williamson had a deeper pocket than Liggett (and Liggett could not turn successfully to the capital markets for a loan), Brown & Williamson's predatory attack could not prompt Liggett to raise its generics prices. Indeed, because Brown & Williamson stood to loose more than Liggett through predation, Liggett might have relished its rival engaging in such a self-defeating tactic. Robert Bork's remark about predation is apposite: "It looks like the best method of predation is to convince your rival that you are a likely victim and lure him into a ruthless price-cutting attack."[55]

There is another reason why an attempt by Brown & Williamson to discipline Liggett would have backfired. By its own account, Liggett "was on the verge of going out of business"[56] in 1980 just before it moved into generics. If true, this implies that the tacitly collusive arrangement Liggett alleged to be operative in the cigarette industry was not working for Liggett; Liggett was losing money. Generics turned out to be Liggett's protection from bankruptcy court. Why, then, would Brown & Williamson have supposed that predatory losses inflicted on Liggett in generics would have prompted Liggett to return meekly to the fold? It is problematic to suppose that Liggett could have been disciplined into abandoning a product line in which it enjoyed great success for one that was unremunerative.

Of course, regardless of the particular predation theory offered by Liggett, it is not impossible for an equally efficient Liggett to succumb to predatory pressure by Brown & Williamson. On one hand,

[54] This is especially true if Liggett had a comparative advantage over Brown & Williamson in the production of generic cigarettes.

[55] Robert H. Bork, *The Antitrust Paradox* 152 (Basic Books, 1978) ("Bork, *Antitrust Paradox*").

[56] The words are actually those of Brown & Williamson, but they are cited approvingly by Areeda in his petition for certiorari filed on behalf of Liggett. Areeda petition at 5 (cited in note 15). Burnett, who served as an expert economic witness for Liggett, reported that "Liggett had formulated a range of contingency plans for liquidation in the event its sagging corporate fortunes could not be reversed . . ." and that Liggett was "on the verge of failure in the late 1970s." Burnett, *Predation* at 262, 267 (cited in note 7).

Liggett may be uncertain whether it is as efficient as Brown & Williamson. Alternatively, Liggett may have insufficient internal funds to defend itself against Brown & Williamson's predation and may be unable to acquire capital from external sources.[57] We consider each possibility in turn.

If Liggett is so uncertain of its efficiency relative to its rivals that it chooses to withdraw in the face of a predatory attack by Brown & Williamson, antitrust law should hesitate to second-guess. But Liggett chose to raise its rebates and retain sales during Brown & Williamson's alleged predation. This reveals, accurately it would seem from the trial record and post-trial events in the cigarette industry, that Liggett did not believe that Brown & Williamson held a decisive efficiency advantage.[58] Further, Liggett did indeed have access to internal funds to fight a predatory price war had such a war been raging. During the period of alleged predation, Liggett was owned by Grand Metropolitan, PLC.[59] Grand Met is a firm of substantial means, described by one of Liggett's economic experts as a "large, diversified British firm."[60]

In contrast, if Liggett possessed insufficient funds of its own, Liggett's failure to invest in fighting an allegedly predatory Brown & Williamson cannot be read as evidence that Liggett really believed that Brown & Williamson was a more-efficient rival, or that Brown & Williamson was pricing below cost. If Liggett knew that it was as efficient as Brown & Williamson and that Brown & Williamson was pricing below cost, but Liggett's internal funds were inadequate to wage a counter-predatory effort, Liggett could (and, presumably, would) have sought to borrow the funds. External capital sources should have been willing to loan Liggett these funds.[61] If Liggett

[57] See, for example, Baker, *Predatory Pricing* at 591 (cited in note 48) ("If imperfections in the market for capital cause the prey to have less access to financial capital than the predator, then the predator may reasonably expect to use its 'deep pockets' in the traditional way to drive the prey to exit.") (footnotes omitted).

[58] One cost of allowing firms to bring predation actions against rivals is that filing suit may be a less expensive way for firms to subdue vigorous competitors than investing one's funds in a price-cutting counterstrategy. Suppose Liggett knows that remaining in generics promises sufficient profit to justify spending its own funds fighting a price war with Brown & Williamson. Further suppose that Liggett cannot sue Brown & Williamson for predation. Then, Liggett will spend its own money fighting Brown & Williamson. But suppose now that Liggett can sue Brown & Williamson for predation. The least-cost way for Liggett to fight the price war with Brown & Williamson might then be to file a predation suit against Brown & Williamson rather than challenge Brown & Williamson by means of price competition.

[59] We address below the effects on Brown & Williamson's alleged predation of Grand Met's wishes to sell Liggett.

[60] Burnett, *Predation* at 273 (cited in note 7).

secured such a loan, Brown & Williamson's predation attempt would fail and Liggett would survive.

That a target firm may in a particular case be unable to obtain adequate funding to wage a counter-predatory effort cannot be denied. Liggett's request for a loan will be refused if Liggett fails to convince fallible capital markets that Brown & Williamson is really no more efficient than Liggett. But the very same capital-market imperfection necessary to clear a path to success for predators in such situations renders court assessments of predation claims untrustworthy. That is, the same real-world scarcities of knowledge that cause capital-market imperfections simultaneously cause imperfections in the knowledge of courts and antitrust-enforcement agents. A court that decides against Brown & Williamson would be second-guessing the collective assessment of experts in capital markets. It is difficult to imagine that court personnel possess knowledge and insight about markets superior to that which is achieved by specialist participants in markets—participants who earn profits when they assess markets accurately and who suffer losses when they assess markets inaccurately. To make this assumption is to abandon what Harold Demsetz has labelled "the trust behind antitrust." It is to assume—wrongly—that courts know better than market participants what are, and what are not, the most profitable avenues for investments.[62]

> 61 Investors should be willing to back the intended victim [of predation], because it would be the more profitable survivor, having sustained smaller losses during the fight. . . . True, the victim may fail, but the loan itself reduces that risk, and the bank, with a diversified portfolio of loans, could charge a suitable rate of interest and be indifferent to the remaining risk.

Easterbrook, *Predatory Strategies* at 269-70 (cited in note 34). See also Bork, *Antitrust Paradox* at 147-48 (cited in note 55) ("If the potential victim would find resistance to predation a profitable use for his liquid assets, a lender should find it equally profitable to lend the required capital."); George J. Stigler, *Imperfections in the Capital Markets,* in George J. Stigler, ed, *The Organization of Industry* 113 (R.D. Irwin, 1968) (arguing that the exceptional fungibility of capital makes it among the most likely of goods to flow to its most highly valued uses).

62 Demsetz, *Trust Behind Antitrust* at 47-48 (cited in note 17):

> One of the most important reasons for trusting in competition is that there is little basis for faith that outsiders—be they government planners, judges, lawyers, or academics—possess the knowledge and the motivation required to fine-tune on behalf of consumers. A complex economy made up of many specialists is productive precisely because each need deal only with a relatively small part of the world; the actions of these specialists, disciplined by competition and motivated by prospects of gain, linked together and made consistent by market prices, offer a superior method for utilizing knowledge in behalf of the consumer. Denial of this premise opens the door to centralized regulation of business activity.

C. Specific Allegations Supporting Liggett's Predation Hypothesis

'Simultaneous Recoupment.' The most substantial problem affecting predators is the difficulty of recouping predatory losses. As a rule, predators cannot begin recouping these losses until after predation is halted. To recoup, the predator's expected stream of monopoly profits must be discounted by an appropriate rate of interest[63]—a rate that reflects uncertainty about future market conditions. The farther off in the future recoupment begins, the greater is the likelihood that market conditions at the time of recoupment will differ significantly from the period of predatory losses. This fact curtails the predator's chances for successful recoupment. As argued above, the *Brooke* Court recognized the importance of recoupment, and ruled that predation plaintiffs must show recoupment to be a genuine possibility for defendants before such cases can move forward.

While not disputing the importance of recoupment for purposes of assessing predation claims, Liggett argued that Brown & Williamson's predation tactics did not fit the traditional mold. Liggett insisted that Brown & Williamson recouped its predatory losses as these losses were being incurred. Therefore, recoupment was alleged to be less of a problem for Brown & Williamson than for a

See also Frank H. Easterbrook, *The Limits of Antitrust,* 63 Tex L Rev 1, 24-25 (1984) (emphasis in original):

> The point is not that business losses perfectly penalize business mistakes, but that they do so better than the next best alternative. *The* fundamental premise of antitrust is the ability of competitive markets to drive firms toward efficient operation. The entire corpus of antitrust doctrine is based on the belief that markets do better than judges or regulators in rewarding practices that create economic benefit and penalizing others. The common belief that if markets are imperfect then something else must be better is a logical fallacy. One need not pretend that markets work perfectly to see that they are better than judges at penalizing inappropriate conduct. Business executives do not respond flawlessly to a decline in profit, but judges do not respond to profit at all.

See more generally, F.A. Hayek, *The Use of Knowledge in Society,* 35 Am Econ Rev 519 (1945); F.A. Hayek, *Competition as a Discovery Procedure,* in F.A. Hayek, ed, *Studies in Philosophy, Politics, Economics, and the History of Ideas* 179 (Simon and Schuster, 1978).

[63] *Brooke,* 113 S Ct at 2589 ("The plaintiff [in a predatory-pricing case] must demonstrate that there is a likelihood that the predatory scheme alleged would cause a rise in prices above a competitive level that would be sufficient to compensate for the amounts expended on the predation, including the time value of the money invested in it."). See also Kenneth G. Elzinga and David E. Mills, *Testing for Predation: Is Recoupment Feasible?,* 34 Antitrust Bull 869, 870 (1989), as cited in *Brooke,* 113 S Ct at 2589.

conventional predator. The Court erred, in Liggett's view, in ruling that Brown & Williamson's prospects for future recoupment were so remote as to make Liggett's predation allegation insupportable.

How could a predator simultaneously recoup? William Burnett, Liggett's expert economic witness, explains Brown & Williamson's simultaneous recoupment:

> Since prices for B&W's branded cigarettes were already above competitive levels, every unit of B&W branded product lost to Liggett generics constituted a loss of substantial margins and profits that was immediate. If the rate of loss of *branded* sales could be reduced as a consequence of its conduct with respect to *generics,* the payback or recoupment of monies lost through predatory pricing would be rapid. In the absence of the price-cutting actions in the generics category, B&W's losses to generics would have been even greater. This "simultaneous recoupment," as it was termed at the trial, meant that price-cutting "investments" made at a specific time were recouped very quickly through a reduction in the loss of branded sales (and margin) that would have occurred absent these investments.[64]

To impart credence to its simultaneous-recoupment hypothesis, Liggett insisted that Brown & Williamson predatorially lowered prices on generics without lowering the *list* price for generics and that this move kept consumers from shifting even more heavily into generics from full revenue brands. Brown & Williamson allegedly accomplished this feat by offering large *rebates* to its cigarette customers (tobacco wholesalers and retail chains), causing them to switch from Liggett's generics to Brown & Williamson's generics. According to Liggett, this diversion did not expand sales of generic cigarettes because the rebates were not passed along to smokers in the form of lower prices. Thus, the losses Brown & Williamson suffered as a result of selling its generics below cost were simultaneously "recouped" in the form of retarding, or at least not accelerating, the decline in sales of full revenue brands.

This novel hypothesis depends on wholesalers and retail chainstores refraining from passing cost savings downstream. These cost savings somehow fail to prompt more intense competition in the distribution of generic cigarettes; therefore, generic-cigarette demand is not enhanced. But such a failure is untenable on economic grounds.

[64] Burnett, *Predation* at 271-73 (cited in note 7) (emphasis in original).

Brown & Williamson's and Liggett's rebates on generics raised the net profits from generics relative to the net profits available from full revenue brands. Customers responded to the higher relative profitability of generics by competing more vigorously in marketing generics relative to full revenue brands. They did so either by lowering the price for generics or through non-price inducements to move generics (for example, by offering better terms to retailers, or by paying for better in-store displays of generics).[65] What Liggett asked the courts to accept is that lower wholesale prices, achieved by paying rebates, had no retail consequences.[66] But deeper rebates on generics upstream expanded generic sales downstream.

Liggett argued that the retail price of cigarettes is rigidly determined by list prices. But Liggett's theory overlooks the ability Liggett had to lower the list price of *its* generics in response to Brown & Williamson's escalating rebates. Rather than match Brown & Williamson's rebates—which, Liggett insisted, had no effect on smokers' demand for generics—Liggett could have increased its sales in the discount segment merely by lowering its list price for generics. In this way, Liggett could have thwarted Brown & Williamson's "simultaneous recoupment."

Brown & Williamson's Predation Imposed Larger Losses on Liggett Than on Itself. In addition to being accused of successfully avoiding the recoupment quandary confronting most predatory pricers, Brown & Williamson also was alleged to have dodged another problem encountered by most predators, namely, the necessity of bearing larger losses than their targets. Liggett argued that Brown & Williamson's below-cost volume rebates on generics were offered to Brown & Williamson's customers—but seldom paid. The reason is that, to maintain its market share, Liggett was obliged to respond with its own equally deep below-cost rebates. Thus, unlike Brown & Williamson, Liggett not only offered, but actually paid, destructively deep discounts to wholesalers.

> B&W's *offer* to sell generics at a price below cost forced the great bulk of the losses on Liggett, the target firm. During the eighteen months, July 1984 to December 1985, Liggett sold about 157.4 million cartons of generics, while B&W sold 50.1 million cartons. Liggett, the target, incurred significantly

[65] The amount of promotional expenditures by cigarette manufacturers has increased dramatically since the mid-1980s. See notes 77-78 below.

[66] Wholesalers purchase generics from producers only insofar as wholesalers expect to be able to resell these generics to retailers.

> greater losses than did B&W. Thus, in the period of recoupment, B&W had less to recoup than would a dominant firm targeting a smaller rival.[67]

This argument is not compelling. To avoid these losses, all Liggett had to do was refuse to meet Brown & Williamson's rebate offers for any tobacco wholesaler or large-account retailer, thereby obliging Brown & Williamson to supply the entire demand for generics temporarily abandoned by Liggett.[68] If Brown & Williamson persisted in honoring its deep rebate offers, Brown & Williamson would have inflicted upon itself larger losses than those inflicted upon Liggett (because unlike Liggett, Brown & Williamson would have had to produce in excess of its loss-minimizing quantity). If Brown & Williamson refused to rescind its offers, an equally efficient Liggett could take consolation in Brown & Williamson's obstinate pursuit of a predatory policy—a policy that would have harmed Brown & Williamson more than Liggett. Liggett's failure to refuse to meet Brown & Williamson's large rebates suggests that these rebates did not drive the price of generics below appropriately measured costs.

Brown & Williamson Had a Disproportionate Incentive to Suppress the Generics Market. Some analysts argue that Brown & Williamson had a greater incentive to prey on Liggett because Brown & Williamson's branded sales were disproportionately reduced by generics and Brown & Williamson had a good deal of excess capacity that was thereby threatened. Burnett, for example, notes:

> Brown & Williamson lost branded cigarette sales disproportionately to Liggett's generics, losing an estimated 3.78 billion units in 1983 alone and contributing about 21 percent of the almost 17.9 billion units gained by Liggett. Brown & Williamson's share of all cigarette sales was about 12 percent at the time, so that the firm contributed to generics an amount equal to 1.7 time its market share. . . .
>
> In sum, B&W's share of all cigarettes continued its historic decline, falling from 14.4 percent in 1979 to 11.5 percent in 1983. Its unit sales fell even more rapidly, reflecting both declining industry sales and a falling share, from almost 88.5

[67] Burnett, *Predation* at 271 (cited in note 7) (emphasis in original).

[68] That Liggett's optimal level of generics production might have been zero in the face of deep below-cost rebates by a predator is not out of the question given that Liggett could have taken temporary refuge in the full-revenue market where, it claimed, monopoly profits lay waiting.

> billion units to 68.5 billion units (about 6.2 percent per year) between 1979 and 1983. Brown & Williamson's motivation to retain or regain unit sales was further bolstered by the need to utilize fully its newly constructed, world-class production facility at Macon, GA, which was being phased into production during the early 1980s.[69]

Far from indicating that Brown & Williamson acted with predatory intent, these facts imply that Brown & Williamson was well-situated to benefit from successful participation in the generics segment. On the demand side, smokers' brand loyalty to Brown & Williamson's brands proved (like Liggett's) not to be as high as smokers' loyalties to the brands of other cigarette manufacturers. The disproportionate negative impact of generics on Brown & Williamson's full revenue brands was a market signal that Brown & Williamson had a comparative advantage (relative to firms such as Philip Morris and Lorillard whose brands were disproportionately less affected) of producing and marketing generics rather than branded products. Therefore, contrary to Liggett's assertion, Brown & Williamson had relatively strong incentives to acquire *and maintain* a position in the emerging discount segment.[70]

On the supply side, Brown & Williamson's excess capacity—created by Brown & Williamson's especially large losses to generics, by the general decline in industry sales beginning in 1981, and by its new factory in Macon, Georgia—furnished Brown & Williamson additional incentives to enter generics. In light of the enormous success of generic cigarettes (relative to that of cigarettes as a whole) in the early 1980s, it was natural for a firm with excess production capacity to seek a part of the market that was expanding. Liggett's expert is correct in the above quotation to suggest that Brown & Williamson's excess capacity motivated the company "to retain or regain unit sales." He errs in suggesting that Brown & Williamson's incentive was to squelch generics in order to reinvigorate the market for full revenue brands.

[69] Burnett, *Predation* at 264 (cited in note 7); Areeda petition at 6 (cited in note 15).

[70] This is not to deny that Brown & Williamson would have preferred that the generics market never have developed. Brown & Williamson's expected profit stream may have been highest if the pre-generics market structure in the cigarette industry had never been disturbed. (Thus, it is not surprising that Liggett was able to find statements in internal Brown & Williamson memoranda lamenting the advent of generics.) But, given that Liggett altered the cigarette market by successfully developing a generics line, which was followed by R.J. Reynolds' entry with a 'branded generic' cigarette (Doral), Brown & Williamson then understood that its best option under the circumstances was to enter generics.

Liggett was Especially Vulnerable to Predation because it was Being Sold. Liggett's parent company, Grand Met, wished to sell Liggett during the price war. Liggett argued that this wish imposed upon Grand Met an especially pressing need to have Liggett avoid a prolonged price war with Brown & Williamson. The Court believed that a jury could have found that this was the case.[71]

Such a finding, though, would have ignored an important feature of the way financial-asset prices are determined.[72] Even though Grand Met was seeking to sell Liggett, the market value of Liggett would have positively reflected steps taken by Grand Met to protect Liggett's position in the generics segment had an equally efficient Brown & Williamson been preying on Liggett. Failure by Grand Met to protect Liggett's position in generics (a segment in which Liggett enjoyed great success) would have lowered the price Grand Met could have hoped to secure for Liggett.[73]

Arguing that Grand Met's desire to sell Liggett somehow rendered Liggett especially vulnerable to predatory attack by an equally efficient Brown & Williamson assumes (1) that the market for corporate equity and bonds would consistently underestimate the profitability of Liggett in face of Brown & Williamson's alleged predation; and (2) that Liggett's own parent did not accurately evaluate Liggett's prospects. Both of these assumptions are unrealistic.

Thus, even disregarding the inherent coordination difficulties confronting would-be predatory members of noncollusive oligopolies—for example, even if Brown & Williamson were Liggett's only rival—Liggett's predation charge made little economic sense. Counterstrategies available to Liggett would have prevented monopolization by Brown & Williamson.

[71] *Brooke,* 113 S Ct at 2592 ("There is also sufficient evidence in the record from which a reasonable jury could conclude that for a period of approximately 18 months, Brown & Williamson's prices on its generic cigarettes were below its costs . . . and that this below-cost pricing imposed losses on Liggett that Liggett was unwilling to sustain, given its corporate parent's effort to locate a buyer for the company."). See also Calkins, *More Objectivity* at 386 (cited in note 38).

[72] See Henry G. Manne, *Mergers and the Market for Corporate Control,* 73 J Pol Econ 110 (1965) (explaining that because the price of publicly traded equity reflects all available information about firms' operations, current owners and managers have incentives to manage corporations in ways that maximize long-run profit streams—i.e., capital values—of the firms). For a more recent treatment of this market, see Frank H. Easterbrook and Daniel R. Fischel, *The Economic Structure of Corporate Law* 171-211 (Harv U, 1991).

[73] If the capital markets would have underestimated the financial propriety of Liggett's counter-predatory efforts, Grand Met would have had a stronger incentive to hang on to Liggett, fund Liggett's price war until Liggett was no longer under predatory attack, and then watch the value of Liggett rise.

V. CONCLUSION

As the quip goes, the proof is in the pudding. Nearly a decade has passed since Brown & Williamson's alleged predation attempt. Liggett's predation hypothesis is inconsistent with developments in the cigarette industry subsequent to the alleged period of predation and Brown & Williamson's victory at the trial-court level. Data on the cigarette industry up through 1993 confirm that the Court properly found in favor of Brown & Williamson.

If Liggett's predation hypothesis were correct, industry sales of generic cigarettes should have declined relative to sales of full revenue brands. Also, cigarette producers other than Brown & Williamson should have avoided the discount segment, given that the alleged purpose of Brown & Williamson's entry into generic cigarettes was to stifle the discount segment in favor of full revenue brands. Neither of these market trends occurred.

In 1993, discount cigarettes accounted for seven of the twenty top selling brands. Five of these seven top-twenty "price value" brands—including Philip Morris's "Basic," the top-selling discount brand—were introduced after Brown & Williamson's alleged predation had ended. Four of the seven discount brands were introduced after Liggett lost its suit against Brown & Williamson in the district court.[74] Moreover, since 1985, 27 discount brands have been introduced. Indeed, in 1990 alone, cigarette manufacturers inaugurated seven discount brands. Of the 30 discount brands introduced after 1982, only five are Brown & Williamson products. Liggett itself introduced three discount brands following Brown & Williamson's victory in the district court: "Pyramid" in 1989, and "Jasmine" and "Covington" in 1993.

Consistent with cigarette-manufacturers' rush into the discount segment is the fact that sales of discount cigarettes as a percentage of the total number of cigarettes sold increased six-fold from 1.2% in 1982 to 7.2% in 1985, and then quintupled between 1985 and 1993. In 1993, sales of discount cigarettes accounted for 36.8% of all cigarettes sold. These data are difficult to square with Liggett's claim that Brown & Williamson sought to 'dial down' the discount segment and that Brown & Williamson's low-price sales of generics from July 1984 through December 1985 could determine the fate of the segment. If Brown & Williamson's purpose was to ruin the market for discount cigarettes, it failed impressively.

[74] "Basic" was introduced in 1990. R.J. Reynolds' "Monarch" was introduced in 1992; RJR's "Best Value" in 1989; Philip Morris's "Cambridge" was repositioned as a discount brand in 1986; and American Tobacco Company's "Montclair" was introduced in 1990.

Liggett insisted, however, that the rise in the list prices of cigarettes (both generics and full revenue brands) after December 1985 shows that Brown & Williamson's predation had the desired effect of cowing Liggett into raising prices of discount cigarettes.[75] List prices for all types of cigarettes did indeed rise after 1985,[76] but such price increases contain too little information to support Liggett's interpretation. In particular, Liggett's focus on *list*-price increases never incorporated changes on the supply side of the market, notably increases in promotional expenditures and tax increases.

Barred from much media advertising, cigarette manufacturers increasingly have used non-advertising promotions. Such marketing expenditures include coupons, promotional allowances, sampling distribution, specialty-item distribution, and financial support for public-entertainment events. In 1991, cigarette manufacturers spent more than $3.5 *billion* on promotional expenditures alone, up from $1.4 billion in 1985.[77] Cigarette-manufacturer's promotional disbursements increased by more than 150% between 1985 and 1991.[78] Because promotional expenditures by manufacturers can return a portion of the list price to buyers, list prices do not reveal the true prices paid by consumers for the final product.

Higher excise taxes for cigarettes also account for a large portion of the cigarette-price hike over the past several years. Average excise taxes on cigarettes rose by approximately $2.00 per carton between 1985 and 1993 (from about $3.00 per carton to $5.00 per carton). Moreover, *maximum* excise taxes (i.e., those imposed in the states with the highest rates of excise taxation on cigarettes) rose even more steeply during this period, almost doubling from about $4.00 per carton in 1985 to nearly $8.00 per carton in 1993.[79] When these higher tax rates are combined with the vast increases in promotional outlays by cigarette producers, reliable conclusions about the success of Brown & Williamson's alleged predatory scheme cannot be extracted from observed changes in list prices.

[75] In his dissent, Justice Stevens indicated that he believed this list-price increase to be significant. See *Brooke*, 113 S Ct at 2601-02 (Stevens dissenting) ("[T]he record amply supports the conclusion that the post-1985 price increases in list prices produced higher consumer prices, as well as higher profits for the manufacturers.").

[76] Id at 2601.

[77] Federal Trade Commission Report to Congress for 1991, Pursuant to the Federal Cigarette Labeling and Advertising Act, Tables 3-3D.

[78] Through 1984, cigarette manufacturers spent more on advertising than on promotions. Beginning in 1985, however, the dollar amounts spent on promotions have exceeded those spent on advertising. In 1991, cigarette manufacturers spent more than $3 on promotions for every $1 spent on advertising.

[79] The Tobacco Institute, 28 *The Tax Burden on Tobacco, Historical Compilation* (1993), Tables 7 and 17.

When examined in light of Brown & Williamson's modest market share—which *shrank* from 11.9% in 1985 to 11.0% in 1993—post-1985 trends in the cigarette industry render the plausibility of Liggett's predation hypothesis even more scant. No sound evidence exists to suggest that Brown & Williamson intended to prey on Liggett or that such predation, had Brown & Williamson actually sought to carry it out, would have succeeded.

In *Utah Pie,* the Court showed a fear of vigorous price competition. That era is past. The Court's present skepticism of predation claims, advanced forcefully in *Matsushita* less than ten years ago, is further underscored in *Brooke.*

The Constitutional Conception of the Corporation

Larry E. Ribstein,†

This article traces the constitutional implications of three theories of the corporation: the "corporate person" theory, which views the corporation as a distinct bundle of rights and obligations; the "contract" theory, which strips away corporate personality and exposes the network of underlying contracts; and the "unconstitutional conditions" theory, which is a variant of the corporate person theory to the extent that it accepts personification of the corporation but would limit government's power to coerce firms to relinquish their rights. The article shows how substituting an artificial legal entity for the underlying individuals implies pervasive government power to regulate corporations, and therefore provides a basis for denigrating the constitutional protection of corporate activities. The contract theory, on the other hand, undercuts the rationale for applying a lower degree of constitutional protection to corporate than to individual rights. The article analyzes how these theories affect application of constitutional rules that protect corporate contracts, jurisdictional choice, governance speech, and documents.

I. INTRODUCTION

The corporate form is an important means of creating wealth, and for politicians a source of rents and competition for power. It is not surprising, therefore, that the regulation of corporations raises

† George Mason University Foundation Professor of Law, George Mason University School of Law. Richard Epstein and Nelson Lund provided helpful comments. Research funding was provided by the Sarah Scaife Foundation.

 0-226-28685-1/95/0004-0003$02.00

many issues concerning the constitutional limits of government power. Although these issues generally have been examined through the broad lens of constitutional law, their resolution has in fact often depended on how the corporation is characterized.

Two views of the corporation have emerged in case law and commentary. The "corporate person" theory views the corporation as a distinct bundle of rights and obligations. Under this view, which substitutes an artificial legal entity for the underlying individuals who act through the corporate form, the government's power to create corporations also implies and assumes pervasive government power to regulate corporations. This, in turn, provides a basis for denigrating the constitutional protection of corporate activities.

An alternative theory of the corporation, the "contract" theory, is based on the economic theory of the firm pioneered by Ronald Coase. The economic theory strips away the corporation's personification and exposes the network of underlying contracts, thus eliminating any fundamental distinction between a corporation and other types of long-term contracts. This theory accordingly undercuts the rationale for applying a lower degree of constitutional protection to "corporate" than to individual rights.

This article is the first to demonstrate systematically how these different theories of the corporation lead to different conclusions about the appropriate extent of corporate constitutional rights.[1] It also provides a framework for evaluating corporate constitutional rights by showing how the competing theories rest on different factual assumptions about the real world. The "corporate person" theory assumes that the separation of ownership and control in the corporate firm creates opportunities for abuse of power by corporate managers that must be checked by stringent controls. Courts and commentators use these assumptions to justify denying corporate persons the benefit of the same constitutional rights that natural persons enjoy. The contract theory, on the other hand, emphasizes that the same sorts of incentives and constraints apply in the corporate context as in the rest of the commercial world. It follows that government should be required to provide as much justification for compromising the constitutional rights of corporations as it must for compromising the rights of individuals.

[1] Some of the views set forth in this Article are developed at more length in Henry N. Butler and Larry E. Ribstein, *The Corporation and the Constitution,* (Am Enterprise Inst, 1995) ("Butler & Ribstein, *The Corporation and the Constitution*"). This article differs primarily in its emphasis on the influence that specific theories of the corporation and their underlying assumptions have on corporate constitutional rights.

The analysis in this article is of considerable current interest. In *Austin v Michigan Chamber of Commerce,*[2] the Supreme Court said that the First Amendment permits regulation of corporate political speech in order to control corporations' "state conferred" powers.[3] If the Court continues to apply this "corporate person" reasoning, that reasoning may determine the extent to which the Court's tightening of First Amendment restrictions on regulation of "commercial" speech, most recently in *Ibanez v Florida Board of Accountancy,*[4] will be applied to corporate speech such as proxy statements and prospectuses.[5] That issue is significant in its own right,[6] but it must also be understood in the broader context of other constitutional provisions, including the Contract and Commerce Clauses.

The next part of the article defines and analyzes the assumptions underlying the "corporate person" and "contractual" theories of the corporation. This part also discusses a variation on the corporate person theory espoused by Richard A. Epstein, who accepts the personification of the corporation but would invoke the doctrine of "unconstitutional conditions" to limit government's power to regulate the corporation.[7] The remainder of the article discusses the implications of these views for corporate law.

II. THEORIES OF THE CORPORATION

A. Corporate Person Theory

The most famous expression of the corporate person theory is found in *Trustees of Dartmouth College v Woodward,*[8] which invoked the Contract Clause[9] to invalidate a New Hampshire statute that altered the terms of a British crown charter granted to Dartmouth College. The Court held that the charter was a contract,[10] entitled

[2] 494 US 652 (1990).

[3] See Section IV.A below.

[4] 114 S Ct 2084 (1994).

[5] See generally Part IV below.

[6] See Henry N. Butler and Larry E. Ribstein, *Corporate Governance Speech and the First Amendment,* 43 U Kan L Rev 163 (1994).

[7] Richard A. Epstein, *Bargaining with the State* (Princeton U, 1993) ("Epstein, *Bargaining*").

[8] 17 US 518 (1819).

[9] US Const, Art I, § 10, cl 1.

[10] Thus, Justice Marshall described the Dartmouth College charter as "a contract, on the faith of which, real and personal estate has been conveyed to the corporation. It is then a contract within the letter of the constitution." *Dartmouth College,* 17 US at 644.

like other contracts to protection from impairment by the state government. But the Court also characterized the charter-granting government (in this case, the Crown) as a party to this contract.[11] Chief Justice Marshall described the corporation as:

> an artificial being, invisible, intangible, and existing only in contemplation of law. Being the mere creature of law, it possesses only those properties which the charter of its creation confers upon it, either expressly, or as incidental to its very existence. These are such as are supposed best calculated to effect the object for which it was created.[12]

The description of the corporation as a "mere creature of law" implies that government has created rights that cannot be created by private contract. Marshall's inference was consistent with the practices of the time. During the early history of corporate law, those who wished to establish corporations applied to state legislatures for state charters that granted permission to incorporate. Special chartering, however, has long since been replaced by general incorporation,[13] in which the state's only involvement in creating the corporation is accepting for filing the articles of incorporation. As general incorporation became widely accepted, legal commentators and courts came to view individual contracting parties, rather than the state, as the creators of the corporate entity.[14] The end of special chartering did not, however, mean the end of the corporate person theory. In the first place, at least two important corporate features seem to be explained by state creation rather than private contract—limited tort liability and choice of law.

[11] Id at 627.

[12] Id at 636.

[13] For a discussion of the evolution of American corporate law from special to general incorporation see Henry N. Butler, *Nineteenth Century Jurisdictional Competition in the Granting of Corporate Privileges,* 14 J Leg Stud 129 (1985) ("Butler, *Nineteenth Century Jurisdictional Competition*"); William F. Shughart II and Robert D. Tollison, *Corporate Chartering: An Exploration in the Economics of Legal Change,* 23 Econ Inq 585 (1985) ("Shughart & Tollison, *Corporate Chartering*").

[14] For recent histories of the concept of the corporation tracing these different theories, see William W. Bratton, Jr., *The New Economic Theory of the Firm: Critical Perspectives from History,* 41 Stan L Rev 1471 (1989); Morton J. Horwitz, *Santa Clara Revisited: The Development of Corporate Theory,* 88 W Va L Rev 173 (1985); Carl J. Mayer, *Personalizing the Impersonal: Corporations and the Bill of Rights,* 41 Hastings L J 577 (1990) ("Mayer, *Personalizing the Impersonal*"); David Millon, *Theories of the Corporation,* 1990 Duke L J 201; Note, *Constitutional Rights of the Corporate Person,* 91 Yale L J 1641 (1982); Comment, *The Personification of the Business Corporation in American Law,* 54 U Chi L Rev 1441 (1987).

The parties who create firms cannot insulate themselves from partnership-type tort liability solely by contracting with creditors, but they can do so by filing the articles or certificate of incorporation with the secretary of state or equivalent state official.[15] Requiring an official state act as a prerequisite for corporate limited liability for torts suggests a state subsidy or a privilege reminiscent of the old special chartering procedure.

With regard to choice of law, the corporate person theory sustains the "internal affairs" rule, a special conflicts rule that applies the law of the state of incorporation to certain legal issues. Without the internal affairs rule, corporations would be subject to vague and unpredictable limits on enforceability of contractual choice of law. These limits, which we see applied to other contracts, arise especially from a concern with undermining the sovereignty of the states in which corporations conduct their affairs.[16] By adopting the fiction of a state-created corporate entity, courts can hold that applying the law of the selected state is based on respect for the sovereignty and regulatory protection of that state.

The corporate person theory also survives in the wake of general incorporation through normative arguments for making corporations special objects of regulation. Although these arguments do not rest explicitly on state creation or on the personification of the corporation, the history of the corporate form provides at least one explanation for the willingness of commentators and lawmakers to accept normative arguments supporting extraordinary regulation of corporations.

One normative argument is based on the separation of ownership and control. Adolf A. Berle and Gardiner C. Means argued that non-owner managers, rather than shareholders, effectively control corporate assets.[17] This separation of ownership and control suggests that corporate property will not be used efficiently unless the managers are subjected to special legal constraints. Another normative argument for special regulation of the corporation is that such regulation is necessary to protect non-shareholder "stakeholders," including creditors and employees. Many commentators claim that these stakeholders cannot protect themselves through ordinary contracts, which necessitates either the creation of extra-contractual

[15] See, for example, 8 Del Code § 106 (1991); Model Bus Corp Act § 2.03(a).

[16] See Larry E. Ribstein, *Choosing Law By Contract,* 18 J Corp L 245 (1993) (comparing enforcement of contractual choice of law for corporations and for other types of contracts) ("Ribstein, *Choosing Law By Contract*").

[17] *The Modern Corporation and Private Property* (Macmillan, 1932).

remedies or the enforcement of generalized expectations in the form of "implicit" contracts.[18]

B. Contractual Theory

Under the contractual theory, the corporation is understood as a set of contractual arrangements, which ought to be no more regulated than other contracts are. The contractual theory is, to some extent, a positive description of corporate law. From this standpoint, the contractual theory says that the state's apparent involvement in "creating" and restricting corporations is qualitatively no different than the state's involvement in other types of contracts. The feasibility of exit and the availability of alternative mechanisms for achieving corporate objectives support this conclusion.[19] Government "creates" corporations only in the sense that it "creates" other types of contractual relationships—by enforcing them. If government action is unnecessary to create the important features of the corporation, the corporate person theory can stand only on normative arguments that justify extraordinary government regulation of the corporate form.

1. Positive aspects of the contractual theory

The contractual theory rejects the corporate person theory as an accurate description of the current state of corporate law. Specifically, neither limited tort liability nor the special internal affairs rule for choice of law purposes, indicates that corporations actually receive special privileges that justify treating corporations differently from other contracts.

Limited liability. Limited tort liability supposedly supports the corporate person theory because it appears to be the only prominent

[18] See, for example, Aleta G. Estreicher, *Beyond Agency Costs: Managing the Corporation for the Long Term,* 45 Rutgers L Rev 513 (1993); Ronald M. Green, *Shareholders as Stakeholders: Changing Metaphors of Corporate Governance,* 50 Wash & Lee L Rev 1409 (1993) ("Green, *Shareholders as Stakeholders*"); Marleen A. O'Connor, *The Human Capital Era: Reconceptualizing Corporate Law to Facilitate Labor Management Cooperation,* 78 Cornell L Rev 899 (1993); Katherine Van Wezel Stone, *Policing Employment Contracts within the Nexus-of-Contracts Firm,* 43 U Toronto L J 353 (1993). Recent symposia on the topic appear in 43 U Toronto L J no 3 (1993); 50 Wash & Lee L Rev no 4 (1993).

[19] See Bernard S. Black, *Is Corporate Law Trivial?: A Political and Economic Analysis,* 84 Nw U L Rev 542 (1990); Larry E. Ribstein, *Efficiency, Regulation and Competition: A Comment on Easterbrook & Fischel's Economic Structure of Corporate Law,* 87 Nw U L Rev 254 (1992).

corporate feature that cannot be created by private contract among the parties to the corporation or with third parties. Unlike the corporation's other features, limited liability seems to be contingent on state involvement through the filing requirement.

Limited tort liability, however, does not distinguish corporations from other types of contracts. Most importantly, limited tort liability is fundamentally contractual because of the inherent limits of mandatory rules under a legal system in which a multitude of jurisdictions coexist and in which contracts are generally enforced.[20] Firms could easily escape a state's rule imposing personal liability on shareholders of all corporations formed in the state by incorporating in limited-liability states or by organizing non-corporate limited-liability firms. Suppose, however, that *all* states or the federal government imposed personal liability on corporate shareholders. Or suppose that states imposed personal liability on resident shareholders or on firms doing business in the state.[21] Then, investors could contract for limited liability in other forms by, for example, contributing capital to a partnership as a non-partner creditor.[22] And even if states, or the federal government, could find some way to impose mandatory personal liability that firms could not completely avoid by contract, markets could provide ways to mitigate the effect of the rule through derivative securities and other mechanisms.[23]

In short, since the government cannot wholly prevent firms from contracting for limited liability, it is not in a position to grant a "privilege" of limited liability by accepting a corporate filing. The government can, at most, regulate limited liability in such a way that most firms will find it cost-effective to comply with a filing requirement. In other words, rather than "creating" limited liability by accepting filings, the state merely decides whether to enforce a particular contract—in this case, informal limited liability. This is no different from the state's role in other contracts that involve filings. For example, secured creditors by virtue of making a public filing have less exposure to the misfortunes of their debtor firm than do unsecured creditors in that their security enables them to

[20] See Larry E. Ribstein, *Limited Liability and Theories of the Corporation,* 50 Md L Rev 80 (1991).

[21] It is not clear that such a rule would be constitutionally permitted. See Part III below.

[22] See generally Alan R. Bromberg and Larry E. Ribstein, 1 *Bromberg & Ribstein on Partnership* ch 2 (Little Brown, 1988 & Supp 1992) ("Bromberg & Ribstein, *On Partnership*") (discussing rules regarding the creation of partnership).

[23] See Joseph A. Grundfest, *The Limited Future of Unlimited Liability: A Capital Markets Perspective,* 102 Yale L J 387 (1992) ("Grundfest, *Limited Future*") (analyzing potential market responses to pro rata tort liability of corporate shareholders).

ignore risks to non-secured assets. Without filing, creditors could enforce their security interests through the more costly mechanism of direct contracts with other creditors. Similarly, while a marriage certificate confers the legal consequences of marriage, many of these consequences, such as rights on breakup, are available by contract, and perhaps by default under the law of partnership[24] or of unincorporated non-profit associations.[25]

To be sure, limited tort liability affects third parties who are not in contractual privity. But this means only that enforcing the liability limitation involves potential externalities. This is true for many, if not most, other contracts or private arrangements. For example, there may be externalities even under individual liability because of the rule of fresh start in bankruptcy.[26] Yet courts do not suggest that individuals' commercial dealings are not "contracts" because they are subject to this inherent "state-created" limitation on enforceability. Although states may choose not to enforce limited liability, this decision does not affect limited liability's underlying contractual nature. Indeed, if the mere existence of externalities were itself grounds for significant state interference, the result would have to apply to many other contractual and non-contractual relationships. Like shareholders' limited liability, for example, other corporate rules are default rules that arise without actual bargaining. Limited tort liability arguably differs only in the difficulty affected parties face in bargaining around the rule.[27] Under Coasian logic, it is these bargaining costs that create the potential externalities that arise from limited tort liability. There is no precise dividing line on the continuum of bargaining costs that delineates the point at which the costs become so high that the relationship should not be considered contractual. Analogously, marriage creates consequences under the inheritance and other laws that potentially

[24] See generally Bromberg & Ribstein, *On Partnership* § 2.10 (cited in note 22) (discussing spousal relationships as partnerships).

[25] See Uniform Unincorporated Nonprofit Association Act (1992). The Act defines "nonprofit association" as "an unincorporated organization consisting of [two] or more members joined by mutual consent for a common, nonprofit purpose." Id § 1(2). Indeed, gay couples who lack the legal right to marry in California are registering in California as unincorporated associations. See *Memorandum to Commissioners on Uniform State Laws from ABA Ad Hoc Committee on Uniform Unincorporated Nonprofit Associations Act* at 5 (July 28, 1992) (quoting letter from California Bar Association Committee).

[26] See Thomas H. Jackson, *The Fresh Start Policy in Bankruptcy Law,* 98 Harv L Rev 1393 (1985).

[27] See Stephen M. Bainbridge, *In Defense of the Shareholder Wealth Maximization Norm: A Reply to Professor Green,* 50 Wash & Lee L Rev 1423, 1429-30 (1993) (discussing bargaining cost aspect of limited tort liability) ("Bainbridge, *A Reply to Professor Green*").

affect third parties. It does not necessarily follow that the state should be able pervasively to interfere in the marriage relationship.

Thus, it does not follow either from potential externalities inherent in limited tort liability or from the filing prerequisite to obtaining limited liability that the corporation is not entitled to the same treatment under the Constitution as other contracts. The extent to which potential externalities justify regulation is a normative question. In other words, the constitutionality of regulating the corporation cannot be justified merely by pointing out that the government has chosen to regulate this kind of contractual relationship in a particular way, such as by imposing a filing requirement.

Internal affairs rule. The corporate person theory also appears to explain the special internal affairs rule for corporations. This theory reconciles sovereignty principles with contractual choice of law through the fiction of a state-created entity. As with limited tort liability, this reasoning implies that a special government action is necessary to create the corporate "privilege" of the internal affairs rule. But, as with limited liability, the creation of the entity is not necessary to effect something like an internal affairs rule. Contractual choice-of-law clauses are, in fact, widely enforced.[28] Moreover, some major commercial states have passed choice-of-law statutes that instruct courts to enforce these clauses.[29] A choice of law clause in a contract that comes within one of these statutes would be enforced in a way that is comparable to the internal affairs rule.[30]

2. Normative aspects of the contractual theory

If government involvement in the creation of corporate features does not itself justify the corporate person theory, this theory must rest on normative arguments based on the need to protect shareholders and non-shareholder "stakeholders."

The shareholder-protection argument for regulating the corporation is derived from the Berle-Means theory. According to this argument, the separation of ownership and control implies that the managers who control corporations would lack appropriate incentives to use corporate resources efficiently absent special government regulations. In other words, the invisible hand of the market,

[28] See generally Ribstein, *Choosing Law By Contract* (cited in note 16).

[29] See generally Larry E. Ribstein, *Delaware, Lawyers and Choice of Law,* 19 Del J Corp L 999 (1994) (discussing statutes in California, Delaware, New York and Texas) ("Ribstein, *Delaware, Lawyers and Choice of Law*").

[30] Id (discussing the interrelation between the internal affairs rule and the Delaware choice of law statute).

which guides other property to its highest and best uses, does not apply to corporations. It follows that the usual presumption in favor of private contractual arrangements also should not apply.

The economic theory of the firm provides a powerful response to the Berle-Means concern with the separation of ownership and control.[31] Shareholders are not helpless victims, but people who shop for investments from among many types of business forms and competing state laws. Given the wide variety of investment choices, it follows that the business forms that survive are those that achieve the optimal reduction of agency costs consistent with other wealth-maximization objectives. This intuition is supported by substantial theory and evidence concerning agency-cost-control devices in firms and by efficient pricing in securities markets. In general, therefore, the contractual theory asserts that there is no reason to assume that special regulatory intervention is necessary when the corporate form is used. Although markets may not operate perfectly, they perform at least as efficiently in controlling corporations as they do with respect to other kinds of contracts.

Many advocates of special regulation of the corporate form no longer appear to emphasize the argument that corporations do not maximize shareholder wealth. Indeed, if there had been any theoretical doubt about that proposition, the takeover boom and significant takeover premia of the 1980s laid it to rest. During the period of the takeover boom the concern about the separation of ownership and control was replaced by a concern for "stakeholders"—in particular, the creditors, employees and others whose interests seem to have been ignored in the market for corporate control.[32] Contractarians have argued in response that contracts and competitive forces constrain managers to act in the interests of stakeholders, and that in any event holding managers to generalized duties to all of the interests in the corporation ultimately does more harm than good.[33] Moreover, even if managers are not constrained by law

[31] For a review of the literature and its relevance to corporate law, see Henry N. Butler and Larry E. Ribstein, *Opting Out of Fiduciary Duties: A Response to the Anti-Contractarians,* 65 Wash L Rev 1 (1990).

[32] See note 18 and accompanying text.

[33] See, for example, Bainbridge, *A Reply to Professor Green* (cited in note 27); William J. Carney, *Does Defining Constituencies Matter?* 59 U Cin L Rev 385 (1990); Ronald Daniels, *Stakeholders and Takeovers: Can Contractarianism be Compassionate?,* 43 U Toronto L J 315 (1993); Jonathan R. Macey, *An Economic Analysis of the Various Rationales for Making Shareholders the Exclusive Beneficiaries of Corporate Fiduciary Duties,* 21 Stetson L Rev 23 (1991); Jonathan R. Macey and Geoffrey P. Miller, *Corporate Stakeholders: A Contractual Perspective,* 43 U Toronto L J 401 (1993); Larry E. Ribstein, *Takeover Defenses and the Corporate Contract,* 78 Georgetown L J 71, 142-50 (1989).

or contract not to injure stakeholders, they do have a moral incentive not to injure consumers and bystanders.[34] The broad business judgment rule leaves managers free to act morally.[35]

The debate between the corporate person theorists and the contractarians continues to shift ground. When takeover defenses, anti-takeover statutes and other impediments to takeovers became effective, some concern shifted back to shareholders. The law and commentary turned to whether the law could reduce agency costs by, for example, empowering institutional investors.[36] But while the specific concerns shift, the general thrust of the debate remains the same. Both contractarians and those who believe that corporations are wards of the state agree that there are many interests connected with corporations that need to be balanced. The two sides differ in that contractarians conclude that enforcing contracts will achieve the most efficient balance, while those who emphasize the assumptions underlying the corporate personality theory argue that contracts in this context do not work, and that the law must continually readjust these interests to achieve the correct balance. Each side of the debate would support different conclusions in balancing government interests against constitutional rights.

C. Unconstitutional Conditions

Richard Epstein presents an alternative view of corporate constitutional rights that is, in effect, an amalgamation of the corporate person and contractual theories. Consistent with the corporate person theory, Epstein views incorporation and a corporation's transaction of business outside of its incorporating state as privileges or subsidies states grant to business. Epstein says that "the law has

[34] See James M. Buchanan, *Choosing What to Choose,* 150 J Inst & The Econ 123 (1994).

[35] Some commentators question this view. See Green, *Shareholders as Stakeholders* at 1419-20 (cited in note 18) (arguing that senior managers at Union Carbide would have had a "hard time" making a case under the business judgment rule for more stringent safety measures at the Bhopal plant); Lawrence E. Mitchell, *Groundwork of the Metaphysics of Corporate Law,* 50 Wash & Lee L Rev 1477 (1993) (proposing a rethinking of corporate law to free managers of profit constraint). Notwithstanding this argument, it seems highly unlikely that corporate managers could not make a case for expenditures to prevent loss of life even under a strict shareholder-benefit model of corporate law by citing the long-term implications of such a loss to corporate reputation.

[36] See, for example, Bernard S. Black, *Agents Watching Agents: The Promise of Institutional Investor Voice,* 39 UCLA L Rev 811 (1992); Bernard S. Black, *The Value of Institutional Investor Monitoring; The Empirical Evidence,* 39 UCLA L Rev 895 (1992); John C. Coffee, Jr., *Liquidity versus Control: The Institutional Investor as Corporate Monitor,* 91 Colum L Rev 1277 (1991).

conferred limited liability on corporate shareholders"[37] and that "[t]here is in general no obligation for the state to supply a system of limited liability for individuals who wish to undertake joint ventures."[38] He also notes the "state's power to exclude foreign corporations."[39] Although he does not articulate the nature of this power, presumably it is related to the state's lack of an obligation to grant limited liability to foreign corporations. Epstein therefore accepts the corporate person view that corporations are state-created entities.

Epstein, however, appears to reject the normative arguments underlying the survival of the corporate person view. In particular, he notes the benefits to society from facilitating aggregations of capital through limited liability.[40] Epstein would protect these benefits through the doctrine of unconstitutional conditions. He argues that the states, in granting benefits to corporations, exercise coercive monopoly power. Accordingly, firms' acceptance of the conditions that states place on corporate privileges cannot be assumed to be efficient bargains. Rather, the control that states exercise over incorporation and foreign corporation triggers political bargaining for competitive advantage that erodes the social gains that the privileges generate,[41] which is just what happened when incorporation could be obtained only by applying to state legislatures for special charters.[42] Epstein would solve this problem through a constitutional rule forbidding states from selecting the firms that obtain these privileges.

Epstein gives two specific examples of the application of unconstitutional conditions in the corporate context. First, he says that corporations should be entitled to full First Amendment rights regarding political speech.[43] Second, Epstein would apply the doctrine of unconstitutional conditions to strike down discriminatory treatment of foreign corporations under the Due Process and Equal Protection Clauses of the Fourteenth Amendment.[44] Epstein's theory may also have applications in the context of the Contract Clause. Enforcing "reservation of powers" provisions in state corporation laws effectively permits states to condition the incorporation priv-

[37] See Epstein, *Bargaining* at 108 (cited in note 7).

[38] Id at 109.

[39] Id at 115.

[40] Id at 108.

[41] Id at 110. Epstein appears to assume a prisoners' dilemma in which the firms cannot practicably cooperate to maximize their joint gains.

[42] Id. See also Richard Epstein, *Unconstitutional Conditions, State Power and the Limits of Consent*, 102 Harv L Rev 5, 28-31 (1988).

[43] Epstein, *Bargaining* at 113-14 (cited in note 7).

[44] Id at 119-20.

ilege on a waiver of Contract Clause rights. This would give rise to the sort of costly rent-seeking that Epstein argues should be prevented by application of the unconstitutional conditions doctrine.[45]

Because Epstein's theory crosses the state-creation aspects of the corporate person theory with the normative arguments underlying the contractual theory, it potentially conflicts with both standard views of the corporation. In accepting the corporate person theory, Epstein also must accept the basic framework of state power to create corporations. This requires one to ask precisely which aspects of the state's power would be limited by the unconstitutional conditions doctrine. Indeed, Epstein acknowledges that government should have some power over corporate persons. For example, Epstein supports minimum capitalization restrictions on limited liability because they make practical sense and because they do not give too much discretion to government officials.[46] Yet defenders of special restrictions on corporate speech would argue that these, too, are necessary constraints on corporate power. Epstein's theory does not provide a clear basis for distinguishing the two types of rules.

Epstein's theory also potentially conflicts with the contractual theory. If corporate rules fundamentally are the product of private contract rather than state action in the sense that the parties to firms can escape "mandatory" rules,[47] constitutional protections are unnecessary and potentially inefficient limits on contracting.

The protections are unnecessary because there would be no coercion under Epstein's theory. For example, if limited liability is readily available without having to comply with filing requirements, the states could not condition corporate features on firms' willingness to accept limitations on their constitutional rights irrespective of the application of the unconstitutional conditions doctrine.

Moreover, broad invalidation of corporate rules under the unconstitutional conditions doctrine could even inefficiently limit contracting. Suppose, for example, that a corporation statute limits political activities by executives on behalf of firms incorporated under the statute. A firm that incorporates under this rule effectively contracts to constrain this kind of executive conduct. A firm may elect this term as a way of limiting what it views as a form of agency cost. Invalidating the term would nullify this sort of standard-form

[45] See Richard A. Epstein, *Toward a Revitalization of the Contract Clause,* 51 U Chi L Rev 703 (1984) (advocating rent-seeking theory of the Contracts Clause).

[46] Epstein, *Bargaining* at 112 (cited in note 7).

[47] See note 23 and accompanying text.

contract.[48] Even if corporate rules are not fully contractual, the availability of exit and of fungible forms means that it may be more efficient to allow corporate law to evolve through competition among incorporating states than to impose inefficient constitutional restrictions.[49]

D. Summary and Implications: The Role of Theories of the Corporation in Determining Constitutional Rights

The choice among the contractual, corporate person, and unconstitutional conditions theories of the corporation has critical implications for the nature and extent of corporate constitutional rights.

The corporate person theory sees a special place for government regulation of the corporation, for it suggests that the government does not have to go as far in justifying infringement of corporate constitutional rights as it does when regulating other ways in which people contract with one another. Indeed, the corporate person theory implies a presumption favoring government regulation that does not, itself, require empirical support. For example, most *evidence* supports the proposition that the effects of corporate takeovers on workers are minimal.[50] Nevertheless, corporate person theorists continue to assert that worker protection is necessary.[51]

[48] This point does not apply to limits on political activity involved in the Supreme Court cases discussed below in Part III because these were imposed by the federal government or by states in which the activities occurred, rather than by the state that was selected by contract as the state of incorporation.

[49] See Part III below.

[50] See Sanjay Bhagat, Andrei Shleifer and P. Vishny, *The Aftermath of Hostile Takeovers* 1 (National Bureau of Economic Research Working Paper No. 276, 1989) (finding that layoffs can at most explain 10-20% of the average premium in a hostile takeover, and finding only "trivial" job loss in a survey of hostile takeover battles during the period 1984-1986, with most of the affected jobs being white collar jobs lost as a result of consolidation of headquarters); Blackwell, Marr and Spivey, *Plant-Closing Decisions and the Market Value of the Firm,* 26 J Fin Econ 277 (1990) (plant-closing decisions were correlated with relatively low earnings rather than takeover activity); Charles Brown and James L. Medoff, *The Impact of Firm Acquisitions on Labor,* in Alan J. Auerbach, ed., *Corporate Takeovers: Causes and Consequences* (U Chicago, 1988) (studying takeovers of smaller firms); Stephen Kaplan, *The Effect of Management Buyouts On Operating Performance and Values,* 24 J Fin Econ 215 (1989) (for management buyouts studied during the period 1980-1986, employment increased a median .9%). For evidence supporting the stakeholder-injury theory, see Ippolito and James, *LBOs, Reversions and Implicit Contracts,* 47 J Fin 139 (1992) (finding strong relationship between an LBO and subsequent pension termination).

[51] For example, some commentators assert that workers are protected by "implicit contracts" with management. See, for example, the O'Connor and Stone articles cited in note 18. Since these are not actual contracts, this is simply an assertion, consistent with the corporate person theory, that worker protection is normatively justified irrespective of contract.

Similarly, they assert the *theory* that limited tort liability will cause corporate managers to externalize costs,[52] despite the existence of theoretical arguments showing that imposing personal liability on shareholders would not make tort creditors much better off.[53]

The corporate contract theory, on the other hand, characterizes corporations like any other contracts. Under this theory, any government regulation that constrains the exercise of constitutional rights would have to be justified to the same extent as it would with respect to other types of contracts.

Finally, the unconstitutional conditions theory would free corporations from inefficient mandatory rules, but at the substantial price of invasive supervision by the courts. This theory thus requires the assumption that it is better to let courts decide which rules should apply than to ensure that firms themselves can choose the applicable rules by constitutionally protecting the security of contracts and exit from inefficient mandatory rules.

Henry Butler and I have elsewhere made the normative case for the contractual theory of the corporation.[54] In this paper I do not attempt to establish that any particular theory *should* be applied, but rather to articulate these theories and then to show the roles these theories play in applying specific constitutional provisions to corporations. But the seemingly modest goal of merely demonstrating the availability of alternative approaches has important normative implications. Once the courts and commentators clearly recognize that corporations can be subjected to a lesser degree of constitutional protection than other contracts only by accepting the corporate person rather than the contractual theory, they will be forced to confront the need to make a normative case for rejecting the contractual theory. This recognition alone would significantly advance a debate which, until now, has relied on assumptions rather than on analysis or evidence.

[52] See Green, *Shareholders as Stakeholders* at 1415 (cited in note 18); Henry Hansmann and Reinier Kraakman, *Toward Unlimited Shareholder Liability for Corporate Torts,* 100 Yale L J 1879 (1991).

[53] See Frank H. Easterbrook and Daniel R. Fischel, *The Economic Structure of Corporate Law* ch 2 (Harvard U, 1992); Janet Cooper Alexander, *Unlimited Shareholder Liability Through A Procedural Lens,* 106 Harv L Rev 387 (1992) (emphasizing procedural problems of unlimited tort liability); Grundfest, *Limited Future* (cited in note 23) (arguing that capital markets would negate effects of unlimited shareholder liability); Larry E. Ribstein, *The Deregulation of Limited Liability and the Death of Partnership,* 70 Wash U L Q 417 (1992) (noting collection problems and incentives to minimize tort risks under a limited liability regime).

[54] For a summary of the arguments and the relevant literature see Butler & Ribstein, *The Corporation and the Constitution* ch 1 (cited in note 1).

II. CHANGES BY THE INCORPORATING STATE: THE CONTRACT CLAUSE

The Contract Clause of the Constitution, states that "No state shall . . . pass any . . . Law impairing the Obligation of Contracts."[55] This provision poses a crucial test for the two theories of the corporation. Under the contractual theory, states should enforce the contracts that comprise the corporation. Under the corporate person theory, on the other hand, the state should have significant power to dictate—and, therefore, change—corporate terms. This part of the article shows that while the corporation has been recognized as a contract for purposes of the Contract Clause it has been denied the full protection of the Clause by arguments consistent with the corporate person theory.

A. The Contract Clause in General

Constitutional protection of contracts discourages state government officials from earning "rents," such as campaign contributions and other benefits, by engineering wealth redistributions to interest groups.[56] Rent-seeking expenditures incurred merely in redistributing wealth from weaker to stronger interest groups are unlikely to be outweighed by any positive results of the expenditures.[57] That is probably the situation when government action impairs contracts, thereby redistributing wealth from the parties who stand to gain, ex post, from enforcement of the contract to those who stand to lose. As a result, contract impairing legislation is rarely, if ever, Pareto optimal in the sense of creating winners without making anyone worse off. Contract impairment may be Kaldor-Hicks efficient if the social benefit from the legislation exceeds the losses to those injured by the impairment. But that is unlikely to be the case, since contract-impairing legislation necessarily frustrates presumptively efficient private bargains.

The most important early Contract Clause case is *Trustees of Dartmouth College v Woodward.*[58] In an opinion by Chief Justice

[55] Art I, § 10, cl 1.

[56] See Richard Epstein, *Toward a Revitalization of the Contract Clause,* 51 U Chi L Rev 703, 714 (1984); Douglas W. Kmiec and John O. McGinnis, *The Contract Clause: A Return to the Original Understanding,* 14 Hastings Const L Q 525 (1987); Jonathan R. Macey, *Promoting Public-Regarding Legislation Through Statutory Interpretation: An Interest Group Model,* 86 Colum L Rev 223, 242-50 (1986); Cass R. Sunstein, *Naked Preferences and the Constitution,* 84 Colum L Rev 1689 (1984).

[57] See Gordon Tullock, *The Welfare Costs of Tariffs, Monopolies and Theft,* 5 West Econ J 224 (1967).

[58] 17 US 518 (1819).

[59] 290 US 398 (1934).

Marshall, the Supreme Court invalidated under the Contract Clause a New Hampshire statute that altered the terms of a British crown charter granted to Dartmouth College. The Contract Clause then flourished as a significant protection of property right for over a century until *Home Bldg. & Loan Ass'n v Blaisdell,*[59] in which the Court held that the "reservation of essential attributes of sovereign power is . . . read into contracts as a postulate of the legal order."[60] For forty years thereafter the Contract Clause was rarely invoked to overturn a state statute.[61] However, in *United States Trust Co. v New Jersey,*[62] the Court struck down under the Contract Clause a New Jersey statute that impaired the rights of bond holders by repealing a covenant that had restricted use of bond funds. The Court reasoned that it was unnecessary to impair the contract in order to serve the state's goals of encouraging mass transportation to conserve energy and protect the environment. A year later, in *Allied Structural Steel Co. v Spannaus,*[63] the Court again invalidated under the Contract Clause a state statute that altered existing pension contracts by requiring an employer who terminated a plan or left the state to fund pensions for employees with at least ten years' service even if the employees' rights had not vested under the original terms of the plan. The Court emphasized, among other things, that the impairment was severe[64] and that the act narrowly focused on a single company.[65] Although several recent Supreme Court cases have denied Contract Clause protection,[66]

[60] Id at 435. The reservation of power argument first appeared in Justice Johnson's dissent in *Fletcher v Peck,* 10 US 87 (1810). For a discussion of the history of this idea in the Supreme Court, see Robert L. Hale, *The Supreme Court and the Contract Clause: III,* 57 Harv L Rev 852, 872-83 (1944).

[61] The Supreme Court invalidated only two state laws on contract clause grounds during this period. See Note, *A Process-Oriented Approach to the Contract Clause,* 89 Yale L J 1623, 1623 (1980).

[62] 431 US 1 (1977).

[63] 438 US 234 (1978).

[64] Id at 245.

[65] Id at 247-48.

[66] See *Energy Reserves Group, Inc. v Kansas Power & Light Co.,* 459 US 400 (1983) (upholding a state statute regulating gas prices that impaired a clause in plaintiff's contract with a utility company that escalated prices up to the state ceiling); *Exxon Corp. v Eagerton,* 462 US 176 (1983) (upholding a state severance tax statute that prohibited producers from passing the tax through to consumers); *Keystone Bituminous Coal Ass'n v DeBenedictis,* 480 US 470 (1987) (upholding a statute providing for liability for subsidence from coal mining that impaired contractual waivers of liability for surface damage). The Court's most recent Contract Clause case, *General Motors Corp. v Romein,* 503 US 181 (1992), provides little indication of the Court's direction on the Contract Clause. The case involved a complex and unusual situation in which a state legislature first passed a statute that affected workers' rights to benefits under existing collective bargaining agreements, and then passed

lower courts continue to apply the Clause to strike down state legislation.[67]

B. Corporate Person Theory

In *Dartmouth College,* the Supreme Court characterized corporations as contracts. Chief Justice Marshall described a corporate charter as:

> a contract, on the faith of which, real and personal estate has been conveyed [by the donors] to the corporation. It is then a contract within the letter of the constitution. . . . It is more than possible, that the preservation of rights of this description was not particularly in the view of the framers of the constitution, when the clause under consideration was introduced into that instrument. . . . But although a particular and a rare case may not, in itself, be of sufficient magnitude to induce a rule, yet it must be governed by the rule, when established, unless some plain and strong reason for excluding it can be given. It is not enough to say, that this particular case was not in the mind of the Convention, when the article was framed. . . . The case being within the words of the rule, must be within its operation likewise, unless there be something in the literal construction so obviously absurd, or mischievous, or repugnant to the general spirit of the instrument, as to justify those who expound the constitution in making it an exception.[68]

The Court, however, has embraced a critical aspect of the corporate person theory by viewing the contract as one with the state rather than among private parties. The state's involvement in the corporate charter triggers the most important limitation on the application of the Contract Clause to the corporation—statutory "reserved power" provisions. Justice Story concurred in *Dartmouth College,* noting that "rights legally vested in a corporation, cannot

another statute retroactively removing the retroactive effect of the first statute. The Court held that the first statute did not give General Motors constitutionally protected contract rights that were impaired by the second statute.

[67] See, for example, *In re Walker,* 959 F2d 894 (10th Cir 1992) (striking down state statute on exemptions for IRA's); *Association of Surrogates & Supreme Court Reporters v New York,* 940 F2d 766 (2d Cir 1991) (striking down state impairment of public employees' contracts); *Northshore Cycles, Inc. v Yamaha Motor Corp., U.S.A.,* 919 F2d 1041 (5th Cir 1990) (striking down law requiring manufacturer to repurchase distributor's inventory).

[68] 17 US at 644-45.

be controled or destroyed by any subsequent statute, unless *a power for that purpose be reserved to the legislature in the act of incorporation.*"[69] Following Justice Story's suggestion, the states routinely came to insert in their corporation statutes just such a reservation of power. For example, the Delaware statute provides:

> This chapter may be amended or repealed, at the pleasure of the General Assembly, but any amendment or repeal shall not take away or impair any remedy under this chapter against any corporation or its officers for any liability which shall have been previously incurred. This chapter and all amendments thereof shall be a part of the charter or certificate of incorporation of every corporation except so far as the same are inapplicable and inappropriate to the objects of the corporation.[70]

These provisions have been applied to permit new statutory provisions to change existing corporate contracts.[71] Consistent with the corporate person theory, since states can grant corporate features, they can also make the grants conditional on corporations' accepting the states' reservations of power, just as if states were granting licenses or franchises.

The normative assumption underlying the corporate person theory that corporations should be subject to special regulation because they pose threats to shareholders and stakeholders also relates to the application of the Contract Clause. Under this assumption, assertions of "sovereign power" under *Blaisdell* for justifying impairment are relatively easy to justify.

C. The Contract Theory

Under the contract theory of the corporation, the corporation is a set of contracts among the parties to the firm—shareholders, employees, creditors and others. The Contract Clause should be as applicable to these contracts as to any others.

[69] Id at 708 (emphasis in original).

[70] 8 Del Code § 394 (1991).

[71] See, for example, *Looker v Maynard,* 179 US 46 (1900) (requirement of cumulative voting for directors); *Miller v New York,* 82 US 478 (1872) (change in ratio of city-appointed directors); *Mobile Press Register, Inc. v McGowin,* 124 S 2d 812 (Ala 1960) (preemptive rights no longer conferred by statute, but must be provided for in certificate); *Adair v Orrell's Mutual Burial Ass'n, Inc.,* 201 SE2d 905 (NC 1974) (requirement that mutual burial association pay benefits in cash to any official funeral director and not merely the association's own funeral director).

A good illustration of this principle is the potential application of the Contract Clause to state anti-takeover statutes. In *CTS Corp. v Dynamics Corp. of America*[72] the Court upheld on Commerce and Supremacy Clause grounds an Indiana anti-takeover statute, which provided that "control shares" obtained by hostile tender offers would be nonvoting unless a majority of disinterested shareholders voted to make them voting shares at the next regularly scheduled shareholder meeting, or at a special meeting called by the tender offeror within fifty days of the offer. It follows from the corporate contract theory that such statutes are unconstitutional under the Contract Clause because they impair shareholders' contractual rights to transfer control. The impairment is not ameliorated by the shareholders' ability to opt out by selling their shares or reincorporating. The new statute reduces the present value of expected future returns for any corporation for which the anti-takeover statute is an inefficient term. This reduction in value is reflected in the market price of the stock. Because reincorporation requires costly mobilization of shareholder votes, any costs imposed by an anti-takeover statute will be tolerated if they are less than the costs of reversing the standard by reincorporating. More importantly, the statute itself frustrates exit through reincorporation by inhibiting acquisition of control to effect this result. Moreover, the contract impairment is a severe one. Any change in the degree of management entrenchment is likely to be a significant change in the contract because of the importance of the market for corporate control to corporate governance.

Under the contract theory, the state's purported justifications of the impairment probably cannot withstand scrutiny. The main purported justification for state anti-takeover provisions has been protection of shareholders of target corporations. This was a basis on which the Supreme Court upheld the Indiana statute in *CTS* under the Commerce Clause.[73] However, under the contract theory, the state's role *vis-à-vis* anti-takeover statutes is simply to minimize transaction costs by establishing standard forms. Problems relating to takeovers should be resolved by the shareholders' contract and not by forcing protection from takeovers on the share-

[72] 481 US 69 (1987).

[73] The Court said: "A State has an interest in promoting stable relationships among parties involved in the corporations it charters, as well as in ensuring that investors in such corporations have an effective voice in corporate affairs." 481 US at 91.

holders.[74] In other words, while the state should be able to enact new default rules that shareholders can vote to adopt, they should not be able impose takeover protection on existing firms without shareholder vote.[75]

The contract theory also raises serious questions about Justice Story's reserved power argument. If the state does not create corporations, it should not be able to limit the terms of their creation. On the other hand, reserved power provisions might be justified under the contract theory by the argument that the parties to firms *choose* to incorporate in states whose laws contain these provisions. Because shareholder's corporations cannot foresee future developments, and because shareholder amendment can be costly, shareholders may wish to empower incorporating states to make state-of-the-art modifications in the corporate contract. Perhaps corporations should be able to decide whether this benefit is worth the risk of potential wealth-redistributive legislation. Corporate statutory terms are priced in the financial markets, and states can compete for chartering business by offering "tight" statutes without reserved-power provisions, or by offering "loose" or "flexible" statutes and protecting firms against opportunistic change by providing a reputational bond.[76]

D. Unconstitutional Conditions

As we have seen, the corporate person theory justifies reserved power clauses as inherent in states' power to grant corporate features such as shareholders' tort immunity. The unconstitutional conditions theory directly challenges the argument that the government can condition granting of privileges on the waiver of constitutional rights. Just as the government's power to sell special charters may give rise to costly abuse, the same may be true if the

[74] The states arguably do have an interest in protecting employees and others in the state from exit by important citizens as a result of takeovers. See Lyman Johnson and David Millon, *Missing the Point About State Takeover Statutes*, 87 Mich L Rev 846, 848 (1989) (arguing that the purpose of state anti-takeover laws is to protect nonshareholders). However, regulating transfers of stock is irrelevant to preventing movement of assets.

[75] See Henry N. Butler and Larry E. Ribstein, *The Contract Clause and the Corporation*, 55 Brooklyn L Rev 767, 795-98 (1989); Henry N. Butler and Larry E. Ribstein, *State Anti-Takeover Statutes and the Contract Clause*, 57 U Cin L Rev 611 (1988).

[76] See Roberta Romano, *Law as a Product: Some Pieces of the Incorporation Puzzle*, 1 J L Econ & Org 225 (1985).

government is not prevented from conditioning the tort subsidy on waiver of the Contract Clause, particularly since the avoidance of rent-seeking costs is at the heart of the constitutional protection.

Once again, however, the unconstitutional conditions theory may conflict with the contract theory. As I noted in the previous section, reserved power provisions could be considered contractual in the sense that they are selected as part of the general corporate statutory package. To be sure, lawmakers may have little incentive to compete to provide "tight" statutes that do not include reserved power provisions. Legislators may gain little political support from maximizing franchise tax revenues because taxpayers are not a cohesive political group, and managers (who do have political power) favor reserved power provisions, while shareholders cannot easily coordinate to force reincorporation. Thus, other states may not be able effectively to compete with Delaware,[77] and the expected costs resulting from the use of the reserved power are in any case unlikely to be high for any given corporation.[78] On the other hand, it remains the case that firms do have a choice of many corporate statutes and non-corporate forms, and investors have their choice of firms. Thus, it is not clear that constitutionally forcing firms to accept "tight" statutes is superior to permitting them to form under "loose" statutes, even in a market that consists only of loose statutes.

In conclusion, application of the Contract Clause to the corporation depends critically on which theory of the corporation the Court accepts. The only qualification of this point is that "reserved power" clauses might be justified even under the contract theory. The strength of this justification depends, however, on the extent to which corporations' choice of the incorporating state is constitutionally protected, an issue to which I now turn.

III. PROTECTING CHOICE OF LAW

Broad enforcement of contractual choice of law through something like the "internal affairs rule" has important practical effects on corporate law.[79] The power to choose the applicable law makes even outwardly mandatory rules effectively contractual. Indeed, as dis-

[77] Delaware's ability to "bond" its law may be a unique advantage that other states cannot readily duplicate. See id. See also Ribstein, *Delaware, Lawyers and Choice of Law* (cited in note 29) (emphasizing role of lawyers in state competition).

[78] For more detailed presentation of these points, see Butler & Ribstein, *The Corporation and the Constitution* at 45 (cited in note 1).

[79] The scope of application of the internal affairs rule is unclear. For present purposes it is enough to point out that the rule should apply the law chosen by the parties to the corporate charter. Thus, the incorporating state's law should apply

cussed at the end of Part II, enforcing jurisdictional choice may even trivialize attempted governmental impairments of contract because states are encouraged to compete for incorporation business by offering strong promises that they will not excessively tamper with their statutes. Conversely, non-enforcement of contractual choice of law reinforces mandatory rules and the application of the corporate person theory. This part shows how enforcement of contractual choice of law in general, and the "internal affairs rule" in particular, depends on which theory of the corporation is applied.

A. The Constitution and Choice of Law

The Constitution can protect choice of law both *directly* and *indirectly.* Direct protection involves mandating application of the contractually selected rule. The Commerce Clause[80] can provide *direct* enforcement by requiring states to apply a single rule to multistate transactions to avoid burdening interstate commerce with multiple potentially inconsistent regulations[81] or by preventing states from exporting regulatory costs.[82] The Constitution could also require or preclude application of the contractually selected rule through the Full Faith and Credit Clause,[83] which requires courts to respect the sovereignty of other states with a regulatory interest in the transaction. The Due Process Clause,[84] too, may have a bearing on contractual choice of law by protecting contracting parties from unexpected application of legal rules from remote

only to the types of matters covered by the charter, particularly including governance matters. It should not necessarily bind those who are not parties to the corporate charter, including creditors and employees, except to the extent that these parties expressly agree to accept the law of the incorporating state.

[80] See US Const, Art I, § 8, cl 3 (giving Congress the power "[t]o regulate Commerce . . . among the several States"). This provision has been interpreted as inferentially restricting state power. See *Cooley v Board of Wardens,* 53 US 299 (1851) (holding that grant of power to Congress forbids some but not all state regulation affecting interstate commerce, and upholding state statute imposing pilotage fee as within state's power).

[81] See Harold W. Horowitz, *The Commerce Clause as a Limitation on State Choice of Law Doctrine,* 84 Harv L Rev 806 (1971). For examples of such cases, see *Kassel v Consolidated Freightways Corp.,* 450 US 662 (1981) (striking down regulation of truck length); *Bibb v Navajo Freight Lines, Inc.,* 359 US 520 (1959) (striking down regulation of mudguards); *Southern Pacific Co. v Arizona,* 325 US 761 (1945) (striking down regulation of train length).

[82] See text accompanying note 102 below.

[83] US Const Art IV, § 1 (providing that "Full Faith and Credit shall be given in each State to the public Acts, Records, and judicial Proceedings of every other State").

[84] See US Const, Amend XIV, § 1 ("No State shall . . . deprive any person of life, liberty, or property, without due process of law").

jurisdictions. Finally, the Supremacy Clause of the Constitution[85] is potentially relevant to direct enforcement of choice of law. Whether federal law should preempt the parties' choice of a particular state law depends not only on an interpretation of a particular federal law, but also on underlying principles of federalism, which require that the benefits of exit from mandatory rules and jurisdictional competition be balanced against the costs of potential external effects.[86] As with the other constitutional issues examined in this Article, the outcome of this balancing process regarding corporate law depends on which theory of the corporation one applies.

Indirect enforcement of contractual choice of law, on the other hand, involves ensuring that states cannot force corporations that transact business locally to incorporate locally. The Constitution indirectly protects the internal affairs rule to the extent that it prevents states from discriminating in regulation and taxation on account of a firm's state of incorporation. This sort of protection is recognized primarily under the Privileges and Immunities[87] and Equal Protection Clauses.[88] It relates primarily to the application of the unconstitutional conditions theory discussed below in Section D.

B. Corporate Person Theory

The corporate person theory *directly* protects the internal affairs rule by rationalizing selection of the law of a particular state under constitutional theories based on the states' constitutional power to regulate an interstate transaction (Commerce Clause), the sovereignty of the regulating state (Full Faith and Credit), and the legitimate expectations of the parties to the transaction (Due Process).

The Supreme Court squarely recognized the corporate person theory in the Commerce Clause context in *CTS Corp. v Dynamics*

[85] US Const Art VI, cl 2:

> This Constitution, and the Laws of the United States which shall be made in Pursuance thereof; and all Treaties made, or which shall be made, under the Authority of the United States, shall be the supreme Law of the Land; and the Judges in every State shall be bound thereby, any Thing in the Constitution or Laws of any State to the Contrary notwithstanding.

[86] See Frank H. Easterbrook, *The State of Madison's Vision of the State: A Public Choice Perspective,* 107 Harv L Rev 1328, 1344-46 (1994); Frank H. Easterbrook, *Federalism and European Business Law,* 14 Int Rev L & Econ 125 (1994).

[87] See US Const, Art. IV, § 2, cl 1 ("The Citizens of each State shall be entitled to all Privileges and Immunities of Citizens in the several States.").

[88] See US Const, Amend XIV, § 1 ("No State shall . . . deny to any person within its jurisdiction the equal protection of the laws.").

Corp. of America,[89] in which it held that an interstate tender offer could be regulated by the law of the state of incorporation. The Court reasoned in part that states that create corporations can control their attributes.[90] Thus, the corporate person theory supports direct constitutional protection of the internal affairs rule by providing a basis (which does not apply to other types of contractual choice of law[91]) for selecting the law of an incorporating state.

The corporate person theory arguably justifies both mandating and permitting contractual choice of law under the Full Faith and Credit Clause. Once again, the significance of the corporate person theory becomes manifest in the contrast between the internal affairs rule and enforcement of non-corporate contractual choice of law. Ordinarily, a contract between private parties to apply a particular state's law does not necessarily trump another state's regulatory interest in the transaction. But the selected state's sovereignty and regulatory power might be implicated if the state is deemed to have "created" the corporation that results from the parties' contract. In particular, the Court has held that, because a fraternal benefit association is a creature of state law, it therefore must be construed under the law of the formation state.[92] This suggests that states may be compelled under Full Faith and Credit in some circumstances to apply the law of the incorporating state, but *only* because the corporation is a separate person.[93] Similarly, a forum state may be constitutionally able to apply the law of the incorporating state where it would not necessarily be able to apply the law selected in a non-corporate contract.[94]

The corporate person theory apparently has an opposite effect on *indirect* protection of contractual choice of law. Because a corporation is only an artificial person, it may be denied protection from

[89] 481 US 69 (1987).

[90] Id at 90-91.

[91] See generally, Ribstein, *Choosing Law By Contract* (cited in note 16).

[92] See *Order of United Commercial Travelers v Wolfe*, 331 US 586, 609 (1947).

[93] The status of such cases is unclear in light of the more recent leading case of *Allstate Insurance Co. v Hague*, 449 US 302 (1981), in which the Court held that a forum court could apply its law as long as it has some reasonable basis for doing so. See Russell J. Weintraub, *Who's Afraid of Constitutional Limitations on Choice of Law?* 10 Hofstra L Rev 17 (1981) (*Hague* indicates that the court will not give close constitutional supervision to conflicts decisions). See also William Winslow Crosskey, *Politics and the Constitution in the History of the United States* 555 (U Chicago, 1953) (noting prior to *Hague* that the Court has done under Full Faith and Credit merely what it would have done under the modern Due Process Clause).

[94] See Note, *Contractual Choice of Law: The Case for a New Determination of Full Faith and Credit Limitations*, 71 Tex L Rev 1019 (1993) (arguing that state statutes mandating enforcement of contractual choice of law clauses are unconstitutional under the Full Faith and Credit Clause).

discrimination that would be accorded individuals. Thus, corporations have not been protected by the Privileges and Immunities Clause.[95] In the leading case of *Paul v Virginia*,[96] the Court reasoned that corporations were the "mere creation of local law," and that they depended on principles of comity to be able to do business outside their states of incorporation.[97] As discussed below in Section D, however, the unconstitutional conditions theory provides a basis for indirectly protecting the internal affairs rule within the corporate person characterization.

The corporate person theory, which holds that corporations are creatures of *state* law, also justifies enforcement of state law rather than preemption by federal law under the Supremacy Clause. In *CTS*, the Court held that a state anti-takeover statute that applied to firms incorporated in the enacting state was not preempted by federal takeover legislation.[98] The Court said: "The longstanding prevalence of state regulation in this area suggests that, if Congress had intended to pre-empt all state laws that delay the acquisition of voting control following a tender offer, it would have said so explicitly."[99]

Ironically, this reliance on state law conflicts with the normative underpinning of the corporate person theory, which presumes in favor of pervasive regulation of the corporation. As long as state, rather than federal, law applies, firms can easily escape regulation by choosing their state of incorporation. Thus, commentators who favor strong regulation of the corporate form tend to favor federal regulation.[100] By accepting the theory of state creation, the Court provides an important condition for moving corporate law closer to the contractual model.[101]

[95] See *Hemphill v Orloff*, 277 US 537, 548-50 (1928); *Paul v Virginia*, 75 US 168 (1868); *Smith Setzer & Sons v South Carolina Procurement Review Panel*, 20 F3d 1311 (4th Cir 1994).

[96] 75 US 168 (1868).

[97] Id at 181.

[98] See text accompanying notes 89-90 above.

[99] 481 US at 86.

[100] The leading article is William L. Cary, *Federalism and Corporate Law: Reflections Upon Delaware*, 83 Yale L J 663 (1974). For a more recent article echoing Cary's concerns in support of federal regulation see Joel Seligman, *The New Corporate Law*, 59 Brooklyn L Rev 1 (1993). For an Australian perspective reviewing the American debate, see Ian M. Ramsay, *Company Law and the Economics of Federalism*, 19 Fed L Rev 169 (1990).

[101] This tension between the state-creation and normative aspects of the corporate person theory might be reconciled by interpreting *CTS* as applying state law only to avoid an anti-regulatory application of the Williams Act. However, the Court reached an analogous conclusion in holding that federal law did not provide the basis for a monitoring duty by the law firm of a federally supervised savings and loan. See

C. Contract Theory

If corporations are characterized as contractual relationships, any rule that ensures enforcement of contractual choice of law in this context would have to apply to other types of contracts. Accordingly, abandoning the theory that the incorporating state has a special interest in the contract would also forfeit the internal affairs rule's special claims to direct protection under the Commerce and Full Faith and Credit Clauses. But the Commerce Clause does provide a constitutional basis for compelling enforcement of both corporate and non-corporate contractual choice of law. In particular, the Commerce Clause would make unconstitutional states' refusals to enforce choice-of-law clauses that amount to efforts by regulating states to impose the costs of their statutes on firms based outside the state.[102] Under this theory, constitutional enforcement of the internal affairs rule is required not because there is something special about corporate law, but because choice-of-law clauses generally should be enforced.

The contract theory has similar implications regarding the Supremacy Clause. Under the contract theory, pervasive regulation of the corporation is presumptively unwarranted. The contract theory accordingly would lead to narrow constructions of federal laws that otherwise would trump the law of the state of incorporation. That is so regardless of whether the federal law would provide more or less stringent standards than the state law, since the contract theory emphasizes the parties' choice of law rather than the nature of the regulation.[103]

It is less clear under the contract theory whether to apply the federal statute over a state law other than that of the incorporating

O'Melveny & Meyers v FDIC, 114 S Ct 2048 (1994). On the other hand, the lower courts have generally held that federal banking law does *not pre-empt more stringent* state standards. See, for example, *FDIC v Bierman*, 2 F3d 1424 (7th Cir 1993); *FDIC v Canfield*, 957 F2d 786 (10th Cir 1992), vacated on reh'g, en banc, 967 F2d 443 (10th Cir 1992); *FDIC v McSweeney*, 772 F Supp 1154 (SD Cal 1991), aff'd, 976 F2d 532 (9th Cir 1992); *FDIC v Isham*, 782 F Supp 524 (D Colo 1992); *FDIC v Black*, 777 F Supp 919 (WD Okla 1991). The tension disappears in cases involving a conflict between federal law and the law of a state other than the incorporating jurisdiction. For example, federal law can provide more stringent standards for regulating the sale of securities than those provided by states in which the securities are sold without conflicting with the state creation theory.

[102] See Butler & Ribstein, *The Corporation and the Constitution* ch 3, at 135-38 (cited in note 1); Ribstein, *Choosing Law By Contract* at 291-94 (cited in note 16).

[103] For example, in *Amanda Acquisition Corp. v Universal Foods Corp.*, 877 F2d 496 (7th Cir 1989), Judge Easterbrook, although a strong opponent of limits on takeovers, nevertheless upheld a strong state anti-takeover statute against a Supremacy Clause challenge.

state (such as a state securities statute) or even a retroactive statute of the incorporating state.[104] Yet even in these situations broad application of the federal law usually interferes with the possibility of exit even more than does the state law. Accordingly, application of federal law generally is disfavored under the contract theory regardless of the nature of the state law that would be preempted.

D. Unconstitutional Conditions

The unconstitutional conditions theory relates to indirect constitutional protection of contractual choice of law. Although, as discussed above in Section A, the Court has denied foreign corporations the protection of the Privileges and Immunities Clause, it has limited states' power to regulate or tax foreign corporate persons differently from domestic firms.[105] These limitations are best reconciled with *Paul* by Richard Epstein's theory that, even if states can deny corporations *all* of the privileges and immunities of citizens, they cannot unconstitutionally condition the privileges they do grant.[106] Epstein reasons that the states should not be able to exact consent to discriminatory conditions as the cost of the privilege of transacting business as a foreign corporation. Since the states can impose their regulations on firms solely on the basis of where the latter transact business, national firms lack enough power of exit to combat the coercive power of the privilege-granting states.[107] This would leave firms at the mercy of state legislators'

[104] The latter was the case regarding the statute in *Amanda.* Indeed, Judge Easterbrook noted a possible Contract Clause argument in that case. See *Amanda,* 877 F2d at 505.

[105] See *Western & Southern Life Ins. Co. v State Board of Equalization,* 451 US 648, 667-68 (1981) (holding that "whatever the extent of a State's authority to exclude foreign corporations from doing business within its boundaries, that authority does not justify imposition of more onerous taxes or other burdens on foreign corporations than those imposed on domestic corporations, unless the discrimination between foreign and domestic corporations bears a rational relation to a legitimate state purpose").

[106] See Epstein, *Bargaining* at 117-25 (cited in note 7). In the *Western & Southern* case, see note 105, the Court reconciled the cases permitting states to deny the privilege of foreign incorporation with those prohibiting lesser restrictions by holding that the evolution to general incorporation had eroded the idea of special privileges that provided the underpinning for *Paul.* But without a theory, like Epstein's, that explains why the lesser discrimination may be worse than the greater prohibition, the Court's reasoning seems to undercut the states' power to deny the foreign incorporation privilege.

[107] Epstein, *Bargaining* at 115-16 (cited in note 7).

powers to tax or regulate foreign corporations at the behest of their in-state competitors.[108]

This approach potentially conflicts with the contractual theory. Under the contractual theory, the place of incorporation matters only in the sense that the parties to the firm have chosen the law, rather than that the firm itself is formed by non-residents. Accordingly, there may be significant political opposition within states to stringent penalties against foreign corporations. This differentiates regulation of foreign *incorporation* from regulation of foreign *business*, such as the anti-chain-store legislation involved in the famous case of *Louis K. Liggett Co. v Lee.*[109] Indeed, states' attempts to discriminate against foreign corporations are unlikely to be effective in the long run. As long as application of the contractual theory results in enforcement of non-corporate contractual choice of law, firms can mitigate states' indirect interference with the internal affairs rule by forming non-corporate firms, such as limited liability companies, that are not subject to taxation or regulation of foreign *corporations.*[110] Although states could tax or regulate those firms as well, they cannot completely isolate forms of contract for special tax or regulatory treatment. This suggests that indirect protection of choice of law through constitutional protection of foreign incorporation is unnecessary.[111]

The application of the unconstitutional conditions theory in the Supremacy Clause context demonstrates the odd consequences of this theory's emphasis on the act of incorporation. The theory apparently would constrain only the law of an incorporating state, because only such a law would make restricting constitutional rights a condition of the granting of corporate privileges. It seems to follow that federal law would not be subject to the theory unless

[108] Id at 120-21.

[109] 288 US 517 (1933).

[110] States might even be able to form as local corporations while contracting to be bound by the law of another jurisdiction. See Ribstein, *Choosing Law By Contract* (cited in note 16).

[111] The early history of the corporate form arguably supports this. See Shughart & Tollison, *Corporate Chartering* (cited in note 13) (discussing spread of general incorporation). Butler, *Nineteenth Century Jurisdictional Competition* at 129 (cited in note 13) stresses the role of *Paul v Virginia* in facilitating this spread. However, it is unlikely *Paul* had a significant effect, since, as discussed in the text accompanying notes 96-97, that case actually denied corporations "privileges and immunities" protection. Even if *Paul* hastened the spread of general incorporation, this might have occurred later even without constitutional impetus. Perhaps the most important underlying cause of state competition is the fact that the Commerce Clause prevented states from interfering with the growth of interstate business by imposing trade tariffs. See William J. Carney, *The Political Economy of Competition for Corporate Charters* (unpublished manuscript 1994).

the federal government decided to grant corporate charters. But the preemption issue should be the same for any imposition of federal standards, whether or not the federal government grants charters. In other words, it should make no difference whether federal law imposes fiduciary standards under such statutes as the securities laws or under a separate corporation law. The underlying problem is one of enforcement of mandatory rules and not of potential coercion through control of the incorporation privilege. Indeed, because it interferes with exit, enforcement of federal rules is the *only* problem in corporation law, again whether or not the federal government is an incorporator. Conversely, the availability of exit makes reliance on state law the solution rather than the problem.

In the final analysis, therefore, corporations' jurisdictional choice is best ensured by characterizing corporations as contracts and constitutionally protecting contractual choice of law than by unique constitutional protections for corporate persons.

IV. CORPORATE SPEECH

As sources of significant wealth and power, corporations are vulnerable to political manipulation. Thus, it is important to consider whether corporations' power to speak out against such manipulation is protected by the First Amendment. The corporate person theory suggests that corporate speech is produced by artificial legal entities, and therefore should not be accorded the same First Amendment protection as speech by individuals. Under the contract theory, on the other hand, the corporate facade disappears, revealing the individual speakers behind the curtain. Moreover, while the corporate person theory assumes that there are dangers associated with corporate speech that justify withdrawing First Amendment protection, the contract theory would apply the same presumption of freedom that applies to any other type of speech. Under the contractual theory, much of the regulation of corporate campaign speech and securities-related disclosure may be unconstitutional under the First Amendment.

A. First Amendment in General: Commercial vs. Political Speech

The extent of First Amendment protection depends on whether the speech is characterized as "political," and fully protected, or "commercial," and entitled to a lower level of protection under the commercial speech doctrine created in *Virginia State Board of Pharmacy v Virginia Citizens Consumer Council,*

Inc.[112] The distinction between "commercial" and non-"commercial" speech is far from clear. Prominent commentators have advocated distinguishing "political" and "commercial" speech on the ground that the framers intended the First Amendment to protect only speech relevant to our representative form of government.[113] While the Supreme Court has indicated that commercial speech may include the broad category of speech "related solely to the economic interests of the speaker and its audience,"[114] more recently it apparently has narrowed the category to speech that proposes a commercial transaction.[115] Thus, advertising seems clearly "commercial." But even the most blatantly commercial advertising is a form of expression of ideas regarding choices that are just as important to most people as the selection among political candidates.[116] Nor is there a clear distinction between advertising that sells a specific product, more "political" advertising that is intended to influence public opinion concerning regulation of the company's products,[117] and political advertising concerning a candidate's philosophy. For example, cigarette advertisements that focus on the pleasures of smoking can be viewed as taking a position in the de-

[112] 425 US 748 (1976).

[113] See Alexander Meiklejohn, *Free Speech and its Relation to Self-Government* (Harper, 1948); Vincent Blasi, *The "Checking Value" in First Amendment Theory,* 1977 Am Bar Found Res J 521; Robert Bork, *Neutral Principles and Some First Amendment Problems,* 47 Ind L J 1 (1971); Thomas H. Jackson and John Calvin Jeffries, *Commercial Speech: Economic Due Process and the First Amendment,* 65 Va L Rev 1 (1979).

[114] *Central Hudson Gas & Elec. Corp. v Public Service Comm'n of New York,* 447 US 557, 561 (1980).

[115] See *Board of Trustees of State Univ. of New York v Fox,* 492 US 469, 473-74 (1989); *Bolger v Youngs Drug Prods. Corp.,* 463 US 60, 66-67 (1983). See also *City of Cincinnati v Discovery Network, Inc.,* 113 S Ct 1505 (1993) (assuming but not deciding that this is the test).

[116] See Nicholas Wolfson, *Corporate First Amendment Rights and the SEC* (Greenwood, 1990) ("Wolfson, *Corporate First Amendment Rights*"); Ronald H. Coase, *The Market for Goods and the Market for Ideas,* 64 Am Econ Rev 384 (Papers & Proceedings, May 1974); Ronald H. Coase, *Advertising and Free Speech,* 6 J Legal Stud 1 (1977). See also Aaron Director, *The Parity of the Economic Market Place,* 7 J L & Econ 1 (1964).

[117] Such advertising has been characterized as commercial. See *National Comm'n on Egg Nutrition v FTC,* 570 F2d 157 (7th Cir 1977) (upholding FTC order prohibiting an egg industry trade association from making certain statements about the health value of eggs, and characterizing speech as commercial); *In re R.J. Reynolds Tobacco Co.,* 111 FTC 539 (1988) (administrative agency ruling that RJR's attacks on the federal government's position that there is a link between smoking and heart disease were commercial speech); *Quinn v Aetna Life & Casualty Co.,* 96 Misc 2d 545, 409 NYS2d 473 (Sup Ct 1978) (insurer's advertisements blaming high insurance premiums on large tort damage awards were commercial speech). For an analysis of this cases criticizing the commercial/non-commercial distinction, see Alan Howard, *The*

bate on tobacco regulation.[118] The distinction may be murkiest for corporate speech such as proxy statements, which deal with important issues of corporate policy and may appear just as "political" as speech by candidates for political office.

In analyzing how theories of the corporation help influence corporate constitutional rights, it is enough to accept the broad outline of the distinction between speech or related activities connected with political campaigns, which is uncontroversially "political," and all other speech. However, even within the established commercial/political distinction, it is worth noting that much speech connected with corporate governance and other corporate activities could be characterized as political because its suppression presents risks of excessively curbing valuable speech and of self-interested regulation by incumbent politicians that are comparable to the risks that arise when conventionally "political speech" is at issue.[119] Moreover, as noted briefly below, the theory of the corporation that the courts apply when considering the regulation of corporate speech bears on whether the corporation's speech should be characterized as commercial or political.

If the regulated speech is characterized as "commercial," the standard doctrine protects lawful and non-misleading speech from regulation unless it "directly advances" a "substantial" government interest and is "not more extensive than is necessary to serve that interest."[120] The Court has made it clear in some of its recent commercial speech cases that this test requires a careful cost/benefit analysis. In other words, it is not enough for the government to show only that a substantial purpose is furthered in some way by the restriction. In *City of Cincinnati v Discovery Network*,[121] for

Constitutionality of Deceptive Speech Regulations: Replacing the Commercial Speech Doctrine with a Tort-Based Relational Framework, 41 Case Wes Res L Rev 1093 (1991).

[118] A recent magazine advertisement portrays desks hanging out office windows. The copy reads: "Have you noticed finding a place to smoke is the hardest part of your job? For a great smoke, put in for a window office. Benson & Hedges 100's. The length you go to for pleasure. " *Entertainment Weekly*, July 15, 1994 at 9. The advertisement also includes the Surgeon General's warning, mandatory disclosure of "tar" and nicotine content, and an "800" number to call for information on "a welcome sign for people who smoke." Only a small part of this advertisement deals with the unique pleasures of Benson & Hedges (primarily, its length), while the rest is either commentary on the political environment in which smokers find themselves or is directly mandated by the government.

[119] See generally Butler & Ribstein, *The Corporation and the Constitution* (cited in note 1).

[120] *Central Hudson Gas & Elec. Corp. v Public Serv Comm'n*, 447 US 557, 566 (1980).

[121] 113 S Ct 1505 (1993).

example, the Court invalidated a city's removal of 62 newsracks that distributed magazines consisting primarily of advertising. The Court reasoned that the city's purpose of improving the appearance of its streets was not sufficiently furthered by singling out 62 "commercial" newsracks from a total of 1500 to 2000 newsracks on public property. In other words, the city could not select one firm's newsracks for its beautification campaign merely because these newsracks were "commercial." Similarly, in *Edenfield v Fane,*[122] the Court struck down a ban on solicitations by C.P.A.'s, reasoning that the state had not shown a sufficient likelihood that permitting such solicitation would compromise the independence of C.P.A.'s or result in fraud or overreaching.[123] Finally, in *Ibanez v Florida Board of Accountancy* the Court struck down a governmental board's censure of a C.P.A. for using a "Certified Financial Planner" designation, reasoning that the board had failed to show that the C.P.A.'s use of the designation without the board's required disclaimer was either inherently or potentially misleading.[124]

The important Supreme Court cases dealing specifically with corporate speech all involve clearly "political" speech. The Court began, in *First National Bank of Boston v Bellotti,* by invalidating under the First and Fourteenth Amendments a Massachusetts statute that prohibited certain business corporations from making contributions or expenditures " 'for the purpose of . . . influencing or affecting the vote on any question submitted to the voters, other than one materially affecting any of the property, business or assets of the corporation.' "[125] The Court reasoned that speech that is otherwise protected does not lose its protection because the speaker is a corporation—that speech is protected not merely as a property right, but as a part of the guarantee of liberty to all natural and artificial persons.[126] The Court also held that the statute could not be sustained by any compelling state interest in preventing corporations from unduly influencing referendum votes, to offset state-

[122] 113 S Ct 1792 (1993).

[123] The Court distinguished prior cases that had sustained bans on lawyer solicitations on the grounds that C.P.A.'s lack lawyers' persuasive skills and that C.P.A.'s deal with sophisticated business people. See id at 1797-98.

[124] 114 S Ct 2084 (1994). In one recent case the Court did uphold a commercial speech restriction—in this case a federal ban on television lottery advertising in states that have no state lottery. See *United States v Edge Broadcasting Co.,* 113 S Ct 2696 (1993). The Court reasoned that the ban served a government interest in carefully balancing the rights of lottery and non-lottery states.

[125] 435 US 765, 765 (1978) (quoting the Massachusetts statute at issue) (alteration in original).

[126] Id at 778-80.

conferred advantages such as limited liability,[127] or to protect shareholders from use of their investments in corporations to support views with which they disagreed.[128]

Despite this strong beginning on corporate speech, the Court has preserved full speech rights only for non-profit "ideological" corporations. In particular, in *Federal Election Comm'n v Massachusetts Citizens For Life, Inc.* ("*MCFL*")[129] the Court held that a federal prohibition on the use of corporate treasury funds for expenditures in a federal election would unconstitutionally burden the exercise of First Amendment rights. In invalidating the law as applied, the Court narrowly focused the application of the First Amendment by emphasizing that the newsletter was published by a nonprofit corporation organized to oppose abortion. In *Austin v Michigan Chamber of Commerce,*[130] however, the Court held that a Michigan statute's prohibition on the use of corporate treasury funds for expenditures for or against candidates for state office was not unconstitutional under the First and Fourteenth Amendments as applied to a newspaper advertisement placed by the Michigan Chamber of Commerce. The Court distinguished *MCFL* on the grounds that the Chamber of Commerce, although non-profit, was not formed for the express purpose of promoting political ideas; that the Chamber conferred nonpolitical benefits on its members; and that the Chamber could be used to funnel money from business corporations.

Questions remain as to how these cases will be applied to less blatantly "political" speech. In *SEC v Wall Street Publishing Institute, Inc.,*[131] the Court held that the First Amendment did not prevent the SEC from invoking the Securities Act of 1933[132] to enjoin publication of monthly magazines that failed to disclose that the publisher (an investment adviser regulated by the SEC) received consideration in the form of free text from the subject firms. Although the Court characterized the speech as more like a news story than clearly "commercial," it reasoned that a rule enacted in the context of extensive federal regulation should be sustained even without weighing its merits. In *Long Island Lighting Co. v Barbash,*[133] an issuer sought to apply proxy disclosure rules to an advertisement concerning the question of municipal ownership of a

[127] Id at 791 n 30.
[128] Id at 791-95.
[129] 479 US 238 (1986).
[130] 494 US 652 (1990).
[131] 851 F2d 365 (DC Cir 1988).
[132] 15 USC § 77q(b) (1988).
[133] 779 F2d 793 (2d Cir 1985).

utility. The court avoided the First Amendment issue by holding that the issuer was entitled to discovery on the question whether the advertisement was a covered solicitation.[134] Finally, in *Lowe v SEC*,[135] which involved the question whether the SEC could prohibit unlicensed publication of an investment newsletter, a majority of the Court avoided the First Amendment question by holding that the Investment Advisers Act regulated only face-to-face professional advice.[136]

In general, these cases suggest that the application of the First Amendment to corporate speech is very much an open question. Accordingly, the following discussion does not assume a particular categorization of corporate speech, but applies the analyses of both the political and commercial speech cases.

B. The Corporate Person Theory

Under the corporate person theory, speech is attributed to the corporate entity rather than to individuals. Although *Bellotti* held that speech is protected even if uttered by artificial persons, the post-*Bellotti* cases on corporate political speech showed that it is easier to deny First Amendment rights if the speech is attributed to an artificial person. These cases accepted several standard arguments for limiting corporate constitutional rights under the corporate person theory.

First, the Court has endorsed the traditional corporate-person argument that, because states create corporations, they may restrict their speech. Justice Rehnquist had reasoned in his *Bellotti* dissent that the right to engage in political speech is merely a privilege states can choose not to confer on their legal creations. In a variation on this view, Justice White's *Bellotti* dissent articulated a rationale for limited constitutional protection of corporate speech that is at least superficially similar to Rehnquist's state-creation theory. Justice White reasoned that states ought to be able to prevent corporations from using their state-conferred advantages to

[134] For another case in which the court held that a newspaper advertisement in connection with a politically-tinged proxy contest was held not to be a solicitation, see *Brown v Chicago, Rock Island & Pacific Railroad*, 328 F2d 122 (7th Cir 1964). See also Comment, *Solicitation under the Proxy Rules: The Need for a More Precise Definition of Solicitation*, 8 Sw U L Rev 1019 (1976).

[135] 472 US 181 (1985). *Wall Street Publishing* distinguished *Lowe* on the ground that the former did not involve a pre-publication restraint.

[136] Three concurring justices said that First Amendment prohibited application of the Act to broad restraint of a publication without regard to its quality, whether or not the speech was characterized as commercial.

dominate the political process.[137] This could be described as the "Frankenstein" theory of corporate speech: The state should be able to build limits into its creatures to prevent them from destroying their creators.[138] Although the *Bellotti* majority firmly rejected the state-creation argument,[139] the Court retreated from this position in *Federal Election Commission v National Right to Work Committee* (*"NRWC"*),[140] reasoning that the statute at issue in that case protected against the use of "substantial aggregations of wealth amassed by the special advantages which go with the corporate form of organization."[141] *Austin* reinforced the application of corporate-person reasoning by emphasizing the "unique *state-conferred* corporate structure that facilitates the amassing of large treasuries."[142]

Second, some members of the Court have reasoned that government restrictions on corporate political speech are justified under the First Amendment by the need to protect shareholders

[137] 435 US at 809-10.

[138] See Carl E. Schneider, *Free Speech and Corporate Freedom: A Comment on First National Bank of Boston v Bellotti,* 59 S Cal L Rev 1227, 1257 (1986) (comparing corporate privileges to state's creation of nuclear power). "Frankenstein" was used in another sense by David L. Ratner, *Corporations and the Constitution,* 15 USF L Rev 11, 29 (1980) (referring to the Court's recognition of corporate free speech rights as endowing the corporation with human characteristics). For a recent expression of this theory, see Mayer, *Personalizing the Impersonal* at 658-59 (cited in note 14) (footnotes omitted):

> The corporate exercise of first amendment rights frustrates the individual's right to participate equally in democratic elections, to pay reasonable utility rates, and to live in a toxin-free environment. Equality of constitutional rights plus an inequality of legislated and de facto powers leads inexorably to the supremacy of artificial over real persons. . . .
>
> The corporate drive for constitutional parity with "real" humans comes at a time when legislatures are awarding these artificial persons superhuman privileges. Besides perpetual life, corporations enjoy limited liability for industrial accidents such as nuclear power disasters, and the use of voluntary bankruptcy and other means to dodge financial obligations while remaining in business.
>
> The legal system thus is creating unaccountable Frankensteins that have superhuman powers but are nonetheless constitutionally shielded from much actual and potential law enforcement as well as from accountability to real persons such as workers, consumers, and taxpayers.

[139] See 435 US at 778-80 nn 14-15.

[140] 459 US 197 (1982) (holding that Congress constitutionally could prohibit a non-profit corporation from mass soliciting from non-"members" political contributions to a segregated fund).

[141] Id at 207.

[142] *Austin,* 494 US at 660 (emphasis added).

from having to support managers' views with which they disagree.[143] This is consistent with the Berle-Means concern with the separation of ownership and control.

Third, the Berle-Means "separation" reasoning also is implicit in the *Austin* Court's argument that restrictions on political speech are constitutionally justified by the state's interest in protecting against "corruption" in the form of "the corrosive and distorting effects of immense aggregations of wealth that are accumulated with the help of the corporate form and that have little or no correlation to the public's support for the corporation's political ideas."[144] This is partly an argument that corporations may be enabled to prevail over the views of others because they control large amounts of wealth.[145] But having explicitly rejected a broad theory that all views must receive equal hearings in *Buckley v Valeo*[146]

[143] Justice White made this argument in his *Bellotti* dissent. In *NRWC*, Justice Rehnquist, writing for a unanimous Court, said that one of the purposes of federal restrictions on campaign contributions is to protect corporate shareholders or union dues contributors "from having that money used to support political candidates to whom they may be opposed." 459 US at 208 (citing *United States v CIO*, 335 US 106, 113 (1948)). And Justice Brennan's *Austin* concurrence emphasized the state's "compelling interest in preventing a corporation it has chartered from exploiting those who do not wish to contribute to the Chamber's political message." 494 US at 675. See also Victor Brudney, *Business Corporations and Stockholders' Rights under the First Amendment*, 91 Yale L J 235 (1981) (advocating protection of speech rights of minority shareholders). The *Bellotti* majority, however, noted that corporate shareholders are free to decide where to invest their money. 435 US at 794.

More recent cases suggest that the "compelled speech" argument may have limited application. *Barnes v State Farm Mutual Automobile Insurance Ass'n*, 16 Cal App 4th 365, 20 Cal Rptr 2d 87 (1993), held that *Bellotti* and its reasoning applied to a policy holder in a mutual insurance company who claimed to have a First Amendment right to object to the company's use of funds for political activities. The court rejected the plaintiff's attempt to distinguish *Bellotti* on the basis of the compulsory nature of automobile insurance, reasoning that plaintiff still had the option to choose his insurer. Finally, the Supreme Court recently held that the "must-carry" provisions of the Cable Television Consumer Protection and Competition Act of 1992 do not compel cable operators to endorse messages in violation of the First Amendment. See *Turner Broadcasting System, Inc. v Federal Communications Comm'n*, 114 S Ct 2445, 2465-66 (1994).

[144] 494 US at 660.

[145] For recent discussions of this and other reasons for limiting campaign spending see *Symposium on Campaign Finance Reform*, 94 Colum L Rev 1125 (1994).

[146] The Court said in *Buckley*, 424 US 1, 48-49 (1976): "[T]he concept that government may restrict the speech of some elements of our society in order to enhance the relative voice of others is wholly foreign to the First Amendment." For a recent article rejecting the "equality" theory of the First Amendment, see Nicholas Wolfson, *Equality in First Amendment Theory*, 38 SLU L J 379 (1993).

and in *Bellotti,*[147] the *Austin* Court apparently was focusing on a problem specific to *corporate* campaign activities. Insofar as it relates particularly to corporations, the "corruption" argument asserts that, because managers' use of resources contributed by shareholders and others to finance their views is not effectively constrained by other corporate participants, the corporate form confers unique power on corporate managers.

Finally, the "corruption" reasoning just described reflects the stakeholder-protection aspect of the corporate person theory. Under this reasoning, managers' power affects not only shareholders, but also employees, consumers and others. Thus, non-shareholder "constituents" should have direct access to corporate governance processes through shareholder proposals and other proxy disclosures.

It follows from this analysis that, under the corporate person theory, the First Amendment permits broad regulation of speech by corporations, including even clearly political speech. Ironically, however, these same arguments may make it more difficult to apply the lower commercial speech standard. The more that courts and legislatures help non-shareholder constituencies to use corporations to espouse political agendas unrelated to corporations' immediate economic goals, the more likely it is that regulation of corporate governance speech will be subject to the higher standard of justification that is applied in the political speech cases, rather than to the commercial speech standard.[148]

This point is illustrated by the application of the shareholder proposal rule,[149] which ensures public access to corporate proxy

[147] *Bellotti,* 435 US at 788-92. Justice Powell wrote that there was no evidence that "corporate advocacy threatened imminently to undermine democratic processes," and did not find the argument "inherently persuasive or supported by the precedents of this Court." Id at 789, 790. Powell quoted the language from *Buckley* set out in note 146 in opposition to the argument that corporate speech may "drown out" other viewpoints. Id at 790-91. And he noted that the equality argument had been accepted only in the "special context of limited access to channels of communication," id at 791 n 30 (citing *Red Lion Broadcasting Co. v FCC,* 395 US 367 (1969)), and had been rejected even in the more persuasive context of candidates' access to newspaper space, id (citing *Miami Herald Publishing Co. v Tornillo,* 418 US 241 (1974)).

[148] For other arguments that the politicization of the corporate form justifies applying First Amendment protection, see Wolfson, *Corporate First Amendment Rights* at 145-46 (cited in note 116); Wolfson remarks in Henry N. Butler, *Edited Transcript of Symposium on the First Amendment and Securities Regulation,* 20 Conn L Rev 383, 454 (1988) ("from the [American Law Institute's and SEC's] standpoint, full first amendment protection of proxy speech is a hoisting of their petard with a vengeance").

[149] SEC Rule 14a-8, 17 CFR § 240.14a-8.

statements.[150] The rule has often been used for blatantly political purposes. For example, in *New York City Employees' Retirement System v Dole Food Co., Inc.*,[151] the court enjoined Dole Food Company from excluding a proposal to examine government health care plans that was made on behalf of its shareholder, the New York City Employees' Retirement System. Other recent cases have required corporations to include a shareholder proposal requiring the company to report on equal employment and affirmative action policies[152] and held that a company had misstated its record on the environment in response to a shareholder proposal urging adoption of the "Valdez principles."[153] Also, courts and commentators have reasoned that managers should be required to make disclosures in proxy statements and other disclosure materials as to matters of social policy.[154]

C. The Contract Theory

Under the contract theory of the corporation, the separate corporate entity disappears for constitutional purposes and the speech is attributed to those immediately responsible for it. Generally this will be the managers who speak or prepare the speech rather than the shareholders who may fund the speech with their investments.[155] That is true whether managers speak on their own behalf or on behalf of the corporation, and whether or not the speech is authorized. Speakers generally do not, and should not, have to trace the source of the funds supporting the speech in order to be entitled to

[150] See Wolfson, *Corporate First Amendment Rights* at 122-24 (cited in note 116) (noting the political nature of proxy proposals).

[151] 795 F Supp 95 (SDNY 1992), dismissed as moot, 969 F2d 1430 (2d Cir 1992).

[152] *Amalgamated Clothing and Textile Workers Union v Wal-Mart Stores, Inc.*, 821 F Supp 877 (SDNY 1993).

[153] See *United Paperworkers Int'l Union v International Paper Co.*, 985 F2d 1190 (2d Cir 1993).

[154] See *SEC v Joseph Schlitz Brewing Co.*, 452 F Supp 824 (ED Wis 1978) (requiring disclosure of corporate misconduct); Larry E. Ribstein, *Business Associations* 340-41 (Matthew Bender, 2d ed 1990); Russell B. Stevenson, Jr., *The SEC and the New Disclosure*, 62 Cornell L Rev 50 (1976); Russell B. Stevenson, Jr., *The SEC and Foreign and Foreign Bribery*, 32 Bus Law 53 (1976).

[155] This conclusion has been questioned by commentators. See Charles R. O'Kelley, *The Constitutional Rights of Corporations Revisited: Social and Political Expression and the Corporation after First National Bank v. Bellotti*, 67 Georgetown L J 1347 (1979) (Supreme Court's initial recognition of constitutional rights of corporations based on rationale of protecting property invested by incorporators in the firm); David L. Ratner, *Corporations and the Constitution*, 15 USF L Rev 11 (1981). The attribution to managers also was questioned by Justice White in his *Bellotti* dissent. See *Bellotti*, 435 US at 805.

First Amendment protection. Moreover, it may be difficult to interpret the managers' contract concerning the extent of their speech rights.[156]

Nor should authorized speech on behalf of the corporation be attributed to the shareholders, since passive shareholders in public corporations cannot be regarded in any meaningful sense as controlling or monitoring corporate activity.[157] Most individuals either hold diversified portfolios of investments or invest in corporations indirectly through institutions such as mutual funds. Accordingly, they care little about the internal affairs of individual companies or statements or expenditures made by their managers. Because shareholders are residual claimants, while creditors and others rely on the corporation's performance of specific contractual obligations, the shareholders' contracts seem to differ from those of other corporate claimholders in a way that arguably makes shareholders uniquely responsible for managers' speech. But shareholders do not "approve" managers' corporate speech except in the attenuated sense that they can sue errant managers for breach of fiduciary duty or vote them out of office for conduct that is significantly contrary to shareholders' interests. Moreover, other claimants may be able to check managerial conduct. For example, creditors may have significant monitoring rights, particularly in insolvent or nearly insolvent firms.[158]

Even if the corporation were disaggregated and its speech attributed directly to managers, the corporate person theory would pre-

[156] The business judgment rule provides broad latitude for corporate political activity. See *Shlensky v Wrigley*, 95 Ill App 2d 173, 237 NE2d 776 (1968) (sustaining a business decision motivated partly by non-business objectives). See also *A.P. Smith Manufacturing Co. v Barlow*, 13 NJ 145, 98 A2d 581, appeal dismissed, 346 US 861 (1953) (charitable gift held not ultra vires).

[157] See Armen A. Alchian and Harold Demsetz, *Production, Information Costs, and Economic Organization*, 62 Am Econ Rev 777, 789 n 14 (1972).

[158] See Wolfson, *Corporate First Amendment Rights* at 111, 123 (cited in note 116) (questioning whether creditors should be distinguished from shareholders since both groups are investors who merely differ with respect to the form of their contracts). Workers, too, may have considerable say through their power to strike or quit. Indeed, the corporate person theory of the corporation goes so far as to support legal rules requiring managers to represent the interests of non-shareholder "stakeholders." See, for example, *Herald Co. v Seawell*, 472 F2d 1081 (10th Cir 1972) (defensive stock issuance upheld partly on ground that the target, a large urban newspaper, was a "quasi-public institution"). Perhaps as large institutional shareholders become more active in corporate governance, corporate speech can be more closely identified with specific shareholders. See, for example, Bernard S. Black, *Shareholder Passivity Reexamined*, 89 Mich L Rev 520 (1990). But new trends in shareholder monitoring have not developed to the point where large shareholders can be identified with specific corporate activities.

sume in favor of regulation of corporate speech in order to protect shareholders and stakeholders for the reasons discussed above.[159] Conversely, the contract theory would not presume that legal regulation protecting these interests is justified. To the contrary, refusing to enforce managers' speech rights would infringe shareholders' rights contractually to empower managers to speak. To be sure, managers' and shareholders' interests are likely to diverge regarding speech. Managers may advocate pet causes that do not relate to the corporation. Or they might advocate wealth transfers to their own firms from others, although shareholders would regard such transfers as merely shifting wealth within their portfolios while imposing deadweight transfer costs.[160] But the contract theory assumes that the parties to the corporation, like parties to other types of contracts, can protect themselves by investing in corporate governance devices that minimize this divergence of interest, and that these contracts are subject to the same sort of market discipline that applies to other contracts.[161]

It follows from this analysis that the "corruption" argument for regulating corporate speech is unfounded. If corporate managers' power is constrained by contract, corporate power may represent voter support at least as well as the "ideological" firms that are favored under the corporate political speech cases.[162] Nor is regulation of the corporate form warranted to protect non-shareholder "stakeholders." It follows that regulation ensuring stakeholders a role in corporate governance and special protection from corporate

[159] See Section IV(B). Some commentators would deny full First Amendment protection to corporate agents because it does not sufficiently represent the expression of autonomous speakers to warrant First Amendment protection. See C. Edwin Baker, *Commercial Speech: A Problem in the Theory of Freedom,* 62 Iowa L Rev 1, 34-40 (1976); C. Edwin Baker, *Realizing Self-Realization: Corporate Political Expenditures and Redish's The Value of Free Speech,* 130 U Pa L Rev 646 (1982). See also Lawrence E. Mitchell, *Groundwork of the Metaphysics of Corporate Law,* 50 Wash & Lee L Rev 1477, 1486 (1993) (arguing that corporate actors should not "be granted the panoply of rights that persons in our society have been granted" because they are only acting out their limited role in the corporation rather than acting fully autonomously).

[160] See Robert G. Hansen and John R. Lott, Jr., *Externalities and Corporate Objectives in a World with Diversified Shareholder/Consumers or, Why Do We Continue to Teach Value Maximization as the Proper Corporate Objective?* (Working Paper, January 1993).

[161] For a detailed discussion of market discipline of contracts relating to corporate speech and the costs and benefits of mandatory rules, see Butler & Ribstein, *The Corporation and the Constitution* at 64-67 (cited in note 1).

[162] See text accompanying note 129 above. For more detailed public choice analyses of the relative power of for-profit and "ideological" firms, see Butler & Ribstein, *The Corporation and the Constitution* at 71-74 (cited in note 1); Larry E. Ribstein, *Corporate Political Speech,* 49 Wash & Lee L Rev 109, 138-40 (1992).

commercial speech is not entitled to a presumption of validity under the First Amendment.

The contract theory may, therefore, make it difficult to justify regulation of corporate political speech under the First Amendment. Moreover, the contract theory may make it difficult to justify regulation of other types of corporate speech, even if such speech is characterized as "commercial." Since the contract theory would treat corporate speech like any other speech, the Supreme Court's recent decisions in *Ibanez, Edenfield,* and *Discovery Network* would apply to all corporate speech.

The commercial speech cases, for example, would apply to the regulation of prospectus disclosures. The Securities Act of 1933[163] requires the delivery of a prospectus containing certain disclosures to purchasers of securities distributed by issuers; forbids most written communications unless accompanied or preceded by a 1933 Act statutory prospectus;[164] and forbids any speech, truthful or not, about the securities for a significant period of time before at least a preliminary version of the statutory prospectus is available.[165] The Act also imposes liability for misstatements about these securities.[166] Communications concerning new securities issues closely resemble advertising, which is conventional commercial speech.[167] Assuming the speech regulated by the 1933 Act should be given no more protection than ordinary commercial speech, some aspects of mandatory prospectus regulation under federal and state law raise serious concerns under the First Amendment. Consider the 1933 Act's prohibition on certain *truthful* statements that are made before the statutory prospectus is available and the Act's requirement that a statutory prospectus accompany most written statements. This effectively outlaws general advertising of securities and forces

[163] 15 USC § 77a et seq (1988).

[164] More precisely, the statute forbids the use of a "prospectus," which is broadly defined in the Act to include most written communications. Securities Act of 1933, § 2(10), 15 USC § 77b(10) (1988).

[165] Securities Act of 1933, § 5, 15 USC § 77e (1988).

[166] Id §§ 77k, 77*l*(2), 77q(a) (1988).

[167] See Note, *The Federal Securities Laws, the First Amendment and Commercial Speech: A Call for Consistency,* 59 St John's L Rev 57 (1984) (distinguishing third party communications and prospectuses advertising securities on the ground that latter are less likely to be chilled by government regulation). For an argument that prospectus regulation involves regulation of the conduct of issuing securities, see Allen D. Boyer, *Free Speech, Free Markets, and Foolish Consistency,* 92 Colum L Rev 474, 484-86 (1992). This is wrong: issuance of securities is clearly governed by state corporate law. Securities law governs only disclosures on public offerings of stock. For arguments that prospectus regulation should not be classified as commercial speech regulation, see Butler & Ribstein, *The Corporation and the Constitution* at 101-102 (cited in note 1).

most issuers to rely on elaborate securities syndications. This is much more extensive regulation than applies to any other type of advertising, including such analogous products as franchises and land sales.[168]

The analogies between prospectus regulation and the recent commercial speech cases are obvious. Prospectus regulation resembles the blanket prohibition on accountant solicitation that the Court struck down in *Edenfield* despite the state's claim that the ban was necessary to prevent fraud.[169] Prospectus regulation also resembles the blanket prohibition on commercial newsracks the Court struck down in *Discovery Network,* and the elaborate disclaimer that was required to describe the "specialist" accrediting agency in *Ibanez.* To be valid under the First Amendment, the government would have to show that there was some special justification for these broad prohibitions—that is, that investors are more likely to be misled as to securities than as to other products, including other investment products, and that the prospectus delivery requirement would protect them. Thus, the government must show that the sorts of investors who are most likely to be misled by overbearing salesmen are likely either to read or to learn much from the prospectus.[170] It also must show that the possibility that requiring delivery of prospectuses will prevent some people from making bad investments is outweighed by the large costs imposed on issuers and on the market. For example, the Court in *Ibanez* held that the Accountancy Board failed to show that the required disclaimer was

> an appropriately tailored check against deception or confusion. . . . This much is plain, however: The detail required in the disclaimer currently described by the Board effectively rules out notation of the "specialist" designation on a business card or letterhead, or in a yellow pages listing.[171]

[168] See Michael E. Schoeman, *The First Amendment and Restrictions on Advertising of Securities Under the Securities Act of 1933,* 41 Bus Law 377 (1986) (also concluding that the 1933 Act is unreasonably broad and therefore unconstitutional under *Central Hudson*).

[169] See *Edenfield v Fane,* 113 S Ct 1792, 1799 (1993):

> But where, as with the blanket ban involved here, truthful and nonmisleading expression will be snared along with fraudulent or deceptive commercial speech, the State must satisfy the remainder of the *Central Hudson* test by demonstrating that its restriction serves a substantial state interest and is designed in a reasonable way to accomplish that end.

[170] See Homer Kripke, *The SEC, the Accountants, Some Myths and Some Realities,* 45 NYU L Rev 1151 (1970).

[171] *Ibanez,* 114 S Ct at 2090-91.

Although some regulation of corporate commercial and political speech may be constitutional, the important point is that the same rules that apply to speech generally, including the rules recently applied in *Discovery, Network,* and *Edenfield,* should be applied to corporate speech regulation. In other words, there should be no special presumption that such regulation is valid based on the market failure assumptions underlying the corporate person theory.

D. Unconstitutional Conditions

Although an important, and apparently direct effect of characterizing a corporation as an artificial entity has been to denigrate First Amendment protection of corporate speech, Richard Epstein has argued for a contrary result while staying within the corporate person model. Epstein has argued that, to subject corporations to a denial of First Amendment rights is to impose an unconstitutional condition on the "privilege" of incorporation.[172] This argument was also implicitly accepted by Justice Scalia in his *Austin* dissent.[173]

Epstein's theory conflicts to some extent with the contractual theory because it provides a basis for invalidating restrictions on corporate speech imposed by the incorporating state.[174] To be sure, corporations could be hurt by such rules if, for example, they are imposed ex post to impair contracts, or if non-incorporating states refuse to enforce the rules that would apply under the statute of the state of incorporation. However, the contract theory would deal with such problems under the Contract and Commerce Clauses, while otherwise relying on corporate contracts and incorporating state law to define shareholder rights.

VI. CONCLUSION

This article has shown how the determination of corporate constitutional rights depends critically on which theory of the corpora-

[172] See Epstein, *Bargaining* at 112-14 (cited in note 7).

[173] See *Austin,* 494 US at 680:

> Those individuals who form that type of voluntary association known as a corporation are, to be sure, given special advantages—notably, the immunization of their personal fortunes from liability for the actions of the association—that the State is under no obligation to confer. But so are other associations and private individuals given all sorts of special advantages that the State need not confer, ranging from tax breaks to contract awards to public employment to outright cash subsidies. It is rudimentary that the State cannot exact as the price of those special advantages the forfeiture of First Amendment rights.

[174] See text accompanying note 43 above.

tion is applied. These theories are more than mere metaphors, but entail different assumptions about the need for government regulation, and therefore about whether interference with constitutional rights is justified. The corporate person theory assumes that pervasive regulation of the corporate form is justified. By contrast, the corporate contract and unconstitutional conditions theories imply the need for significant constitutional limitations on the regulation of corporations.

The theories of the corporation have potential implications for the application of consitutional rules other than those discussed in this article. For example, consistent with the corporate person theory, the Court has limited corporations' protection against self-incrimination under the Fourth[175] and Fifth Amendments[176] on the theory that corporations are artificial entities. However, under the contract theory individuals would not lose Fourth and Fifth Amendment rights merely because they work for corporate firms. For example, the Fifth Amendment could be applied in appropriate cases to protect an individual from having to turn over documents which incriminate that individual even if she has custody of the records as a corporate agent. To be sure, this might allow corporations to escape some government control because they can choose agents who can claim privilege.[177] But given the assumptions underlying the contract theory, owners have market incentives not to insulate their agents from the law. Finally, the unconstitutional conditions theory would protect corporate persons from being coerced into relinquishing their constitutional rights in order to obtain corporate

[175] See *United States v Morton Salt Co.*, 338 US 632, 642 (1950), in which the Court said:

> [C]orporations can claim no equality with individuals in the enjoyment of a right to privacy. . . . They are endowed with public attributes. They have a collective impact upon society, from which they derive the privilege of acting as artificial entities.

[176] See *United States v Kordel*, 397 US 1 (1970); *Hale v Henkel*, 201 US 43 (1906) (reasoning that the corporation was a separate entity for Fifth Amendment purposes although not for purposes of applying the Fourth Amendment). By contrast, the privilege aginst self-incrimination is available to protect against requests for personal, as distinguished from corporate, records. See *Wilson v United States*, 221 US 361 (1911). The privilege has also been denied to non-corporate associations that are considered collective entities. See *Bellis v United States*, 417 US 85 (1974) (law firm); *United States v White*, 322 US 694 (1944) (labor union). But it has been denied even to one-person corporations. See *Braswell v United States*, 487 US 99 (1988).

[177] Cf *United States v Kordel*, 397 US 1 (1970) (denying Fifth Amendment protection on the ground that, since officer claiming privilege could have appointed an agent who had no fear of self-incrimination to answer the interrogatories, the interrogatories did not force him to incriminate himself).

privileges. But it follows from the contract analysis that corporate "entities" should *not* be entitled to Fifth Amendment rights because this might frustrate the firm's contracts. The parties to the firm might choose to neutralize the self-incrimination privilege and facilitate legal surveillance by giving custody over documents to a custodian who could not assert a privilege in connection with proceedings against the corporation.

In general, while the unconstitutional conditions and contract theories rest on similar normative assumptions about the appropriate role of government regulation, they start from contrasting characterizations of the positive law of corporations. The unconstitutional conditions theory assumes that states *do* create corporations, and that this power must be restricted by the Constitution. On the other hand, the contractual theory sees corporations fundamentally as the product of contract. It follows from this theory that, as long as contracting is protected by the Contract Clause and the possibility of exit is assured by the Commerce Clause, *state* corporation law should be mostly free from constitutional interference.

Interpreting Health Care Cost Containment Legislation: *Good Samaritan Hospital v Shalala* and Relative Institutional Competence

Simonetti Samuels[†]

Good Samaritan Hospital v Shalala *provides an occasion for examining the roles of courts, Congress, and HCFA (the agency that implements the financing mechanisms for federal health care programs) in the interpretation of health care cost control legislation. The* Good Samaritan *majority held that the statute at issue did not require HCFA to provide retroactive case-by-case review of its financing determinations. This conclusion, which was reached through the application of the* Chevron *framework, respected the agency's technical expertise in the field of health care financing. The wide discretion granted to HCFA, however, increases the possibility of agency capture by special interests, with resulting welfare losses. The dissent's application of* Chevron*, which would have required retroactive case-by-case review, is more consistent with the economic insight that judicial supervision of the agency may be the only practicable device for limiting the efficiency losses caused by agency capture.*

I. INTRODUCTION

In an early attempt to slow upwardly spiraling health care costs in the Medicare program, Congress passed legislation allowing the

[†] Director, Health Law Research Institute, Case Western Reserve University School of Law. The author would like to thank those individuals without whose help this paper could not have been written. For invaluable comments and suggestions, I thank Peter C. Carstensen, Richard A. Epstein, Neil K. Komesar, and two anonymous referees. Additionally, I thank Nelson Lund not only for his editorial guidance but also for his epic patience and persistence. For endless hours of diligent research and support, I thank J. Tobias Fizzell, David D. Augustin, and Luis Machado. Of course, any remaining errors and omissions are my own.

 0-226-28685-1/95/0004-0004$02.00

Secretary of the Department of Health and Human Services (HHS) to set cost limits on payments to health care providers under the Medicare program.[1] Originally, providers were reimbursed for the total costs of treating Medicare patients as long as they were not "substantially out of line" with costs at like institutions. After the Social Security Amendments of 1972, cost limits were developed.[2] Because the regulatory agency had little knowledge of the underlying cost structure of the health care industry, these constraints were at first crudely developed and had little effect in restraining cost growth. As the knowledge base and experience of the regulator grew, however, methodological refinements permitted the regulator to lower the cost limits with increasing boldness, so that eventually they imposed a binding constraint upon providers.[3] In response, high-cost providers were faced with the following choices: become more efficient and lower costs; attempt to qualify for one of the established exceptions or exemptions; lobby the regulatory agency for an adjustment in the payment methodology; and/or seek a "retroactive corrective adjustment" after the fact.

In recent years, the Supreme Court has twice reviewed the scope of authority delegated by Congress to the Secretary of HHS in making retroactive adjustments to Medicare cost limits. In *Bowen v Georgetown University Hospital*,[4] the Court held that the relevant statute gave the Secretary authority only to make adjustments on a case-by-case basis, rejecting the agency's claim that it was permitted to promulgate retroactive Medicare cost-limit rules. More recently, in *Good Samaritan Hospital v Shalala*,[5] the Court deferred to the agency's interpretation of the statute, holding that the Secretary did not have to provide hospitals an opportunity to show that they were entitled to payments above the regulatory cost limits and that the Secretary could limit adjustments to "year-end book balancing."[6] Justice Souter's dissent, however, which was joined by Justices Stevens and Scalia, interpreted the statutory provision to require the promulgation of rules to permit providers the opportu-

[1] Social Security Amendments of 1972, Pub L No 92-603, § 223, 86 Stat 1329, 1393 (1972).

[2] The prospective payment system (PPS), discussed below, has now for the most part replaced the use of cost limits with respect to hospital inpatient reimbursement. Cost limits, however, continue to play a role in establishing the maximum reimbursement level for skilled nursing facilities, home health agencies and some categories of hospitals.

[3] These cost limits were applied to the cost of routine care, not the total cost per admission.

[4] 488 US 204 (1988).

[5] 113 S Ct 2151 (1993).

[6] Id at 2161-62.

nity to seek adjustments when a provider's aggregate Medicare reimbursement is below "the actual reasonable costs of providing services to Medicare beneficiaries."[7]

Good Samaritan provides an occasion for examining the appropriate role for the regulator[8] in the interpretation and implementation of health care cost containment legislation, and for analyzing the institutional capacities of Congress and the courts in monitoring agency performance. Once Congress made the decision to engage in command-and-control style regulation of the health care industry under the Medicare program, serious questions about the best way to control the regulatory agency have necessarily been raised. The Justices purported to disagree in *Good Samaritan* about whether the relevant statutory language is ambiguous, and thus on whether deference should be extended to a reasonable interpretation of ambiguous language by the agency. Whatever one thinks about that dispute as a legal matter or as a matter of contending theories of statutory construction—issues that I do not address in detail in this article—one also needs to evaluate the consequences to which the two interpretive approaches lead. By deferring to the agency's interpretation of the statute, the *Good Samaritan* majority tacitly concludes either that the agency is in a better position than the judiciary to effect congressional intent, or more likely, that if the agency deviates from congressional intent, Congress is in a better position than the Court to remedy the problem. The position taken by the dissenting judges is consistent with a less sanguine view of the agency's ability to interpret the statutory provisions at issue correctly, as well as a less optimistic evaluation of Congress' ability to monitor the regulatory process. If this view is correct, the dissent's approach to interpreting the statute would lead to a salutary increase in judicial intervention in the regulatory process.

The outcome in *Good Samaritan* thus raises an important question for health care policymakers, which is likely to become increasingly significant if Congress begins making serious efforts to control health care costs in the large segments of the market that are not yet heavily regulated. Should Congress give an agency like the Health Care Financing Administration (HCFA), the regulatory agency that implements the Medicare and Medicaid programs, the kind of discretion that *Good Samaritan* confers in the context of Medicare and Medicaid?

[7] Id at 2167 (Souter dissenting).

[8] The regulator in question is the Health Care Financing Administration (HCFA), an agency within HHS.

This article provides an economic and legal analysis of the issue. Part II identifies the goals and problems in setting cost limits and explains how agency interpretation of congressional legislation can stray from these goals. Part III examines both the need for wide discretion so agencies can meet the technical challenges in developing cost containment regulation and the social losses that can result from granting the agency this latitude. The potential benefits and pitfalls of congressional monitoring and judicial review are explored in Part IV. Part V concludes by suggesting that a greater recognition of institutional trade-offs by the Court might have led to a more satisfying result in *Good Samaritan.*

II. DEFINING THE SCOPE OF HCFA's AUTHORITY IN HEALTH CARE COST CONTAINMENT LEGISLATION

A. Background: Goals of Cost Limit Legislation

Prior to the adoption of cost limits, hospitals were reimbursed under the Medicare program on the basis of costs, subject only to the requirement that they not be "out of line" with those of other similar providers. While arguments over reimbursement were common, Medicare expanded access to health care for the elderly, and the hospital sector of the economy grew.

Concerned with the rapid growth in health care costs, Congress gave the Secretary of HHS authority to set prospective limits on costs reimbursed under the Medicare program in 1972.[9] Cost limits served to introduce the concept of limiting hospital inpatient payments to the costs of an "efficient" hospital. Specifically, this legislation requires:

> [T]he establishment of limits on the direct or indirect overall incurred costs or incurred costs of specific items or services or groups of items or services to be recognized as reasonable based on estimates of the costs necessary in the efficient de-

[9] Pub L No 92-603, § 223(b), 86 Stat 1329 (1972) (codified at 42 USC §§ 1395x(v)(1)(A)). The Medicare program was originally enacted in 1965 as Title XVIII of the Social Security Act, Pub L No 89-97, 79 Stat 291 (1965), codified at 42 USC §§ 1395 - 1395ccc. Medicare comprises Part A for inpatient hospital coverage, nursing facilities, home health and hospice services, and Part B for outpatient services, physician services, diagnostic test, and durable medical equipment. Part A automatically covers individuals who are age 65 or over and are eligible for retirement benefits. Enrollment in Part B is voluntary, though 95% of those who are covered under Part A elect to pay the premium for Part B. Part A is financed through payroll taxes, Part B through premiums and through general revenue.

livery of needed health services to individuals covered by the insurance programs established under this title.[10]

The first step in understanding cost limits is to recognize the determinants of hospital costs. The cost of a given unit of hospital output will depend on the following parameters: the quality of care; the intensity of treatment necessary for the severity of a given patient's illness; and the price of hospital inputs (such as labor, supplies, and equipment). In theory, an efficient hospital provider would be one that produces a given level of output at the minimum cost using available technology. In practice, it would be far too costly for policymakers to make the necessary measurements directly, so they have to settle for benchmarks that rely instead on the costs of a "representative" hospital. Under the cost-limits scheme at issue here, hospitals are assigned to peer groups. These groupings are based on factors that serve as proxies for the causes of cost variation in hospital output. Comparing actual costs within these categories, a "representative" level of costs is chosen and designated as the benchmark for payment purposes. Hospitals whose costs fall below this level are considered "efficient" and compensated for their total costs;[11] hospitals with costs above this level are deemed "inefficient" and must absorb at least a portion of the excess costs of treating patients.

The goal in developing an efficiency benchmark was to coax the hospital industry into a competitive battle: efficient firms would be rewarded, and high-cost producers would be forced to change production strategy or go out of business. Success in improving the efficiency of hospital providers, and thereby lowering the price of medical care, however, will depend on the ability of the Medicare payment system to identify "efficient" providers. To the extent that the methodology is flawed, inefficient hospitals whose costs fall below the "efficiency" benchmark may be receiving rewards. At the same time, efficient hospitals with costs above the "efficiency" benchmark are penalized.

HHS' first stab at cost limits. Initially, the cost limit methodology was relatively crude and cost limits applied only to the cost of routine (i.e. bed and board) inpatient hospital services. HHS created a benchmark system limiting the reimbursement rate for hospitals based on the per diem cost of treating the average patient by hos-

[10] 42 USC § 1395x(v)(1)(A) (1988).

[11] Under TEFRA and PPS, hospitals with costs below the benchmarks are rewarded for efficiency. See Part II below.

pitals within a specific peer group. First, hospital peer groups were created based on geographic area, per capita income in that area, and number of beds in the hospital.[12] These groupings were established by assigning each hospital a geographic designation. Urban hospitals were classified in the Metropolitan Statistical Area (MSA)[13] in which they were located while rural hospitals were assigned to a single statewide non-urban area. Each geographic area was then divided into levels based on per capita income,[14] and the hospitals were then put into categories by number of beds. Second, the per diem costs for inpatient routine services were ranked for hospitals in each category from highest to lowest. Finally, the per diem reimbursement rate was set as a percentile of the ranked costs.[15] The cost limits for an upcoming payment year were calculated by inflating these base limit amounts by an inflation factor.[16]

In addition to the generously defined limit, the rule provided for a variety of exemptions and exceptions.[17] Sole community hospitals,[18] and provider hospitals certified for Medicare for less than three years, were exempt from cost limits.[19] Other hospitals could qualify for exceptions if they could show that their costs exceeded the cost limits due to the provision of atypical services; extraordi-

[12] These cost limits were published annually beginning in 1974. See Dept of Health, Education, and Welfare, Social Security Administration, Hospital Costs Under the Health Insurance Program, 39 Fed Reg 20168 (1974).

[13] The Office of Management and Budget defines MSAs using demographic criteria, including population and labor commuting patterns. For the complete definition, see Office of Management and Budget, Revised Standards for Defining Metropolitan Areas in the 1990s, 55 Fed Reg 12154 (1990).

[14] Per capita income was used as a proxy for wage differences because it is heavily influenced by wage levels and the data is uniformly available across the country. Dept of Health and Human Services (HHS), Health Care Financing Administration (HCFA), Medicare Program; Schedule of Limits on Hospital Costs for Cost Reporting Periods Beginning on or after October 1, 1978, 43 Fed Reg 43558, 43560 (1978).

[15] Due to concern over punishing "efficient" hospitals (erroneously categorized as inefficient), the limits were initially set at the 90th percentile (later changed to the 80th percentile) of hospitals in the peer group, with an additional cushion tacked on of 10 percent of the mean.

[16] Dept of Health, Education, and Welfare, Social Security Administration, Hospital Costs Under the Health Insurance Program, 39 Fed Reg 20168 (1974).

[17] 42 CFR 413.30(e)-(f) (1994).

[18] "Sole community hospital" is a Medicare payment classification for a hospital that is the only provider in its community. 42 CFR 413.30(e)(1). The policy justification for this exemption is the assumption that, due to the limited extent of demand in their markets, these hospitals face greater variation in demand and therefore cost, and are therefore less likely to exploit scale economies in the production of hospital care.

[19] 42 CFR 413.30(e)(1)-(2).

nary circumstances; more intensive routine care; essential community hospital services; or unusual labor costs.[20] As we will see below, the issue in *Good Samaritan* was whether an additional safeguard was available for retroactive case-by-case review of the cost limit methodology.

Three important refinements to cost limit methodology were adopted in fiscal years 1980 and 1981. First, a hospital "market basket index," which projected price increases in the cost of hospital inputs, was developed as an inflation factor. Second, a teaching adjustment was added to compensate providers for the additional costs associated with the joint production of patient care and medical education.[21] Finally, and most relevant to our discussion below, the area wage index was introduced as a more precise mechanism for adjusting for local variation in labor costs.[22] These refinements in cost limit methodology made the regulator confident that the benchmarks would more accurately separate out efficient from inefficient providers, thereby enabling the adoption of more stringent limits.[23]

TEFRA 1982. Changes were made in the benchmarks in the 1980's to address measurement concerns. The Tax Equity and Fiscal Responsibility Act of 1982 (TEFRA),[24] for example, applied cost limits to hospitals on a per admission or discharge basis, rather than a per diem basis, and included all operating costs associated with inpatient care. TEFRA's limitations expanded the scope of the cost limits to "operating costs of inpatient hospital services," by including—in addition to the routine cost of inpatient care covered by cost limits—ancillary services and special care costs.[25] A case-mix measure was also adopted to control for patient severity differences.

[20] 42 CFR 413.30(f)(1), (2), (5), (6), and (8).

[21] An exception had always been available under 42 CFR 413.30(f)(4) for costs that exceed the limit where the provider could prove that the excess was due to operation of an approved educational program. Adding the teaching adjustment to the cost limits made the adjustment available systematically to all teaching hospitals.

[22] Dept of Health and Human Services, Health Care Finance Administration, Medicare Program; Schedule of Limits on Hospital Inpatient General Routine Operating Costs for Cost Reporting Periods Beginning on or after July 1, 1980, 45 Fed Reg 41868, 41869 (1980).

[23] David M. Frankford, *The Complexities of Medicare's Hospital Reimbursement System*, 78 Iowa L Rev 517, 543 n 93 (1993) ("Frankford, *Complexities*"). For FY 1980 the limits were set at 115% of the group mean. For FY 1981, they were lowered to 112%. Congress stepped in and required limits to be set at no more than 108% for FY 1982. See Omnibus Budget Reconciliation Act of 1981, Pub L No 97-35, § 2143, 95 Stat 357, 798.

[24] Pub L No 97-248, 96 Stat 324 (1982).

[25] See Frankford, *Complexities*, at 566 n 178 (cited in note 23).

TEFRA strengthened cost containment incentives by placing two limitations on the Medicare reimbursement to hospitals. First, a payment ceiling was calculated by grouping comparable hospitals into peer groups analogous to those used in determining cost limits, limiting reimbursement to a determined percentage of the average cost of hospitals in the peer group.[26] A second limit on Medicare reimbursement for hospital operating expenses was created by setting a "target amount"—a limit on per discharge or admission costs for each hospital. Target amounts for the upcoming year were calculated by inflating allowable operating costs from the prior year by the hospital market basket (the measure of cost inflation for hospital inputs).[27] If costs exceeded the target, the hospital was entitled only to a portion of the excess.[28] If hospital costs fell below the target amount, the hospital received actual costs plus a "TEFRA bonus" equal to fifty percent of the difference.[29]

Although Congress had set limits for fiscal years 1983 through 1985, it also instructed HHS to develop a prospective payment system (PPS) by December 31, 1982. PPS was implemented ahead of schedule, so that TEFRA limits were only in effect for a single year.[30]

Medicare PPS. Approximately one month after Congress enacted TEFRA limits, the Secretary announced that a new reimbursement system would soon be adopted for Medicare hospital payment, replacing cost limits.[31] The PPS system that was adopted reimburses hospitals for the average cost of treating a patient with a particular condition. To determine the appropriate payment, costs for inpatient treatment for each "diagnostic related group" (DRG) are identified. These costs are standardized by adjusting for certain factors unrelated to efficiency (such as medical education). Finally, the

[26] For periods beginning between October 1, 1982 and October 1, 1983, "reasonable costs" were set at 120% of the group average; between October 1, 1983 and October 1, 1984, at 115%; and on or after October 1, 1984, at 110%. Pub L No 97-248, § 101(a)(1), 96 Stat at 331-32.

[27] In addition to the market basket estimate for inflation, there was an extra 1% add-on. Id at 333 (adding 42 USC § 1395ww(b)(3)(B)).

[28] Beginning in fiscal year 1985, the target amount became an absolute ceiling on the amount that Medicare would reimburse. Id at 332-33 (adding 42 USC § 1395ww(b)(1)(A)-(B)).

[29] Over time, various caps were placed on the maximum bonus a hospital could receive. Id.

[30] A modified version of TEFRA limits still applies to PPS-exempt hospitals, and these limits were applicable to many hospitals during the PPS phase-in.

[31] Dept of HHS, HCFA, Medicare Program; Prospective Payments for Medicare Inpatient Hospital Services, 48 Fed Reg 39752 (1983).

standardized costs are combined with those of all other similarly situated hospitals (urban or rural) to calculate the reimbursement rate.[32]

In theory, the Medicare prospective payment system is designed to reimburse a hospital fee, determined in advance, equal to the average cost of treating a patient with that condition. While intensity of resource use will vary on a case-by-case basis, these differences theoretically average out as the hospital treats a number of patients over time, and a hospital with average costs will be adequately compensated. Assuming that cost variations are accurately captured in payment adjustments, "efficient" hospitals can profit under PPS, while inefficient hospitals will suffer losses.

In practice, under PPS, a hospital is reimbursed a fixed base rate for each inpatient stay.[33] Originally there were two standard rates: one for hospitals located in rural areas, the other for hospitals in urban areas.[34] As of October 1987, the urban base rate was divided into two urban standard rates: one for hospitals in MSAs with more than 1 million persons (large urban) and the other for all other urban areas.[35] This standard rate is adjusted based upon the severity of illness of the patient treated, measured by the DRG appropriate for the stay, and other factors that affect the cost structure of the hospital, including: area wage levels; the degree of teaching activity; and the percentage of low-income patients served by the hospital. Outlier payments serve to compensate hospitals for unusually expensive cases.[36]

[32] Due to budget neutrality requirements, the standardized amounts were adjusted to result in aggregate expenditures equal to what would have been paid under the previous system.

[33] For a detailed description of PPS, see Social Security Amendments of 1983, Pub L No 98-21, 97 Stat 65, 153 (adding (d) to 42 USC § 1395ww).

[34] Separate rural and urban rates were adopted to prevent the urban hospitals from being financially disadvantaged under PPS. Dept of HHS, HCFA, Medicare Program; Prospective Payment for Medicare Inpatient Hospital Services, 49 Fed Reg 234 (1984). The 1981 Medicare cost report data used to establish PPS standard rates indicated that the average rural hospital costs per case were about 40 percent lower than the urban hospital costs per case. After adjusting for case mix, labor costs, and indirect teaching costs, a 20 percent differential remained unexplained. See Steven H. Sheingold and Elizabeth Richter, *Are PPS Payments Adequate? Issues for Updating and Assessing Rates,* Health Care Financing Review 165 (Winter 1992).

[35] Omnibus Budget Reconciliation Act of 1990, Pub L No 101-508, 104 Stat 1388, 1388-24, requires that separate standard rates for urban and rural hospitals be phased out over the period FY 1991 through FY 1995. By FY 1995 rural and other urban will be collapsed into one category, while large urban will continue to receive a 1.5 percent higher rate. This differential is much smaller than the historical difference.

[36] Karen Davis, et al, *Health Care Cost Containment* 18-20, 30-31 (Johns Hopkins U, 1990) ("Davis, *Health Care Cost Containment*").

While the DRG-based system revolutionized hospital payments under Medicare, it is clear that cost limits already marked a philosophical shift from reimbursing hospitals on a cost basis, to one that reimbursed hospitals based upon a benchmark—the "efficient" hospital.[37] In addition, many of the measurement tools that appeared in the cost limit methodology were carried over into the new prospective payment system. However, establishing a workable definition of efficiency in the inpatient hospital setting still eludes Medicare policymakers.

B. Technical Difficulties in Developing Cost Benchmarks

To provide an overview of potential problems in accurately developing a benchmark for the "efficient" provider, let us return to the variations in cost. For a given unit of hospital output, cost will vary in accordance with the quality of care, the intensity of treatment, and the price of inputs. The first issue is how to define the "unit of output." Under cost limits, hospital output was measured as a day of routine care in the inpatient setting (and later as a patient admission by DRG). For cost limit purposes, ancillary services were ignored.[38]

Since intensity of treatment will vary according to the illness of the patient, some cost variation will be exogenous to the hospital. In the simple world of cost limits, the following factors were intended to control for intensity differences: length of stay, number of beds, and teaching status. Because larger hospitals with resident training programs had historically higher costs, they were assumed to treat sicker patients. It is clear that these rough proxies for intensity would lead to significant measurement problems. These intensity measures could also lead to incentive problems: hospitals could increase total reimbursement amounts by increasing the lengths of their patients' stays.

The other major source of cost variation is input prices. Under PPS, an analogous problem arises as a result of the regulator's inability to accurately measure the severity of illness. Since hospitals receive larger payments for patients in DRGs that require, on average, a greater intensity of treatment, hospitals have an incentive

[37] While it has been hoped that these benchmarks measure "efficient" providers, they are more likely reflecting the representative, or average hospital. For an excellent discussion of the flaws of Medicare reimbursement for hospitals, see Frankford, *Complexities* at 584-85 (cited in note 23).

[38] One author believes that confining cost limits to inter-hospital comparisons of routine care was a primary factor leading to the development of the DRG-based system. Davis, *Health Care Cost Containment* at 19 (cited in note 36).

to alter their coding practices to maximize reimbursements. This phenomenon, called "DRG creep," inappropriately enhances Medicare payments to hospitals.[39] One study estimated that DRG creep increased Medicare payments by 1.9% or $308 million nationally in 1985.[40] Improved monitoring of hospital and physician coding has since reduced miscoding and over-reimbursement of providers.[41]

In 1980, the wage index was introduced.[42] The wage index replaced per capita income as a proxy for cost variation attributable to differences in labor prices. This labor cost adjustment was later incorporated into both the TEFRA and PPS methodologies.

The substantive Medicare payment issue raised in both *Good Samaritan* and *Georgetown* was the wage-index calculation. It is not surprising that the wage-index methodology has been repeatedly challenged by providers: labor costs account for approximately 75% of the operating costs of inpatient hospital care, and variation in Medicare payment across wage-index categories can be significant.[43] The wage index is intended to adjust Medicare reimbursement benchmarks to reflect geographic variation in labor costs. The goal of a wage adjustment is a challenging one: to avoid punishing hospitals for cost variations attributable to higher labor input prices beyond their control, while maintaining the cost-containment objectives of cost benchmarks.

[39] Paul J. Feldstein, *Health Care Economics* 291 (Delmar, 1993) ("Feldstein, *Health Care Economics*").

[40] David C. Hsia, et al, *Medicare Reimbursement Accuracy under the Prospective Payment System, 1985 to 1988*, 268 JAMA 896 (1992).

[41] Id at 898.

[42] Dept of HHS, HCFA, Medicare Program; Schedule of Cost Limits on Hospital Inpatient General Routine Operating Costs for Cost Reporting Periods Beginning on or after July 1, 1980, 45 Fed Reg 41868 (1980).

[43] The wage index is used to adjust cost-limits and the standardized payment amounts under PPS to reflect variations in labor costs. For example, for FY 1991, the wage index for the Omaha, Nebraska MSA was .9007, while the wage index for rural counties in Nebraska was .7010. For each area, the wage index is multiplied by the standard labor amount, and this is added to the non-labor standard payment to give the total prospective payment per Medicare patient. Using the FY 1991 urban standard payments of $2441.33 labor / $1005.80 non-labor, and the rural payments of $2434.74 labor / $784.43 non-labor, the total prospective payment per Medicare patient for a hospital in the MSA is 29% greater than for a hospital in a rural Nebraska county. See Dept of HHS, HCFA, Medicare Program; Mid-Year FY 1991 Changes to the Inpatient Hospital Prospective Payment System, 56 Fed Reg 568, 576-81 (1991), for wage index and standard payment rates. One of the six hospitals in *Good Samaritan*, Memorial Community Hospital, was found to be in the Omaha MSA in 1983 after revisions were made to the 1980 census data. HCFA refused to retroactively apply the higher MSA wage index for the 1980 to 1982 cost reporting periods for Memorial Community Hospital.

Measuring hospital wages. The calculation of a wage index, beginning with its adoption in 1980, has consisted of two basic steps. First, discrete labor markets for hospital workers are identified by geographic area. Second, within these geographic areas, the average cost of hospital labor is calculated. This area wage information is then aggregated to calculate the national average hospital wage, which is necessary for the denominator of the index. The ratio of the average wage for each of these markets to the national average hospital wage permits the calculation of an index designed to measure each area's relative labor costs.[44] The wage index is used to calculate the reimbursement rate of a hospital by multiplying the labor portion of the base rate by the wage index.[45]

As a point of departure for examining the impediments to creating a useful wage index, let us examine the wage index in effect at the time the *Good Samaritan* and *Georgetown* controversies arose. For the cost period in question, the wage index was calculated as follows. MSAs were used to define urban labor markets.[46] Counties not included in MSAs were grouped into statewide rural labor market areas.[47] For each urban and non-urban "labor market," the Bureau of Labor Statistics computed an average monthly hospital salary by summing aggregate salaries for the year and dividing by the sum of the annual number of employees. Prior to October 1, 1982, urban and non-urban national average wages were calculated to create two separate, urban and non-urban, indices. On Sept 30, 1982, the wage index was revised to create a single national wage index for all areas.[48]

[44] The area wage index for any given geographic area can be represented by the following ratio:

average wage within the area/national average wage.

The average wage within the area is calculated using the following ratio:

total salary/total hours worked.

[45] This method of calculating payment amounts has been criticized for overcompensating urban hospitals because both the base rate and the wage index adjust for the higher costs of inputs in urban settings, resulting in substantially higher reimbursement for urban hospitals than their rural counterparts.

[46] See note 13 above.

[47] The most reliable nationwide hospital wage data available at the time was data collected by the Bureau of Labor Statistics. This data base contained quarterly information on aggregate hospital salaries and monthly data on the total number of hospital employees, by hospital. (These data are processed with a significant lag, therefore 1979-1980 wage data were used to calculate 1982-1983 wage indices, for example.)

Due to the composition of the early wage index, data limitations significantly constrained HCFA's ability to fashion a wage index that would provide for equitable payment. These early proxies created a wage index that has been criticized for inaccurately measuring wages, over-reimbursing hospitals that are in areas that staff with a richer skill mix and misspecifying geographic boundaries by using convenient geopolitical definitions (namely, MSAs) that were not designed for this purpose.[49] If the goal of the wage index is to encourage the efficient delivery of Medicare services,[50] refinements to the measurement of average area-specific wages to more accurately reflect the opportunity cost of labor in a given area are desirable.[51]

While many refinements have been made possible by the introduction of new data collected by HCFA,[52] one issue that remains unresolved (and well-debated) is the failure of the wage index to take into account differences in occupational mix. It has been argued that this methodological flaw overcompensates hospitals in richly staffed areas.[53] The bias arises because the current wage index methodology does not adjust hospital labor costs for case-mix variation, quality differences, or labor substitution possibilities across hospitals.

[48] Exceptions were made for rural hospitals with fewer than 50 beds, for children's hospitals, and for long-term care facilities. See Dept of HHS, HCFA, Medicare Program; Schedule of Limits on Hospital Inpatient Operating Costs for Cost Reporting Periods Beginning on or after October 1, 1982, 47 Fed Reg 43296, 43299-300 (1982).

[49] Nancy De Lew, *Geographic Classification of Hospitals: Alternative Labor Market Areas,* 14 (2) Health Care Financing Review 49, 49 (Winter 1992).

[50] The discussion below suggests that this may not be the principal objective.

[51] By definition, a payment benchmark measures an average quantity across individual observations. The wage index therefore does not capture the distinctive costs of each provider and so over- or under-reimburses many hospitals. This bias is likely to increase as a given hospital's profile deviates from the "average" hospital. Over time, payment based upon benchmarks will tend to encourage uniformity across hospitals, and discourage specialization.

[52] In addition to the corrections mentioned above, a series of adjustments have been made to refine which labor costs should be included or excluded from the wage index calculations. For example, additional refinements were designed to separate out costs that were not directly related to the provision of hospital inpatient care (all salaries and hours associated with skilled nursing facilities and all non-hospital cost centers) and to include all relevant administrative costs generated by a home office. Dept of HHS, HCFA, Medicare Program; Changes to the Inpatient Hospital Prospective Payment System and FY 1991 Rates, 55 Fed Reg 35990, 36035 (1990).

[53] See D. Williams, J. Pettengill and C. Lisk, *Adjusting a Wage Index for Geographic Differences in Occupational Mix,* ProPAC Technical Report No 1-90-02 (1990). See also Prospective Payment Assessment Commission, *Report and Recommendations to the Secretary, US Dept of HHS* (1990) and ProPAC, *Report and Recommendations to Congress* (1991).

Case-mix (severity of illness of patients treated) differences will result in variation in the proportion of skilled workers a hospital employs. Generally, if the hospital treats sicker patients, it will require a richer mix of employees, resulting in a higher average hourly wage. To the extent that the Medicare base rate already reflects additional payment for severity differences (bed size under cost limit methodology, case-mix adjustment under PPS), hospitals in wage index areas that (on average) treat more severely ill patients, will be rewarded twice for these severity differences.

Similarly, variation in quality is not controlled for with the current wage index. Presumably, if hospitals in an area provide a higher level quality of care than average, their wage index will be greater, and therefore will reflect more than the opportunity cost of labor. Alternatively, if regional practice patterns dictate the use of more expensive inputs (RNs instead of LPNs, for example), the wage index will compensate these areas at a higher rate than their more cost-effective neighbors.

Finally, the use of average hourly wages (rather than the total cost of labor) does not take into account the possibility of substituting across labor types. Hospitals in areas with relatively inexpensive skilled labor will use a higher proportion of highly skilled workers, which may result in higher per hour wages but lower overall costs of producing hospital care. Thus, the current wage index overstates labor costs in areas where skilled labor is relatively inexpensive.

Clearly, the wage index as applied to cost limits in fiscal years 1981-1982, or as currently applied to the PPS standard payment amounts, provides imperfect proxies for relative labor costs. Of greatest concern from the perspective of encouraging the efficient production of care, the payment system has a built in bias to overcompensate hospitals in areas with a richer skill-mix. To address how well the wage index adjusts for labor cost variation requires an examination of the second component of the wage index calculation, identification of the hospital labor market.

Geographic classification: defining hospital labor markets. The geographic classification component of the wage index designation was also raised as an issue in *Good Samaritan.* The rural hospitals that brought the case claimed that the cost limit methodology did not permit them to demonstrate that they competed for labor in neighboring urban markets, forcing them to offer comparable wages.[54] As a result, their costs exceeded the applicable cost limits. Essentially, from an economic perspective, the hospitals were ar-

[54] *Good Samaritan,* 113 S Ct at 2156.

guing that HCFA's simple urban/non-urban classification did not accurately reflect the labor market in which they were located. However, improving geographic classification for wage index purposes would require adjusting the wage index area boundaries to reflect the "true" geographic markets for hospital labor, rather than relying on the MSA definition.

Unfortunately, economists can describe a hospital's market better in theory than they can measure it empirically. From a theoretical perspective, a local market for hospital labor is simply the area within which the market clearing wage is determined.[55] Workers whose wages are not determined by a given set of supply and demand forces are therefore considered to be in a separate market.

Economists have also developed analytical tools in an attempt to delineate separate markets in the real world. "Price tests" and "shipments tests," for example, are two techniques commonly employed by economists to demonstrate that two geographic areas are within the same economic market. These tests utilize data on prices and on the shipment of goods between areas. These tests have been especially important in the area of antitrust, where a market must be defined before the existence or absence of market power can be assessed.[56] The work of Stigler and Sher-

[55] The market is the set of suppliers and demanders of hospital labor whose trading patterns establish the price of hospital labor.

[56] The Merger Guidelines define a market for antitrust purposes as follows:

> [A] product or group of products and a geographic area in which it is sold such that a hypothetical, profit-maximizing firm, not subject to price regulation, that was the only present and future seller of those products in that area would impose a "small but significant and nontransitory" increase in price above prevailing or likely future levels.

1984 Merger Guidelines § 2.0. This definition has been criticized as "impractical," Thomas W. Dunfee et al., *Bounding Markets in Merger Cases: Identifying the Relevant Competitors,* 78 Nw U L Rev 733, 754-55 (1984), and as "completely nonoperational," George J. Stigler and Robert A. Sherwin, *The Extent of the Market,* 28 J L & Econ 555, 582 (1985) ("Stigler & Sherwin, *Extent of the Market*"). Price and shipments tests are two techniques which have been used to operationalize the Merger Guidelines' theoretical test.

A third empirical method, residual demand estimation, has also been employed in antitrust market analysis, despite the fact that the Merger Guidelines would appear to preclude this method for market definition. See *1992 Merger Guidelines* § 1.0. "A residual demand curve indicates the amount consumers are wiling to purchase at various prices, with the prices of all other products adjusting in accord with prevailing economic forces to the various prices of the product for which the demand curve is constructed." Gregory J. Werden, *History of Antitrust Market Delineation,* 76 Marq L Rev 123 (1992) ("Werden, *History*"). While application of this test to labor market delineation for wage index purposes is analytically appealing, this method's onerous data requirements place serious limitations on its usefulness.

win[57] has been influential in illustrating how price tests can be used to delineate market areas. However, the shipment tests suggested by Elzinga and Hogarty[58] have probably been the most widely used.

Price tests focus on the pattern and trend of prices (which means wages in the case of labor markets) prevailing in different areas. On average, if two areas are in the same economic market, the prices in the two areas should move together, with the difference in price levels limited by the marginal transportation costs. If transportation costs are constant, then differences in the movement of prices in two areas over time suggest that the areas are subject to different supply and demand shocks and therefore represent different markets. Different parts of a market are likely to be more closely integrated the closer the movement of their prices. Significant nonparallel price movements suggest that the two areas are not in the same market unless the discord in price movements can be traced to changes in transportation costs.

Shipments tests focus on the physical movement of goods from one area to another. In the case of labor, this refers to the commuting pattern of employees. The extent to which goods are transported between areas reflects the substitutability of supply. Thus, information about the geographic reach of the market is provided by the level of imports and exports to and from adjacent areas. Substantial shipments between two areas suggest that the two areas are in the same market. For example, two areas are likely to be in the same labor market if there is a substantial amount of commuting by employees from one area to another.

These price and shipment tests have been subjected to criticism in antitrust market analysis,[59] and their application to hospital labor markets is not beyond controversy.[60] In fact, labor markets are particularly difficult to define using these standard economist's tools. Many of the issues in defining labor markets using price tests parallel the problems discussed above in measuring wages. As a result, the observation of a simple wage differential or the lack of

[57] Stigler & Sherwin, *Extent of the Market* (cited in note 56.)

[58] Kenneth G. Elzinga and Thomas F. Hogarty, *The Problem of Geographic Market Delineation in Antimerger Suits,* 18 Antitrust Bulletin 45 (1973).

[59] See, for example, Gregory J. Werden, *The Limited Relevance of Patient Migration Data in Market Delineation for Hospital Merger Cases,* 8 J Health Econ 363 (1989). See also Werden, *History* (cited in note 56).

[60] See, for example, Stigler & Sherwin, *Extent of the Market* at 576 (cited in note 56)

a positive correlation in wage movements is not sufficient evidence on which to conclude that two areas are in different labor markets. Empirically, the usefulness of the price test in hospital labor markets is limited by difficulties in accurately measuring the total transportation costs (both pecuniary and non-pecuniary), the costs of switching jobs, occupational mix differences attributable to both case-mix and quality differences in hospital output, and other determinants of wage differentials. An empirical analysis that does not control for these factors will be biased toward finding that two areas are not in the same labor market; the observed wage differential would appear larger than the "true" differential. Furthermore, changes in these omitted characteristics will mean that the perfect correlation in wage movements that is implied when two areas are in the same market will not be observed, even if two areas are, in fact, in the same market.

Many of these same issues surface in the application of shipments tests because of the need to define the "product" before performing the empirical analysis. Due to the variation in skill mix across hospitals, identifying a standardized unit of hospital labor raises the same the same thorny methodological problems discussed above regarding occupational mix. Additional problems also interfere with the usefulness of this approach. A major criticism that is discussed in the antitrust literature, and is particularly problematic here, is the static nature of the analysis. The absence of workers commuting from an urban to a rural market does not reveal whether commuting patterns might change if the wage differential increased by a small amount. This flaw is particularly troublesome in defining labor markets for Medicare reimbursement purposes because existing travel patterns may not capture the pressure on hospitals in rural areas to keep wages competitive with neighboring urban areas.[61] Further, the dynamic nature of labor markets suggests that while a given community hospital may not compete with its urban neighbor today, it may tomorrow. This problem is further aggravated by the lag time in collecting data for wage index calculations.[62]

[61] Alternatively, unionization in urban areas may drive wages up, thereby attracting workers from outlying rural communities and resulting in broader geographic markets than would exist in a competitive labor market. In the Medicare reimbursement context, this raises the interesting issue of whether Medicare should provide reimbursement for costs attributable to unionization and monopoly power.

[62] When initially developed, there was a significant lag between data collection and wage index updates. Beginning in FY 1993, HCFA has been required to update its hospital wage data annually.

C. Issues in *Good Samaritan*

A variety of data problems have been corrected over time. The earliest data refinement became the subject of the Supreme Court's 1988 decision in *Georgetown.*[63] In updating the wage index for FY 1982, HCFA decided to exclude federal hospital labor cost data from wage index calculations.[64] HCFA believed the index would be more accurate with this exclusion because federal hospitals paid wage on a national pay scale, and therefore wages paid by federal hospitals were not reflective of local wage rates. However, because this change was made to the wage index without prior notice, and time for comments, it was declared invalid.[65] In 1984, after a period for pubic comment, HCFA reissued the wage index for FY 1981 excluding federal data.[66] The Secretary then attempted to recoup payments that had been made in the time during which the index was invalidated. In *Georgetown,* the Supreme Court held that the Secretary could not reissue the previously invalidated wage index because Congress had not authorized retroactive promulgation of the rule, and could not recoup the payments. Thereafter, for periods beginning on October 1, 1982, Medicare payments to hospitals were based upon a wage index that excluded federal hospital data.[67]

In *Good Samaritan,* the hospitals complained that the use of "average salary per worker" to create the wage index disadvantaged areas that employed a greater percentage of part-time employees.[68] This problem arose purely as the result of a data limitation—the Bureau of Labor Statistics did not distinguish between part-time and full-time employees when requesting information on the number of workers employed in the hospital. Since part-time workers naturally earn less than full-time employees in a given year, the "average salary per worker" and the imputed labor costs are then downwardly biased in those areas that employed a greater number of part-time employees. As the plaintiffs pointed out in *Good Samar-*

[63] *Bowen v Georgetown Univ Hospital,* 488 US 204 (1988).

[64] Dept of HHS, HCFA, Medicare Program; Hospital Per Diem Inpatient General Routine Operating Costs, Schedule of Limits, 46 Fed Reg 33637, 33639 (1981).

[65] *District of Columbia Hospital Ass'n v Heckler,* 1984 WL 48798 (D DC 1984). Cost reporting periods between July 1, 1980 and September 30, 1982 were affected by this decision.

[66] Dept of HHS, HCFA, Medicare Program; Reissuance of the Wage Index in the 1981 Schedule of Limits on Hospital Per Diem Inpatient General Routine Operating Costs, 49 Fed Reg 46495 (1984).

[67] Dept of HHS, HCFA, Medicare Program; Schedule of Limits on Hospital Inpatient Operating Costs for Cost Reporting Periods Beginning on or after October 1, 1982, 47 Fed Reg 43296, 43301 (1982).

[68] 113 S Ct at 2156.

itan, a congressionally mandated study indicated that this bias resulted in significant under- and over-payment in some areas.[69]

Finally in 1986, when HCFA was ready to use its own wage data, this methodological error was corrected. In constructing the new wage index, HCFA used hospital salary and fringe benefit data extracted from Medicare cost reports for hospital fiscal years ending in calendar year 1982.[70] This index accounted for part-time employees by calculating wages per hour, rather than per worker, as was done under the old index.

In *Good Samaritan,*[71] six Nebraska hospitals classified as rural for the purposes of Medicare reimbursement filed an administrative appeal challenging the validity of the cost limits used to calculate their reimbursement levels.[72] Pointing to HCFA's 1986 revision of the wage index, the hospitals claimed that the pre-1986 wage index applied by HCFA did not account appropriately for their use of part-time personnel during the years in which they exceeded the cost limits (fiscal years 1980-1983). Further, they argued that rural classification did not provide the hospitals an adequate opportunity to show that their proximity to urban markets increased the wages necessary to retain hospital employees. HHS's Provider Reimbursement Review Board (PRRB), believing that it lacked the authority to award the desired relief, granted the hospital's request for expedited judicial review.[73] The District Court ruled for the hospitals, holding that clause (ii) of 42 USC § 1395x(v)(1)(A) compelled the Secretary to reimburse all reasonable costs, regardless of the cost limits, because the terms of the statute require that regulations:

> provide for the making of suitable retroactive corrective adjustments where, for a provider of services for any fiscal period, the aggregate reimbursement produced by the methods

[69] In 1984, Congress instructed the Secretary to conduct a study to develop a wage index that would account for wage differences of part-time and full-time workers. Deficit Reduction Act of 1984, Pub L No 98-369, § 2316(a), 98 Stat 494, 1081.

[70] Dept of HHS, HCFA, Medicare Program; Changes to the Inpatient Hospital Prospective Payment System and FY 1986 Rates, 50 Fed Reg 35646, 35661 (1985). The method that was eventually adopted was the "gross wage index." It was based on gross salaries and wages paid to all hospital employees including interns and residents, provider-based physicians, and workers employed by the hospital but working in areas other than the inpatient area. Another index was computed that eliminated these interns, etc., but due to difficulties encountered in making such adjustments, HCFA adopted the administratively simpler, but analytically flawed, option.

[71] 113 S Ct 2151 (1993).

[72] The appeal was filed with the Provider Reimbursement Review Board pursuant to 42 USC § 1395oo. See 113 S Ct at 1256.

[73] Id.

of determining costs proves to be either inadequate or excessive.[74]

The U.S. Court of Appeals for the Eighth Circuit reversed, relying on the decision in *Georgetown,*[75] which held that clause (ii) does not permit retroactive rulemaking, and adopting the Secretary's interpretation that clause (ii) allows only for year end book-balancing.[76]

The Supreme Court affirmed the Eighth Circuit. Invoking the familiar *Chevron* paradigm,[77] Justice White's majority opinion held that the language of clause (ii) is not clear on its face, and does not necessarily require that hospitals be afforded an opportunity to establish that they are entitled to reimbursement above the rate set by HCFA. The Court then accepted the interpretation of the Secretary—that clause (ii) allows for only year end book-balancing—on the ground that courts should generally defer to any permissible interpretation of an ambiguous statute espoused by the agency entrusted with its implementation.[78]

Justice Souter's dissent argued that, in the context of the statute, the language of clause (ii) requires regulation providing for case-by-case exceptions to the cost limits.[79] The dissent argued that clause (ii) expressly contemplates corrective adjustments to the aggregate reimbursements produced under the cost limitations, and emphasized Congress' stated "concern that Medicare neither subsidize, nor be subsidized by, non-Medicare patients."[80] Under this reading, clause (ii) would specifically allow providers to seek adjustments on the grounds that total payments as calculated were lower (or higher) than the actual reasonable costs of providing the services.

[74] *Good Samaritan Hospital v Sullivan,* No CV88-L-523, 1990 WL 42393 (D Neb Feb 16, 1990) (order and memorandum).

[75] *Bowen v Georgetown Univ Hospital,* 488 US 204 (1988).

[76] 952 F2d 1017, 1024 (8th Cir 1991).

[77] In *Chevron U.S.A. Inc. v Natural Resources Defense Council, Inc.* 467 US 837 (1984), the Supreme Court developed a two-pronged test for judicial review of agency statutory interpretations. The reviewing court must first ask whether Congress has "directly spoken to the precise question at issue." Id at 842. If it has, then the Court should look no further. If Congress has not definitively addressed the issue, then the Court must ask "whether the agency's answer is based upon a permissible construction of the statute." Id at 842-43. *Good Samaritan* is one of several post-*Chevron* cases in which the justices have disagreed among themselves about the proper application of this two-pronged test. For a review of the cases, see Thomas W. Merrill, *Textualism and the Future of the* Chevron *Doctrine,* 72 Wash U L Q 351 (1994).

[78] 113 S Ct at 2157-59.

[79] Id at 2166.

[80] Id at 2165.

The fundamental issue in *Good Samaritan* was whether HCFA's methodology for establishing cost limits conclusively determines the "reasonable cost" of hospital care, or only creates the presumption that the level of reimbursement is reasonable, subject to retroactive case-by-case review. The hospitals argued that clause (ii) means that corrective adjustments "are required when, for 'a provider,' the 'aggregate reimbursement produced by the methods of determining costs' is too low or too high."[81] The Secretary, on the other hand, interpreted the clause merely to permit year end book-balancing of interim advance payments made to providers within the amount the regulations determined to be "reasonable."

It is tempting to frame the issue as the Court did, as one of statutory interpretation, and use an economic analysis of the Medicare program to ascertain which definition is most consistent with the statutory scheme. Such an analysis, however, would be misleading, for the complexities of the public payment health care system are designed not only to purchase health care services at a "reasonable" price, but to facilitate significant wealth transfers. These wealth transfers arise from the political nature of the Medicare "legislative bargain."

A more fruitful approach is to recognize that each of the entities that share responsibility in developing and overseeing health care cost containment legislation is an "imperfect alternative." The ultimate question, which underlies the concerns voiced by Justice Souter's dissent, is whether HCFA should be provided the level of discretion in interpreting health care cost containment legislation implied by the majority opinion.

III. CONSEQUENCES OF GIVING HCFA BROAD DISCRETION

Once Congress has made the decision to employ a command-and-control approach to regulation, the problem of controlling the regulator necessarily arises. This problem is inherently intractable, and it lies at the root of the real importance of judicial decisions like the one in *Good Samaritan.*

A. The Role of Agency Discretion

Wide discretion provides agencies with the flexibility to use their technical expertise to seek the most efficient solutions to regulatory issues. In favor of a broad delegation of authority to HCFA in

[81] Petitioner's Brief at 14 (quoting *Georgetown,* 488 US at 210).

developing Medicare cost containment rules is the need for innovation in the development of cost benchmarks. The technical nature of economic regulation requires detailed knowledge of the industry structure and the ability to refine regulations as more knowledge is acquired. As discussed above, inappropriate regulation can penalize efficient as well as inefficient providers.

In the context of cost limits, limiting agency discretion could reduce efficiency. This would be true if HCFA rejected retroactive case-by-case review because the costs of such review would outweigh the benefits. As with any general rule, there will be winners and losers, and in some cases efficient providers will be incorrectly identified as inefficient, resulting in undercompensation. Retroactive case-by-case review might reduce these errors, but it is not costless. In addition to administrative costs, the review process might blunt the cost containment incentives of the regulations by providing an opportunity for inefficient providers to use their superior knowledge of local market conditions to procure additional payments. If the motivation of the regulator is to identify the costs of the efficient provider, then presumably the agency charged with implementation will provide case-by-case review when providing review would reduce the likelihood of undercompensation more than increase administrative costs and the likelihood of overcompensating inefficient hospitals. Under this interpretation, deferring to the agency's interpretation of clause (ii) enhances efficiency.

The political nature of such programs may also favor the delegation of authority to the agency. Some agency discretion may be desirable to balance the interests of different parties, for reductions in Medicare reimbursement have a more ambiguous effect on consumer welfare than, for example, reductions in the price of electrical current by a regulated utility. Due to the regulatory constraints under which hospitals operate, as well as the subsidies they receive for providing charity care, the potential responses of a hospital provider to a reduction in Medicare reimbursement include: reducing quality and access for Medicare patients, cost-shifting to privately insured and self-pay patients, and reducing the level of uncompensated care. Reductions in quality and access for Medicare patients can be achieved, for example by reducing the lengths of stay for inpatient treatment. This shifts a portion of the burden of post-hospital care onto the family (or other caretakers) of the elderly patient. Alternatively, ratcheting down reimbursement rates may result in cost-shifting, increasing prices to privately insured or self-pay patients.[82] Finally, hospitals can reduce services that attract un-

[82] David Dranove, *Pricing By Non-Profit Institutions: The Case of Hospital Cost-Shifting*, 7 J Health Econ 47 (1988) ("Dranove, *Pricing By Non-Profit Institutions*").

compensated care patients, patients for which hospitals receive no payments.

These potential responses illustrate the political nature of the Medicare reimbursement system, and the importance of understanding the underlying political bargain when interpreting health care cost containment legislation. The two major pressure groups concerned with Medicare are the providers and the elderly. The primary concern of providers is adequate reimbursement, while the interest of the elderly is in improved quality and access. Over time, as health care costs have increased, there has been an enhanced interest in cost containment by two other stakeholders, the government and businesses, as they have faced increasing health care costs. For the government, concern comes from the growth in the federal budget attributable to the expansion of the government sponsored health care programs. Businesses have also become concerned about the growth in their employees' insurance premiums. This growth in premium payments is caused both by the general increase in health care costs and by the cost shifting between public- and private-pay patients that results from cost containment legislation.

Referring to the HCFA's role in Medicare policy, the Court has subsequently recognized the importance of agency discretion:

> This broad deference is all the more warranted when, as here, the regulation concerns "a complex and highly technical regulatory program," in which the identification and classification of relevant "criteria necessarily require significant expertise and entail the exercise of judgment grounded in policy concerns."[83]

B. The Health Care Financing Administration: Opportunity for Capture

The trend toward increasing the role of administrative agencies in political decision-making has been justified by the increased complexity of regulated activities. While these attributes weigh in favor of providing significant discretion in agency interpretation, economic theory can assist in identifying inherent institutional biases that would recommend narrowing HCFA's responsibility in interpreting of health care cost containment legislation.

Economic theory of regulation. The objective of identifying the costs of the "efficient" provider for reimbursement purposes is con-

[83] *Thomas Jefferson Univ v Shalala,* 114 S Ct 2381, 2387 (1994) (quoting *Pauley v BethEnergy Mines, Inc.,* 501 U.S. 680, 697 (1991)).

sistent with the "public interest" view of regulation. According to this theory, the role of the regulator in developing Medicare regulation includes protecting consumers' interests by lowering prices (and profits) in the health care industry. Establishing and enforcing efficiency benchmarks encourages otherwise monopolistic firms to behave as if they were in a competitive industry and thereby achieves this goal.

Skeptics would suggest that an alternative behavioral model should be considered when assessing the regulator's goals. The economic theory of regulation provides a framework for understanding the role of the regulator in the market for special interest legislation.[84] According to this theory, special interest groups lobby for regulation that will achieve the coalition's desired goals. In exchange for these benefits, the pressure groups provide tangible rewards to those who regulate. This constitutes the demand for regulation. On the supply side, the regulator wishes to maximize his political support (either directly, as with legislators, or indirectly, as with bureaucrats who are answerable to legislators), which requires that other, competing interests be counterbalanced against the interests of the lobbying groups. The theory predicts that compact, cohesive coalitions can be successful in employing the political process to redistribute wealth from other groups whose interests are more diffuse (such as consumers at large and taxpayers). For example, hospitals will lobby for regulation that will insulate them from competition, thereby raising profits. Given competing interests, however, it is unlikely that the regulator will permit the hospital industry to achieve a monopoly level of profits. Rather, some of the consumer surplus will be distributed to other politically influential groups.[85]

Subsequent economic literature has questioned whether political markets are any less competitive than other markets.[86] In the absence of barriers to entry in this market, interest groups would have

[84] See Sam Peltzman, *Toward a More General Theory of Regulation*, 19 J L & Econ 211 (1976) ("Peltzman, *Toward a More General Theory*"). See also Mark V. Pauly, *Positive Political Economy of Medicare, Past and Future*, in *Lessons from the First Twenty Years of Medicare* 49 (Mark V. Pauly, William L. Kissick & Laura E. Roper, eds, U Pennsylvania, 1988) ("Pauly, *Positive Political Economy of Medicare*"); George Stigler, *The Theory of Economic Regulation*, 2 Bell J Econ & Mgmt Sci 3 (1971).

[85] See Peltzman, *Toward a More General Theory* at 211 (cited in note 84). In this way the economic theory of regulation differs from "capture" theory, which would predict that the regulatory body is used by the regulated industry for its own benefit.

[86] See, for example, Herbert Hovenkamp, *Legislation, Well-Being and Public Choice*, 57 U Chi L Rev 63, 100 (1990) ("Hovenkamp, *Legislation, Well-Being and Public Choice*").

little ability to extract rents, since voters would monitor legislators and regulatory agencies to guarantee that their activities maximized social welfare. Asymmetric information, however, may serve as one such barrier.

Agency capture. Using an agency-theoretic approach, recent literature has examined the impact of informational asymmetries on the ability of industry (or other interest groups) to enter into side contracts with regulatory agencies to withhold information from Congress.[87] Under certain conditions, interest groups can "capture" the government decision-making processes, thereby influencing regulatory outcomes. Because of these severe informational constraints, ex post review can remedy only some of the distortions that are introduced by the capture.

In the world of hospital cost containment under Medicare, many of the necessary conditions for successful capture exist. As discussed above, it is difficult to measure the costs of an "efficient" hospital, so that superior knowledge about which cost reductions are technically feasible may yield an informational rent. Under Medicare cost limits (as well as the new prospective payment system), the agency not only identifies which factors will be included in the Medicare payment model, but also decides how unexplained cost variation will be distributed across hospitals. Hospitals may have an incentive to invest resources in assisting the regulator to develop self-serving "refinements" to a complex Medicare payment system that relies upon cost benchmarks.[88]

Though an unregulated system is preferred by the providers, capture allows a second-best solution for them. Even with cost benchmarks below their actual costs of treating public-pay patients, private information and market power in the unregulated private market permit the providers to shift costs from the Medicare patients to the private-payers. This could not occur in a purely competitive market with profit-maximizing sellers; they would simply opt out of providing non-emergency care.[89] But the non-profit nature of many providers suggests that cost-shifting can occur if they

[87] See Jean-Jacques Laffont and Jean Tirole, *The Politics of Government Decision-Making: A Theory of Regulatory Capture,* 106 Q J Econ 1089 (1991).

[88] The benefits to the regulator of such assistance may consist of payments such as: direct monetary bribes, future employment for ex-regulators, personal relationships, restraint from public criticism, and indirect transfers through increased appropriations. Id at 1090-91.

[89] Joel W. Hay, *The Impact of Public Health Care Financing Policies on Private-Sector Hospital Costs,* 7 J Health Politics, Policy and Law 4 (1983).

maximize an objective function other than profit.[90] As evidence that this cost-shifting benefits the provider, hospitals have lobbied to prevent further regulation by an all-payer system that would prevent cross-subsidization between private- and public-pay patients.[91]

This extraction of private-pay hospital profits to cross-subsidize the expanding Medicare services is a form of indirect taxation. This practice, which has been called "taxation by regulation,"[92] is a way for regulatory agencies and Congress to expand a program's scope without increasing direct taxes. The losers in this indirect taxation scheme are the insurers and employers of the private-pay patients. The beneficiaries include the agency (as the increased size of the program made possible by cross-subsidies provides justification for increasing the agency's appropriations and influence) and the legislators who need not vote to raise taxes. The potential for collusion between HCFA and the hospital industry may be further enhanced if the other key interest group, consisting of the elderly who receive Medicare benefits, enjoys improved access and quality as a result of reimbursement enhancements to hospitals. Extraction of benefits in this manner may be particularly effective as they do not require congressional action and may be difficult for competing interest groups to decipher.[93]

The two-force model. Congress has the capacity to punish or reward an agency that deviates from the congressional mandate. In the extreme, Congress can abolish the agency,[94] but more likely

[90] Dranove, *Pricing By Non-Profit Institutions* at 49 (cited in note 82).

[91] See Feldstein, *Health Care Economics* 281-82 (cited in note 39).

[92] Richard A. Posner, *Taxation by Regulation,* 2 Bell J Econ & Mgmt Sci 22, 23 (1971) (one of the traditional (but inefficient) goals of regulation is "to perform the distributive and allocative chores usually associated with the taxing or financial branch of government").

[93] Pauly has challenged the conventional wisdom that the provider lobby is a critical pressure group in forcing administrative decisions contrary to congressional goals. Pauly, *Positive Political Economy of Medicare* at 49, 63 (cited in note 84). He points out that Medicare reimbursement is not merely a transfer payment, but a payment for government sponsored services. Provider power would be evidenced only if payment levels are high enough to create "rents" (or quasi rents) for the largely "nonprofit" hospital sector. Pauly's analysis ignores the greatest potential loss for hospitals from the revelation of accurate cost and technology information—the potential reduction in private pay revenues. Under this scenario, hospitals, the elderly, and HCFA all have an incentive to collude to raise Medicare revenues through "indirect taxation." Hospitals trade off a portion of their private pay surplus in exchange for a payment system that maintains "equity" in payment across hospitals. The elderly and HCFA benefit from this arrangement as the government sector can expand beyond the point where it could through direct taxation.

[94] See Barry R. Weingast, *The Congressional-Bureaucratic System: A Principal-Agent Perspective,* 44 Public Choice 147 (1984).

responses include increasing the appropriations to congressional committees assigned oversight functions with respect to Medicare payment issues, reducing the level of discretion by amending Medicare legislation, or allocating increased responsibility to the judiciary.[95]

Applying Komesar's analysis of bureaucratic behavior and bureaucratic growth to the Medicare context suggests that apparent divergences between congressional mandate and agency interpretation are not accidental. Instead, Komesar explains this divergence with the "two-force model." The first force, minoritarian influence, is definitionally equivalent to the influence of special interest groups identified in the economic or public choice model. The second force Komesar refers to as "majoritarian influence." The actual results of the entire legislative-administrative process then reflect an accommodation of both forces.

The two-force model to health care cost containment legislation might explain the discrepancy between congressional language and agency interpretation that the dissent in *Good Samaritan* perceived. Congress passes legislation that (on its face) is designed to reduce the cost of inpatient care, giving the appearance of victory to employers and non-elderly workers (the majoritarian influence) who are shouldering the ever-increasing burden of health care for the elderly. Through the complexities of the administrative process, however, hidden transfers through cost-shifting can be made to hospitals and the elderly. Congress, by delegating health care cost containment regulations to HCFA, ostensibly satisfies both constituencies.

Though many arguments can be made for granting regulatory agencies wide discretionary powers to promote efficiency and the general public interest, economic theories of institutions imply that this discretion can also create inefficient subsidies to special interest groups. In the two-force model, Congress tolerates the agency using its discretion to implement indirect taxation for the benefit of minoritarian interests. Congress may even be pleased with this use of agency discretion, but Congress does not want to take responsibility for effecting the result itself. In the agency-theoretic model, the regulator thwarts Congress' intentions to the benefit of these interests and the detriment of the general interest. In this case Congress can correct the agency bias through ex post review or through preemptively creating better regulatory institutions.

[95] Neil K. Komesar, *Imperfect Alternatives: Choosing Institutions in Law, Economics, and Public Policy* 93 (U Chicago, 1994) ("Komesar, *Imperfect Alternatives*").

IV. MONITORING AGENCY ACTION

A. Congressional Oversight of Agency Action

Assuming that Congress is less susceptible to capture than the agency, or even that Congress is simply more reluctant to look as though it has been captured (as under the two-force model), the legislature can reduce interest-group influence by placing limitations upon agency discretion. Congress can shape health care regulatory policy by mandating a research study, appointing a Congressional committee to monitor agency activity, or adopting detail-specific legislation. Unfortunately, narrowing the agency's choice set also constrains the agency's ability to apply its technical expertise in developing innovative solutions to complex regulatory problems.

With respect to Medicare cost containment legislation, the advantage of congressional oversight, as compared with judicial intervention, derives from the legislators' first hand knowledge of the political bargain negotiated by the various health care constituencies. As discussed above, Medicare is not solely a government-sponsored health insurance program, it is also a social program. The democratic process—which counts votes, not just dollars—may result in wealth transfers that reduce overall wealth, but may be utility maximizing in some political sense.[96] Congress, rather than an economist or other neutral analyst, may be in the best position to evaluate the agency's interpretation of a statute against the political utility function that emerges from the democratic process.

The mere fact that economic inefficiencies exist, however, does not imply that Congress has chosen that particular level of efficiency in order to satisfy some broader criterion of utility. There are several impediments (in addition to the risk of regulatory capture) that Congress must overcome in monitoring the agency.[97] First, the cumbersome nature of the legislative process hinders Congress' ability to adjust statutory provisions rapidly. Second, Con-

[96] See Hovenkamp, *Legislation, Well-Being and Public Choice* (cited in note 86).

[97] This is especially true in the type of ex post review adopted here. Congress could explore alternatives that establish majoritarian counterbalances to minority capture of the agency, such as establishing a tripartite regulatory system. In the tripartite model, Congress establishes a parallel agency to represent the public interest, which in this case might consist of employers and taxpayers. This parallel agency competes as a third party with the agency and the providers. The third player is empowered by Congress to review information that would otherwise be in the sole possession of the agency. This establishes a triad of interests that limits the agency's ability to collude with providers. See Ian Ayres and John Braithwaite, *Tripartism: Regulatory Capture & Empowerment*, 16 L & Social Inquiry 435 (1991).

gress' limited technical expertise may require agency assistance in developing program details, giving the agency another opportunity to respond to special interest pressures.

Congressional reactions to HCFA's adoption and modification of the wage index illustrates how Congress can respond to agency interpretations with which it is dissatisfied. The history of these reactions also highlights both of the impediments just mentioned.

The technical discussion of the composition of the wage index revealed the historical bias of the Medicare payment methodology to favor urban hospitals.[98] Over time, Congress has been responsive to requests from rural hospitals to adjust the wage index in order to redistribute Medicare reimbursement dollars in a more equitable fashion.

As the plaintiffs explained in *Good Samaritan*, a congressionally mandated study revealed that the failure to adjust for part-time workers resulted in significant under- and over-payment in some areas.[99] While the study identifying the bias was mandated in 1984, HCFA did not modify the wage index to correct for this methodological error until fiscal year 1986.[100]

Congressional activity has also been responsive to complaints about geographical classification issues similar to the one raised in *Good Samaritan*. Congress intervened in geographic classification for wage index purposes for the first time in 1987.[101] Under this legislation, the Secretary was required to reclassify rural hospitals as urban if specific demographic and commuting criteria were satisfied.[102] As a result of this congressional mandate 37 counties were reclassified by the Secretary.[103]

[98] The failure to account for occupational mix favors hospitals with a richer skill mix. Separate urban and rural rates were adopted to recognize the higher costs of urban hospitals which could not be explained by differences in case mix, labor costs or indirect teaching costs. See Part II above.

[99] In 1984, Congress instructed the Secretary to conduct a study to develop a wage index that would account for wage differences of part-time and full-time workers. Pub L No 98-369, § 2316(a).

[100] Dept of HHS, HCFA, Medicare Program; Changes to Inpatient the Hospital Prospective Payment System and FY 1986 Rates, 50 Fed Reg 35646, 35661 (1985). The new wage index accounted for part-time employees by calculating wages per hour, rather than per worker, as was done under the old index.

[101] Omnibus Budget Reconciliation Act of 1987, Pub L No 100-203, § 4005, 101 Stat 1330, 1330-47.

[102] See Table I below.

[103] Dept of HHS, HCFA, Medicare Program; Changes to the Inpatient Hospital Prospective Payment System and FY 1989 Rates, 53 Fed Reg 19498 (1988). In addition, Congress "relocated" one hospital so that it could be classified as urban for payment purposes. Section 4005(a)(2) of OBRA 1987 reads: "For the purpose of Section 1886

In 1989 Congress again intervened to modify the wage index regulation and established the Medicare Geographic Classification Review Board (MGCRB) to consider applications by hospitals for prospective adjustments for wage index purposes and/or standard payment amounts.[104] The Board is composed of five members: two members representing the interests of rural hospitals, at least one member of the Prospective Payment Assessment Commission, and at least one person knowledgeable in cost analysis with respect to inpatient hospital services. Congress turned to HCFA to publish guidelines to be used by the Board in decision making. After much delay, the new regulations were promulgated in final form on June 4, 1991.[105] In contrast to the 1987 reclassification scheme where rural hospitals were treated as urban for both wage index and standard payment amounts, reclassification by the MGCRB may take place for purposes of adjusting the wage index, the standardized amount, or both. In either case, a hospital must demonstrate that it is either proximate to or imports labor from the area to which it seeks reclassification.[106] If it is the goal of the hospital to adjust its wage index, it must show that its wages are more comparable to the wages paid by hospitals in the area to which it seeks reclassification.[107] In this case, reclassification of a hospital is based solely on labor market area. However, if the goal is to receive an adjacent area's standardized payment amount, a hospital must demonstrate

of the Social Security Act, Watertown Memorial Hospital in Watertown, Wisconsin is deemed to be located in Jefferson County, Wisconsin." While Watertown Memorial was actually located in a county that was not one of the 37 counties reclassified by the Secretary, Jefferson County, by coincidence, was.

[104] Omnibus Budget Reconciliation Act of 1989, Pub L No 101-239, § 6003(h), 103 Stat 2106, 2154.

[105] Dept of HHS, HCFA, Medicare Program; Medicare Geographic Classification Review Board Procedures and Criteria, 56 Fed Reg 25458 (1991).

[106] To demonstrate a geographic relationship with the area to which it seeks redesignation, an individual hospital must meet at least one of the following criteria: 1) a rural hospital must be at most 35 road miles from the adjacent area, while an urban hospital must be at most 15 road miles from the adjacent area; or 2) at least 50% of the hospital's employees must reside in the geographic area to which it seeks reclassification. Exceptions apply to RRCs and SCHs. Hospitals applying as a group must show why the county should be considered part of the neighboring area. The group must show that the county meets the standards for redesignation as an urban area, or as an outlying county.

[107] To demonstrate comparable wages with an adjacent area, one of the following conditions must be satisfied: 1) the hospital's average hourly wage is equal to at least 85% of the average hourly wage of the adjacent area; or 2) the hospital's average hourly wage weighted for occupational categories is at least 90% of the average hourly wage of the adjacent area. Hospitals which apply in groups must show that one of these conditions holds in the aggregate.

Table 1. Wage Index Adjustments: 1980 - present

Year	Action	Actor	Procedure/Change	Purpose/Goal
1980	Area wage index adopted	HHS/HCFA	Identification of discrete labor markets for hospital workers, and calculation of average cost of hospital labor within each area.	Avoid punishing hospitals with higher labor input prices.
1982	Federal hospital cost data excluded	HHS/HCFA	Federal hospital labor cost data excluded from wage index calculations due to use of national pay scale by federal hospitals.	Make local area wage index more accurate.
1984	HHS ordered to revise wage index	Congress	HHS ordered to develop a wage index accounting for differences in wages paid to full- and part-time workers.	Avoid underestimating labor costs in areas with more part-time workers.
1986	HCFA begins using its own wage data	HHS/HCFA	New area wage index adopted, using data from Medicare cost reports, and calculating wages per hour rather than per worker.	Implementaion of 1984 congressional mandate.
1987	Reclassification of certain rural hospitals	Congress	HHS required to reclassify rural hospitals if specific demographic and commuting requirements were met.	Draw geographic lines better reflecting urban/rural distinctions.
1988	Wage index protected at reclasssification	Congress	Urban standard payment rates were adjusted rather than lowering the wage rate at reclassification.	Protect certain MSAs by spreading reduction in hospital payments.
1989	MGCRB established	Congress	Review board created to evaluate and decide all requests by hospitals for adjustment of wage index and/or the standard payment.	Correct perceived payment inequities stemming from wage index.
1989	Floor established for area wage index	Congress	Reclassificataion may not lower the wage index for either the new or the previous area in which the hospital is classified.	Minimize impact of reclassification on hospitals in affected areas.

that its costs are comparable to the costs incurred by hospitals in the adjacent area to which it is applying.[108]

In its first year of operation (1991) the MGCRB approved requests of 958 Medicare hospital providers (approximately 20 percent of all hospital providers) to increase their PPS payments through reclassification for wage index and/or standard payment amounts.[109] The large number of approvals suggests that the MGCRB has served to counterbalance the urban hospitals' redistributive advantage, which was derived from the wage index classification scheme.

The fifteen year evolution of the wage index reveals the increased pressure Congress faced from rural hospitals complaining of payment inequities in the Medicare reimbursement system. Congressional responses ranged from mandating a study to setting up a parallel agency to respond to rural hospital concerns. Further, the history indicates that significant innovations in measuring labor cost variations are still needed, which suggests a continuing need for agency discretion in decision-making, despite the potential for agency capture. Finally, it reveals the difficulties Congress must face when assuming an active role in Medicare policy making: the inability of the legislative process to adjust statutory provisions quickly and Congress' limited expertise in developing program details.

Unfortunately, from this chronology it is impossible to determine whether the significant lag in congressional response is attributable to the agency withholding information (as predicted by the agency-theoretic approach) or strategic timing of empty victories to satisfy majoritarian interests (as predicted by the two-force model). Regardless of the motivation, as long as HCFA adheres to a rigid policy of supporting its payment methodology as developed, the influence of ex post congressional adjustments will only have an impact many years later. And, by that time, the politically powerful coalition will presumably have discovered another regulatory profit opportunity.

[108] A hospital demonstrates that its costs are more comparable to the amount it would be paid if it were reclassified when the hospital's case-mix adjusted cost per discharge is at least equal to its current rate plus 75% of the difference between that rate and the rate it would receive if reclassified.

[109] Richard A. Dudgeon and Laurie J. Harmon, *Geographic Reclassification Can Increase Payment—For Now,* Health Care Financial Management 76 (August 1991). The MGCRB reviewed 1,135 applications for reclassification and approved approximately 84%. Id at 78. The high success rate was attributable both to the detailed qualifying criteria specified in the regulatory provisions and to the apparent policy of the MGCRB to liberally interpret these requirements. (The Chairman of the MGCRB reported that "denials usually occurred if a provider clearly failed to meet or to demonstrate that it meets one or more of the required criteria." Id at 80.)

To the extent that Congress is unwilling (in the two-force model) or unable (in the agency-theoretic model) to monitor the regulatory process, minoritarian interests prevail and create inefficiencies that have not been deliberately chosen through the democratic process. It is then necessary to look beyond the political process to the judiciary for help in reducing the distortions that result from regulatory capture.

B. Role of the Judiciary

Good Samaritan raises the issue of the appropriate role of the judiciary in developing health care cost containment policy. Many health law scholars have advocated significant latitude for agency interpretation of statutes, assuming that since the agency is in a better position than the courts to understand both the complexities and political nature of health care policy-making, it is therefore more likely to interpret the statute in a manner consistent with congressional intent.[110] While the factual assumption may be valid, the normative conclusion does not follow. Focusing on judicial competence alone obscures the possibility that there are other reasons for the judiciary to intervene in the regulatory process. A complete analysis must consider both the shortcomings and advantages of alternative institutions in order to evaluate which institution is best suited to address which questions arising from Medicare reimbursement issues.[111] Here, "[t]he trade-off is between a political process that integrates far more information but with a significant risk of bias and an adjudicative process that suppresses information but decreases distortions in its presentations."[112]

The major advantage of the judiciary is its independence. Unlike administrative agencies, judges will be much less susceptible to side payments that encourage the inefficient transfer of resources to concentrated interest groups.[113] Other attributes of the judicial sys-

[110] See, for example, Gerard F. Anderson and Mark A. Hall, *The Adequacy of Hospital Reimbursement Under Medicaid's Boren Amendment*, 13 J Leg Medicine 205, 230 (1992) ("Anderson & Hall, *Adequacy of Hospital Reimbursement*"); Eleanor D. Kinney, *The Role of Judicial Review Regarding Medicare and Medicaid Program Policy: Past Experience and Future Expectations*, 35 SLU L J 759, 791-92 (1991).

[111] Komesar, *Imperfect Alternatives* at 140 (cited in note 95).

[112] *Id* at 141.

[113] For this reason, many scholars have advocated an active role for the judiciary in curtailing the impact of interest group politics. See, for example, Richard A. Epstein, *Takings: Private Property and the Power of Eminent Domain* (Harvard U, 1985); Bernard H. Siegan, *Economic Liberties and the Constitution* (U Chicago, 1980); Martin Shapiro, *Freedom of Speech: The Supreme Court and Judicial Review* (Prentice-Hall, 1966); Erwin Chemerinsky, *The Supreme Court, 1988 Term-Forward:*

tem, it is true, may place limitations upon its ability to effectively counterbalance regulatory distortions in the development of cost containment legislation. In particular, a systemic bias in review and the technical limitations of judicial intervention may make the costs of that intervention greater than the benefits in many circumstances.[114] An analysis of these competing considerations in the context of health-care cost containment suggests, however, that the courts should have a greater role than that assigned by the majority opinion in *Good Samaritan.*

As harmed providers are the most likely to benefit from litigating cost containment provisions, the courts will most often be called upon to correct for majoritarian bias rather than correct the type of bias of concern here: regulatory decision-making capture by concentrated interests. However, to the extent that the courts intervene in the agency's decision-making process and require explicit acknowledgement of Congress' goals, they may reduce the rents from collusion. In *Good Samaritan,* for example, the dissent interpreted clause (ii) to require that HCFA provide for retroactive case-by-case review when providers are over- or under- compensated. Even if only the under-compensated providers challenge their reimbursement, case-by-case review may reduce the potential for regulatory capture indirectly. Ex ante, each provider may have an incentive to collude with the agency and agree to a given payment methodology. This coalition of interests implicitly distributes the rents from capture amongst its members. But ex post, the payment methodology will reward providers that have low costs relative to their reimbursement and will penalize providers that suffer unforeseen cost shocks that raise their costs above the reimbursement level. This redistributes the rents among coalition members and provides the "losers" an incentive to challenge the agreed reimbursement scheme. As a result, the benefits and likelihood of collusion are reduced.

Challenges by providers also serve to disseminate information regarding provider costs and technology more rapidly, thereby reducing potential informational rents. In addition, retroactive case-by-case review subjects the agency to criticism for developing flawed payment methodologies, thus reducing its collusive rents.

The Vanishing Constitution, 103 Harv L Rev 43 (1989); Cass R. Sunstein, *Interest Groups in American Public Law,* 38 Stan L Rev 29 (1985); Richard A. Epstein, *Toward a Revitalization of the Contract Clause,* 51 U Chi L Rev 703 (1984); Cass R. Sunstein, *Naked Preferences and the Constitution,* 84 Colum L Rev 1689 (1984); Jerry L. Mashaw, *Constitutional Deregulation: Notes Toward a Public, Public Law,* 54 Tul L Rev 849 (1980).

[114] Komesar, *Imperfect Alternatives* at 150 (cited in note 95).

While the specific remedy advocated by the dissent cannot reduce minoritarian bias in the development and application of hospital cost limits (because cost limits have been replaced by PPS), review could reduce distortions in setting reimbursement levels for the thousands of home health agencies and skilled nursing facilities still subject to payment on the basis of "reasonable costs." More generally, the dissent's approach, if adopted, would have signaled a willingness by the Court to intervene in the interpretation of future cost containment legislation, thereby reducing the potential gains from side deals that contradict Congress' articulated goals.

The benefits of judicial intervention in interpreting cost containment legislation (including retroactive case-by-case review) must be weighed against the costs associated with substituting the judicial system for political determinations. Whether this intervention is cost beneficial depends on the remedy envisioned. Recent challenges by hospital and nursing home providers to changes in Medicaid reimbursement are helpful in defining the potential role of judicial review in the cost limit context. These cases show that the judiciary tends to limit its scope by focusing on procedural issues.[115]

As part of the Omnibus Budget Reconciliation Acts of 1980 and 1981, the Boren Amendment gave states flexibility in developing alternative payment methodologies for state Medicaid programs that had originally been tied to Medicare cost-based reimbursement principles. While granting program flexibility, the amendment imposed several conditions, including the requirement that payment methodologies be "reasonable and adequate to meet the costs which must be incurred by efficiently and economically operated facilities."[116] The courts have struggled to find their appropriate role in reviewing state programs under this clause. As with the review of cost limits under Medicare, there are significant arguments for deferring to state agencies which administer these programs.[117] In particular, courts may feel they lack the expertise to identify "efficient" providers. The compromise that most courts have reached in reviewing these claims is to focus on whether the state provided the appropriate procedural safeguards in modifying the state Medicaid program, thus avoiding an inquiry into the definition of an efficient facility.[118] Confining the judicial role in reviewing cost-

[115] For a good overview of these cases, see Anderson & Hall, *Adequacy of Hospital Reimbursement* (cited in note 110).

[116] Pub L No 96-499, § 962(A), 94 Stat 2599, 2651 (1980), and Pub L No 97-35, § 2173, 95 Stat 357, 808-809 (1981) (codified at 42 USC § 1396a(a)(13)(A) (1988)).

[117] See Anderson & Hall, *Adequacy of Hospital Reimbursement* (cited in note 110).

[118] Id at 224.

containment legislation to a similar inquiry would reduce the burden for the courts and focus their inquiry in an area where the courts do have a comparative advantage: defining adequate and appropriate process. This is the result advocated by the *Good Samaritan* dissent in the context of cost limits, and it would lead to a more efficient outcome.

Thus, the courts' limited expertise in technical and political issues and the costs of judicial intervention undoubtedly foreclose the possibility of a judicial panacea for the special interest bias in cost containment legislation. Despite these limitations, the judiciary may nonetheless be able to provide a significant facilitating role in preventing unnecessary failures by other institutions. The *Good Samaritan* majority abdicated this role—an abdication that would not have occurred under the dissent's application of the *Chevron* doctrine—and thereby missed an opportunity to promote the more efficient operation of the health care industry.

V. CONCLUSION

A comparative institutional approach suggests that the Health Care Financing Administration, the agency entrusted with deciphering and implementing Medicare and Medicaid legislation, should not be given the broad and unreviewable discretion in interpreting cost limit (and other health care cost containment) legislation that was granted by the majority in *Good Samaritan.* Analysis of health care industry dynamics reveals the need for broad administrative discretion to bring technical competence and political sensitivity to cost containment issues. These same market characteristics, however, also increase the likelihood that there would be gains from agency collusion with health care providers. The *Good Samaritan* dissent interpreted the statute in a manner that would have preserved the advantages of agency discretion, while reducing the potential for inefficiencies resulting from collusion between the agency and the regulated parties. In this respect, the dissent's interpretation—while apparently not based on economic principles or reasoning—is economically preferable to the majority's.

The *Good Samaritan* majority, by framing the issue as one of statutory interpretation under the *Chevron* framework, may have implicitly focused the inquiry too narrowly upon judicial competence. Given the significant social welfare losses that can result from agency capture, and Congress' unwillingness or inability to intervene, the dissent's advocacy of retroactive case-by-case review may provide the only cost beneficial option for limiting efficiency losses attributable to special interest bias. Although the dissent did not challenge the accepted *Chevron* doctrine, the result reached by the dissent was consistent with an important insight that the majority's analysis obscures: while courts may be poorly equipped to make the technical and political judgments required to implement health care cost containment, they may be well positioned to induce other institutions to improve their performance in making the difficult tradeoffs entailed in those judgments.

O'Melveny & Meyers v FDIC: Imputation of Fraud and Optimal Monitoring

A. C. Pritchard,[†]

The imputation-of-fraud rule bars recovery by a corporation from its outside professionals who fail to uncover fraud against third parties committed by the corporation's management. In O'Melveny & Meyers v FDIC, *the Supreme Court refused to adopt a federal common law exception to that rule for transactions undertaken while the corporation was insolvent. This article explains why that exception is justified under traditional standards of state corporate law. Under those traditional standards, creditors become the beneficial owners of the corporation after insolvency. Their aversion to corporate risktaking—such as the commission of fraud against third parties—requires an exception to the ordinary imputation-of-fraud rule in order to induce outside professionals to monitor fraud by the corporation. Enlisting outside professionals to monitor for fraud will curb excessive risktaking by the corporation, thereby minimizing the corporations' cost of credit.*

I. INTRODUCTION

In *O'Melveny & Meyers v FDIC,*[1] the Supreme Court waded into the thicket surrounding the FDIC's ongoing efforts to recover a por-

[†] Bickel & Brewer, Washington, DC. The author thanks Don Boudreaux, Charlie Steen, and two anonymous referees for helpful comments and discussion. Special thanks go to Linda Staples for excellent word processing. The author was employed by the Office of the Solicitor General at the time the *O'Melveny* case was briefed and argued, and assisted in the government's preparation of its position. The views expressed here are solely those of the author, and do not necessarily represent the views of the Department of Justice or the FDIC.

[1] 114 S Ct 2048 (1994).

 0-226-28685-1/95/0004-0005$02.00

tion of the cost of the savings-and-loan bailout from outside professionals who provided accounting and legal services to insolvent thrifts. Specifically, the FDIC, in its capacity as receiver for American Diversified Savings Bank (ADSB), sought to recover tort damages for legal malpractice from the O'Melveny law firm. ADSB had retained O'Melveny to prepare private-placement memoranda for two real-estate syndication projects. Shortly after the deals closed, the FDIC took over ADSB as receiver. As a result of investors' complaints of misleading disclosures in the memoranda, the FDIC was forced to rescind the syndication projects.[2]

The FDIC filed suit, alleging that the law firm negligently failed to make appropriate inquiries into the solvency of ADSB, which at the time of the syndications was in fact insolvent, and as a consequence, incapable of financing the deals. O'Melveny responded to the complaint by asserting that:

> (1) it owed no duty to ADSB or its affiliates to ferret out ADSB's own fraud; (2) the conduct of ADSB's wrongdoing officers must be imputed to ADSB, and that FDIC as receiver, stood in the shoes of ADSB; (3) and that therefore, as an ordinary assignee, FDIC was barred from pursuing any claims against O'Melveny.[3]

O'Melveny's defense was the "imputation-of-fraud" rule: whatever O'Melveny's negligence, the wrongdoing of ADSB's officers barred the thrift's recovery against the law firm for its failure to uncover that wrongdoing. The rights of the FDIC, as receiver of ADSB, could in turn rise no higher than those of ADSB.

The district court agreed with O'Melveny and dismissed the complaint, but the Ninth Circuit reversed. The court of appeals concluded that O'Melveny "had a duty to guide the thrift as to its obligations and to protect it against liability," and that its negligent failure to perform that duty gave ADSB a cause of action. If O'Melveny could have discovered ADSB's insolvency by taking reasonable care, it had a duty to do so.[4] The court further concluded that the fraud of ADSB's officers could not be attributed to the thrift or the FDIC to bar recovery, because the officers had acted adversely to the thrift, in that "conduct aggravating a corporation's insolvency and fraudulently prolonging its life does not benefit that corporation."[5] Finally, the court held that federal common law, rather than

[2] Id at 2052.

[3] *FDIC v O'Melveny & Meyers*, 969 F2d 744, 747 (9th Cir 1992).

[4] Id at 749.

[5] Id at 750.

state law, should govern whether the knowledge of fraud by a thrift's officers should be imputed to the corporation.[6]

The Supreme Court reversed. The Court did not determine whether the officers' fraud should be imputed to ADSB; instead, it simply rejected the Ninth Circuit's holding that federal law controlled.[7] The Court held that there was no "general federal common law," and remanded to the court of appeals to determine the relevant state-law rule.[8]

Justice Stevens, while concurring in the majority's opinion, wrote separately to note that a state court would be free to adopt as a matter of common law, an imputation-of-fraud rule protecting the corporation's creditors.[9] Federal courts, by contrast, "must do their best to estimate how the relevant state courts would perform their lawmaking task, and then emulate that sometimes purely hypothetical model."[10]

I will not address here the choice between federal and state law addressed by the Supreme Court majority.[11] Instead, I will discuss the substance of the underlying imputation-of-fraud rule, which must be resolved regardless of whether state or federal law applies. This discussion may shed some light on the hypothetical state-court lawmaking task posed by Justice Stevens, which the lower federal courts are now undertaking in the aftermath of *O'Melveny.* Must outside professionals use reasonable care to "ferret out" wrongdoing by a corporation's officers when those officers have defrauded third parties, or should the officers' fraud be imputed to the corporation to bar malpractice recovery for negligent legal or accounting services? To rephrase the question in economic terms: should outside professionals be enlisted as "monitors" to uncover, and deter, conduct that could potentially impair the corporation's ability to pay its obligations?

To answer this question, I review the corporate form's allocation of the risk of insolvency among various claimants to the corporation's assets. Broadly speaking, creditors of the corporation—bondholders, lenders, trade creditors, employees, and tort victims—are

[6] Id at 751 ("It is by now clear beyond doubt that federal, not state, law governs the application of defenses against FDIC.").

[7] 114 S Ct at 2056.

[8] Id at 2053.

[9] Id at 2056.

[10] Id.

[11] I also will not address whether managerial fraud should bar recovery against innocent, rather than negligent, third parties. The established rule in these cases bars recovery by the corporation. See Brief for the Federal Deposit Insurance Corporation, *O'Melveny & Meyers v FDIC,* No. 93-489 at 19-25 (corporation cannot recover from innocent third parties who owed corporation no duty.).

promised payment in full of the corporation's obligations to them. Should the corporation become insolvent, these promises will be breached. Shareholders, by contrast, receive no promise from the corporation of any return on their investment, or even that they will recoup their initial investment. Upon dissolution, shareholders are entitled only to the residual after all creditors have been paid in full. By purchasing shares, stockholders have assumed the risk that they will receive nothing. Insolvency, therefore, impairs no promise of the corporation to its shareholders. As a result of these contractual arrangements, creditors have more to lose than shareholders when a corporation becomes insolvent. Accordingly, creditors and shareholders will have very different attitudes regarding the risk of corporate insolvency.[12]

I then explore how corporate law attempts to resolve the tensions that inevitably arise from claimants' differing tolerance for risk of insolvency. Specifically, I explore the relationship between claimants' tolerance for risk and optimal monitoring of the corporation's agents, i.e., its officers and directors. Given their different risk tolerance, it follows that creditors and stockholders will disagree on the role of outside professionals in guarding against undue risktaking by the corporation's managers. Creditors would like more monitoring (and hence, less risk), while shareholders would prefer less monitoring (and more risk). I model fraud as a form of risktaking by the corporation's managers, and argue that creditors and stockholders would choose different levels of monitoring for fraud by outside professionals based on their differing preferences for risktaking by the corporation. The imputation-of-fraud rule can help resolve this conflict.

I conclude that whether or not the fraud of the corporation's managers should be imputed to the corporation depends on who

[12] "Risk" here denotes the probability that the corporation will not be able to pay its creditors and investors. Some creditors, such as bondholders and lenders, can convert the risk of default into a fixed cost through diversification. In the parlance of finance theorists, diversification eliminates the firm-specific "risk" of default because variance around expected returns has been eliminated. For a thorough econometric discussion of securities fraud risk measured as dispersion about expected returns, see Charles H. Steen, *The Econometrics of "Fraud-On-The-Market" Securities Fraud,* 4 J Leg Econ 11 (1994) ("Steen, *Fraud-On-The-Market*") (employing event study methodology to test for excess returns due to allegedly fraudulent communications by firms which were sued for fraud-on-the-market pursuant to Rule 10b-5, 17 CFR § 240.10b-5 (1993)). This article does not address the implications of corporate fraud for holders of a diversified portfolio, but instead focuses on limiting the agency costs of fraud committed by the individual corporation. Diversification converts the firm-specific risk of corporate fraud to a fixed rather than variable cost, but it cannot eliminate the problem.

can claim the status of residual claimant to the corporation's assets at the time of the fraudulent transaction. If the corporation is solvent at the time of the transaction, the fraud of the officers should be imputed to the corporation, because the shareholders, with their greater preference for risk, are the residual claimants. Conversely, if the corporation is insolvent, managerial fraud should not be imputed to the corporation, because more risk-averse creditors are now the residual claimants. In determining whether managers' fraud was "adverse" to the corporation, courts should look to who owns the corporation at the time of the fraud. By adjusting the monitoring duties of outside professionals to correspond with the risk preferences of the claimants owning the corporation's residual value, the rule minimizes the corporation's cost of credit, without unduly interfering with the shareholders' ability to take on risk. The imputation-of-fraud rule thereby maximizes the corporation's value.

II. THE IMPUTATION-OF-FRAUD RULE: PRE- AND POST-INSOLVENCY

Before *O'Melveny,* the imputation-of-fraud rule received little attention in the federal courts. The Seventh Circuit produced the two seminal cases in the area, applying the imputation-of-fraud rule to bar recovery for pre-insolvency transactions, but not for post-insolvency transactions. Those cases provide a useful starting point for placing the imputation-of-fraud rule into the doctrinal framework of corporate law.

The first, *Cenco Inc. v Seidman & Seidman,*[13] involved a massive fraud by Cenco's managers to inflate the value of the corporation's inventories. The managers' fraud benefitted the company (at least until it was uncovered) by allowing the corporation to acquire other firms on the cheap via inflated stock, and to borrow at lower rates than it would have been able to if the corporation had been accurately valued.[14] After the fraud was uncovered, Cenco faced massive liability for securities fraud.[15] In response, Cenco sued its auditor, Seidman & Seidman, for common-law negligence in failing to uncover the fraud. Writing for the Seventh Circuit panel, Judge Posner noted that the question had not been the subject of a reported case.[16] After finding that Illinois law should be applied under

[13] 686 F2d 449 (7th Cir 1982).
[14] Id at 451.
[15] Id.
[16] Id at 454.

the doctrine of ancillary jurisdiction, he determined that Cenco's shareholders would be the beneficiaries of any judgment in favor of Cenco. Judge Posner reasoned that "such a judgment would be perverse from the standpoint of compensating the victims of wrongdoing" because the corrupt managers held Cenco shares, and also because the shareholders had selected the board of directors that failed to stop the fraud.[17] Deterrence concerns also counseled against Cenco's recovery: "[I]f the owners of the corrupt enterprise are allowed to shift the costs of wrongdoing entirely to the auditor, their incentives to hire honest managers and monitor their behavior will be reduced."[18] Accordingly, the court held that Cenco's claim was barred as a matter of law.

In a subsequent case, *Schacht v Brown,* the Seventh Circuit reached the opposite result.[19] The managers of Reserve Insurance Corporation ceded to Societe Commerciale de Reassurance (SCOR) most of Reserve's most profitable business in return for certain commission payments from SCOR, while Reserve secretly guaranteed SCOR against loss from the ceded policies. The agreement gave Reserve the appearance of an increased surplus and a lower liability-to-surplus ratio. The actual effect was to conceal and exacerbate Reserve's insolvency.[20]

After state regulators shut Reserve down, Reserve's liquidator brought a RICO[21] suit against all parties involved, including Reserve's accountants—Coopers and Lybrand, Alexander Grant, and Arthur Anderson—charging that the defendants had fraudulently conspired with Reserve's officers to keep "Reserve operating long past insolvency in a manner which resulted in enormous losses to [Reserve]."[22] The defendants raised *Cenco* as a bar to the liquidator's claim. The Seventh Circuit disagreed, distinguishing *Cenco* on the grounds that: (1) *Cenco* arose under Illinois, rather than federal, law; and (2) the fraud of the managers, rather than benefitting the company as in *Cenco,* prolonged Reserve's insolvency to the detriment of the corporation.[23] The court further reasoned that the corporation's insolvency would prevent shareholders from deriving a benefit from any recovery, and their deterrent incentives would not be

[17] Id at 455.

[18] Id.

[19] 711 F2d 1343 (1983). Judge Wood, who wrote the opinion in this case, was also on the *Cenco* panel.

[20] Id at 1345.

[21] 18 USC § 1961 *et seq.* (1988).

[22] *Schacht,* 711 F2d at 1345-46.

[23] Id at 1347-48.

undercut.[24] The court rejected the defendants' argument that the corporation was benefitted by having had its existence prolonged:

> This premise collides with common sense, for the corporate body is ineluctably damaged by the deepening of its insolvency, through increased exposure to creditor liability. Indeed, in most cases, it would be crucial that the insolvency of the corporation be disclosed, so that shareholders may exercise their right to dissolve the corporation in order to cut their losses. Thus, acceptance of a rule which would bar a corporation from recovering damages due to the hiding of information concerning its insolvency would create perverse incentives for wrong-doing officers and directors to conceal the true financial condition of the corporation from the corporate body as long as possible.[25]

Accordingly, the court overruled the defendants' motion to dismiss the complaint.

The imputation-of-fraud rule that emerges from *Cenco* and *Schacht* is that pre-insolvency managerial fraud against third parties will be imputed to the corporation, and will bar recovery by the corporation for negligence in failing to uncover the fraud, because it benefits the corporation's shareholders. Post-insolvency, managerial fraud will not be imputed the corporation because it harms shareholders by exacerbating the corporation's liability to creditors.

The reasoning on which the *Cenco/Schacht* rule was based is inadequate, though the rule itself can ultimately by defended on grounds different from those offered by the Seventh Circuit panels that decided these cases. It is an empirical question, both pre- and post-insolvency, whether fraud benefits the corporation and its shareholders: it depends on how often the corporation gets caught. *Schacht* offers no reason to believe that detection becomes more likely with the advent of insolvency. More fundamentally, *Schacht*'s assertion that shareholders would want insolvency disclosed so they could cut their losses is backward: shareholders of an insolvent corporation have nothing more to lose, and concealing the insolvency allows shareholders to gamble with the creditors' money. Both *Cenco* and *Schacht* focus on shareholders' interests, failing to account for creditors' interests. *Schacht* ignores the cen-

[24] Id at 1348-49.

[25] Id at 1350 (citations omitted). See also *In re Investors Funding Corp.*, 523 F Supp 533 (SDNY 1980) (same).

tral role that the shift of beneficial ownership from shareholders to creditors upon insolvency plays in determining optimal monitoring rules. A more convincing rationale for the *Cenco/Schacht* rule is available, but it requires a more detailed inquiry into fraud by the corporation and claimants' resulting demand for monitoring by outside professionals. I turn now to that inquiry.

III. THE CORPORATE FORM: PRE- AND POST-INSOLVENCY

While the corporation is solvent, shareholders control the management of the corporation by voting for directors, who in turn choose the managers who run the firm on a day-to-day basis. Shareholders' control, however, is limited. Shareholders must be consulted on major business decisions, such as mergers or sales of the corporation's assets, but managers generally run the corporation's affairs, subject to review only by the board of directors. Shareholders can challenge some management decisions in court, but the overwhelming majority of management decisions are protected from judicial second-guessing by the "business judgment" rule. The business judgment rule "is a presumption that in making a business decision the directors of a corporation acted on an informed basis, in good faith and the honest belief that the action taken was in the best interests of the company."[26] Overcoming this presumption is a high hurdle, and the practical effect is to insulate the overwhelming majority of management decisions from judicial review.[27]

Shareholders willingly contract for such a rule because it encourages management to undertake the risks that in turn generate profits.[28] Under the business judgment rule, shareholders can challenge managers' decisions only when managers have breached their fiduciary duties to the corporation.[29] Absent a breach of fi-

[26] *Smith v Van Gorkom,* 488 A2d 858, 872 (Del 1985).

[27] See *Joy v North,* 695 F2d 880, 885 (2d Cir 1982) (Judge Winter) ("[A] corporate officer who makes a mistake in judgment as to economic conditions, consumer tastes or production line efficiency will rarely, if ever, be found liable for damages suffered by the corporation.").

[28] See id at 886 ("[B]ecause potential profit often corresponds to the potential risk, it is very much in the interest of shareholders that the law not create incentives for overly cautious corporate decisions. Some opportunities offer great profits at the risk of very substantial losses, while the alternatives offer less risk of loss but also less potential profit.").

[29] See *Unocal Corp. v Mesa Petroleum Co.,* 493 A2d 946, 958 (Del 1985) ("[U]nless it is shown by a preponderance of the evidence that the directors' decisions were primarily based on perpetuating themselves in office, or some other breach of fiduciary duty such as fraud, overreaching, lack of good faith, or being uninformed, a

duciary duty, the business judgment rule ties the hands of shareholders in the event that risky decisions later turn out to be mistaken.[30]

Creditors of a solvent corporation have even less opportunity for legal challenges to managers' decisions because they are barred from recovering even when the managers have breached their fiduciary duties. Creditors are seemingly left vulnerable to management decisions that may significantly alter the default risk accepted by creditors when they initially contracted with the corporation. Creditors who can bargain with the corporation factor the risk of default into the contract price, but management may upset that calculus by unilaterally increasing the firm's riskiness after creditors have contracted, which will effectively reduce the contract price.[31]

The corporate form allows creditors to protect against this contingency by providing mechanisms for controlling corporate risktaking: (1) under the default rule, creditors' claims to the corporation's assets are given priority over the claims of shareholders;[32] (2) creditors can limit the range of overreaching through contractual provisions;[33] and (3) fraudulent conveyance law limits the corporation's ability to transfer assets to sharehold-

Court will not substitute its judgment for that of the board."). While managers' fiduciary duties include both a duty of care and a duty of loyalty, see *Smith,* 488 A2d 858 (holding directors liable for failure to reasonably inform themselves before approving a merger proposal), as practical matter, only the duty of loyalty is likely to affect manager's behavior. See 8 Del Code § 102(b)(7) (1991) (authorizing corporations to eliminate damages for breach of the duty of care).

[30] As such, the rule can be thought of as a form of precommitment. Precommitment is the restriction of future choices in order to rationally maximize long-term utility. See Jon Elster, *Ulysses and the Sirens: Studies in Rationality and Irrationality* 36 (Cambridge U, 1979).

[31] See Richard A. Posner, *The Rights of Creditors of Affiliated Corporations,* 43 U Chi L Rev 499, 504 (1976) ("Posner, *Rights of Creditors*") ("After the interest rate has been agreed upon and the loan agreement signed, the borrower may increase the risk of defaulting on the loan by, for example, obtaining additional loans not subordinated to the first or transferring assets to its shareholders or others without adequate consideration.").

[32] *Railroad Co. v Howard,* 74 US 392, 409-10 (1868) ("[T]he rule is well settled that stockholders are not entitled to any share of the capital stock nor to any dividend of the profits until all the debts of the corporation are paid.").

[33] See generally Clifford W. Smith, Jr. and Jerold B. Warner, *On Financial Contracting: An Analysis of Bond Covenants* 7 J Fin Econ 117 (1979) (analyzing bond covenants commonly used to reduce creditors' risks). See also Frank H. Easterbrook and Daniel R. Fischel, *Contract and Fiduciary Duty,* 36 J L & Econ 425, 437 (1993) ("Managers owe fiduciary duties to equity investors, but not debt investors or employees, because these claimants can contract at low cost, while the costs of specification are prohibitively high for the residual claimants.").

ers.[34] Creditors' claim priority ensures that the shareholder's claims will ordinarily provide a "cushion" protecting creditors; if managers breach their fiduciary duties, shareholder lawsuits to hold them accountable will benefit the creditors as well. Of course, shareholders will frequently be more tolerant of risky behavior than creditors would be, especially where shareholders' claims are a small percentage of the firm's value.[35] Some highly risky decisions will seem advantageous to the shareholders, who stand to realize all of the potential profits, but will not seem advantageous to the creditors, who will bear the costs in the event that the decision proves to be wrong. In those cases, creditors cannot rely on the shareholders to act as their monitors, but instead must contract to limit managerial discretion directly.

Contractual protections, however, are an imperfect device for limiting excessive managerial risktaking. Management makes a virtually infinite number of decisions affecting the riskiness of the corporation, and the parties may find it difficult to specify in advance what decisions creditors will be willing to pay to have removed from managerial discretion. This difficulty in contracting has led many commentators to call for the extension of fiduciary duties to creditors (in addition to managers' existing fiduciary duties to shareholders).[36] The call for extended fiduciary duties, however, has been limited to academics; courts have uniformly refused

[34] See generally Robert Charles Clark, *The Duties of the Corporate Debtor to its Creditors,* 90 Harv L Rev 505 (1977) (fraudulent conveyance law and related doctrines help assure that the corporation will retain sufficient assets to pay its creditors).

[35] See John C. Coffey, Jr., *Litigation and Corporate Governance: An Essay on Steering Between Scylla and Charybdis,* 52 Geo Wash L Rev, 789, 806 n 41 (1984) (bondholder likely to attack high-risk transactions). The role of plaintiffs' attorneys in "safeguarding" shareholders' interests may blur this distinction. These attorneys may be more interested in settlement value than maximizing shareholder wealth, which may produce lawsuits even where shareholders would have ratified management's decisions ex ante. The agency costs faced by shareholders in enforcing their rights are non-trivial. See Janet Cooper Alexander, *Do the Merits Matter? A Study of Settlements in Securities Class Actions,* 43 Stan L Rev 497 (1991) (concluding that derivative actions primarily benefit attorneys rather than the shareholders).

[36] See, for example, Lawrence E. Mitchell, *The Fairness Rights of Corporate Bondholders,* 65 NYU L Rev 1165 (1990); Morey W. McDaniel, *Bondholders and Stockholders,* 13 J Corp Law 205 (1988); Note, *Creditors' Derivative Suits on Behalf of Solvent Corporations,* 88 Yale L J 1299 (1979). But see Jonathan R. Macey, *An Economic Analysis of the Various Rationales for Making Shareholders the Exclusive Beneficiaries of Corporate Fiduciary Duties,* 21 Stetson L Rev 23, 41 (1991) ("To the extent that [fiduciary duties] are allowed to trump the terms contained in a contract between a nonshareholder constituency and the firm, such statutes simply transfer wealth from shareholders to these other constituencies."); Dale B. Tauke, *Should Bonds Have More Fun? A Reexamination of the Debate Over Corporate Bondholder Rights,* 1989 Colum Bus L Rev 1, 134 ("Granting [fiduciary] rights to bondholders

to recognize fiduciary duties to creditors while the corporation remains solvent.[37]

The legal rule changes, however, when the corporation becomes insolvent.[38] Contractual protections, of limited value while the corporation was solvent, become decidedly less effective when the corporation becomes insolvent. Contractual remedies are only as good as the corporation's ability to pay a judgment; by definition, insolvent corporations are seriously impaired in their ability to pay judgments.[39] In this situation, corporate law substitutes fiduciary duties for contractual duties. Under the "trust fund" doctrine, the bene-

would tend to induce corporations to minimize socially desirable risk-taking behavior because the taking of risky courses of action, even where justified by expected returns, normally does not significantly benefit bondholders.").

[37] See, for example, *Simons v Cogan,* 549 A2d 300, 304 (Del 1988) (holding that directors of solvent corporation owed no fiduciary duty to holder of convertible debenture: "[A] mere expectancy interest does not create a fiduciary relationship. Before a fiduciary duty arises, an existing property right or equitable interest supporting such a duty must exist."); *Harff v Kerkorian,* 324 A2d 215 (Del Ch 1974), aff'd in part, rev'd in part on other grounds, 347 A2d 133 (Del 1975) ("[U]nless there are special circumstances which affect the rights of the debenture holders as creditors of the corporation, e.g., fraud, insolvency, or a violation of a statute, the rights of the debenture holders are confined to the terms of the Indenture Agreement pursuant to which the debentures were issued.").

Courts have rejected such duties with good reason. Granting fiduciary rights to bondholders would essentially place them in the same position as preferred shareholders, who have long been protected by fiduciary duties. See *Judah v Delaware Trust Co.,* 378 A2d 624, 628 (Del 1977). But if bondholders really wanted to be treated like preferred shareholders, they could simply buy preferred stock. The commentators who call for fiduciary duties to bondholders have uniformly failed to address this market solution to the supposed problem of a lack of fiduciary duties to creditors. Moreover, granting new rights to creditors against the managers would skew managerial decision-making: managers would be liable for increasing risk to bondholders, but bondholders would not have to pay over their gains when managers took decisions that *decreased* bondholder risk. If the goal is optimizing risktaking, liability should run both ways. Finally, denying fiduciary duties to creditors encourages them to compete in monitoring the corporation. See Note, *Creditors' Derivative Suits on Behalf of Solvent Corporations,* 88 Yale L J 1299, 1310 (1979) ("It is small comfort that losses on a given loan may be recovered by charging higher interest rates, since competing creditors who are more successful in anticipating, detecting, and controlling mismanagement can charge lower rates.").

[38] See *Commodity Futures Trading Comm'n v Weintraub,* 471 US 343, 357 (1985) ("Insolvency is a most important and material fact, not only with individuals but with corporations, and with the latter as with the former the mere fact of its existence may change radically and materially its rights and obligations.") (quoting *McDonald v Williams,* 174 US 397, 404 (1899)).

[39] See George C. Triantis, *The Effects of Insolvency and Bankruptcy on Contract Performance and Adjustment,* 43 U Toronto L J 679, 684 (1993) ("Triantis, *Effects of Insolvency*") ("If the investors in the promisor enjoy limited liability and since damages are unsecured claims, the cost of breach to the promisor varies inversely with the degree of insolvency.").

ficial ownership of the corporation shifts at the moment of insolvency from the shareholders to the creditors.[40] This change in the legal rule reflects the change in the economic reality of the corporation: under the traditional priority scheme, creditors, rather than shareholders, now hold the residual claims to the corporation's assets.[41] When the corporation is insolvent, shareholders are left with nothing to claim after debts to creditors have been satisfied from the corporation's assets. As a consequence, managers of insolvent corporations must account to creditors first, and then to shareholders.[42] After insolvency, letting managers' duties continue to run exclusively to shareholders would spell disaster for the creditors. Both before and after insolvency, shareholders are likely to differ with creditors on the appropriate level of risktaking by managers: their main concern will be inducing managers to take on *more* risk, not less.[43] This conflict is increased exponentially at the advent of insolvency. Shareholders, effectively gambling with other peoples'

[40] See *Hollins v Brierfield Coal & Iron Co.*, 150 US 371, 383 (1893) ("Solvent, [the corporation] holds its property as any individual holds his, free from the touch of a creditor who has acquired no lien; free also from the touch of a stockholder who, though equitably interested in, has no legal right to, the property. Becoming insolvent, the equitable interest of the stockholders in the property, together with their conditional liability to the creditors, places the property in a condition of trust, first, for the creditors, and then for the stockholders."); *Graham v Railroad Co.*, 102 US 148, 161 (1880) ("When a corporation becomes insolvent, it is so far civilly dead, that its property may be administered as a trust-fund for the benefit of its stockholders and creditors. A court of equity, at the instance of the proper parties, will then make those funds trust-funds, which, in other circumstances, are as much the absolute property of the corporation, as any man's property is his."). See also Beth A. Brady and Gail A. O'Gradney, eds, 3 *Fletcher Cyclopedia of the Law of Private Corporations* § 849 at 238 (Clark Boardman Callaghan, perm. ed 1994) ("With some exceptions, when the corporation becomes insolvent, the directors are considered as trustees for the corporate creditors.") (footnotes omitted).

[41] See *In re Central Ice Cream Co.*, 836 F2d 1068, 1073 (7th Cir 1987) (Judge Easterbrook) ("Although shareholders outside of bankruptcy must file a derivative suit if they believe that the firm errs in accepting a compromise of pendinglitigation, bankruptcy alters the procedure by which investors of all kinds assert their claims. Creditors outside of bankruptcy may not challenge the firm's decisions; in bankruptcy they may do so, because they are (presumed to be) the principally affected persons, the new residual claimants."). See also Jonathan R. Macey and Geoffrey P. Miller, *Corporate Stakeholders: A Contractual Perspective*, 43 U Toronto L J 401 (1993) (arguing that fiduciary duties should run exclusively to residual claimants).

[42] See *FDIC v Sea Pines Co.*, 692 F2d 973, 977 (4th Cir 1982) ("when a corporation becomes insolvent, or in a failing condition, the officers and directors no longer represent the stockholders, but by fact of insolvency, become trustees for the creditors"). Cf *Pepper v Litton*, 308 US 295, 311 (1939) (fiduciary obligations run to creditors as well as shareholders when corporation is insolvent.).

[43] Frank H. Easterbrook and Daniel R. Fischel, *The Economic Structure of Corporate Law* 340-41 (Harvard U, 1991) ("A manager is undiversified and acts as if risk averse. Much of his human capital and a substantial portion of his other wealth are tied up in a single firm. Lack of diversification induces the manager to work in the

money, would be delighted to literally put the corporation's assets on the table at Vegas—heads, the shareholders win; tails, the creditors lose.[44] Courts recognize this change in incentives by permitting creditors to bring claims against management based upon breach of fiduciary duty when the corporation was insolvent at the time of the alleged misconduct.[45]

Creditors gain other tools when the corporation becomes insolvent. For example, while the corporation is solvent, management has an essentially free hand in transferring the assets of the corporation. Creditors will find it difficult to limit this discretion by contract without unduly fettering management; it will be difficult to predict in advance what assets the corporation will own, or how those assets are best allocated. Fraudulent conveyance law steps in to fill this gap. Transfers made without consideration can be set aside if they render the corporation insolvent.

Fraudulent conveyance law reaches only outright transfers, however; it does not limit risky transactions taken during insolvency which may be equally costly to creditors. Risky transactions taken while insolvent reflect a wealth distribution from creditors to shareholders indistinguishable from the fraudulent conveyance of a physical asset: creditors bear the loss while shareholders enjoy the gain. Accordingly, risky transactions taken while insolvent have a negative expected value for creditors, and a positive expected value for shareholders. As explained in the next section, corporate managers have incentives to undertake such transactions post-insolvency, despite the fact that the creditors have become the residual claimant to the corporation's assets.

IV. CREDITORS, SHAREHOLDERS, AND FIDUCIARY MONITORING FOR FRAUD

Once the corporation becomes insolvent, the *Schacht* rule effectively enlists accountants and lawyers in ferreting out fraud on the

investors' interests; it ties his fortunes to those of the firm. It also makes the manager a singularly poor recipient of additional risk. The more of the inevitable risks of the venture the manager bears personally, the more cautiously he behaves. Yet the effectively risk-neutral investors do not want overcautious managers.").

[44] See Thomas H. Jackson, *The Logic and Limits of Bankruptcy Law* 205 (Harvard U, 1986) ("When a firm is insolvent and has $100,000 in debts and only $80,000 in assets, it is unlikely that it would be in the interests of the creditors to have that $80,000 placed on number 20 at a roulette wheel in Atlantic City, but it clearly would be in the interests of the shareholders to do so.").

[45] *In re STN Enterprises*, 779 F2d 901, 904 (2d Cir 1985) ("[T]he 'majority rule' permits recovery by creditors of an insolvent corporation for mismanagement as if the corporation itself were plaintiff . . . ."); *Geyer v Ingersoll Publications Co.*, 621 A2d 784, 790 (Del Ch 1992) ("[F]iduciary duties to creditors arise when one is able to establish the fact of insolvency.").

creditors' behalf. The shift in the imputation-of-fraud rule after insolvency does not change the formal legal duty of lawyers and accountants: the standard both before and after insolvency remains the ordinary negligence rule of reasonable care. It does not follow, however, that the behavior of fiduciaries will be unaffected by the imputation-of-fraud rule. On the contrary, the expected consequences from failing to exercise reasonable care are dramatically changed. The *Cenco* imputation rule invites fiduciaries to neglect their duty to ferret out fraud by corporate insiders because even if they are negligent, there will be no damages assessed against them for their malfeasance. A rule that is not backed by a monetary sanction is likely to have a very low rate of compliance. There may be some sanctions for malpractice by professionals, such as damage to reputation or the possibility of an ethics inquiry by the bar, but those penalties are slight relative to the prospect of a multi-million dollar tort judgment. Under the *Schacht* rule, that very sobering prospect becomes real after insolvency.

It seems obvious why creditors would want a rule, with an effective sanction, that would enlist fiduciary professionals in the monitoring of corporate insiders for fraudulent behavior. Creditors ordinarily do not have the resources to monitor the internal workings of a corporation on their own, although they will frequently contract for regular audits. Nonetheless, while the corporation remains solvent, ordinary contractual terms suffice to protect the interests of creditors, who require only that the corporation maintain sufficient assets to pay its debts. Creditors may dislike bearing increased risk, but until the corporation cannot pay adverse judgments, creditors are not actually harmed by riskiness.[46]

Contractual obligations lose their effectiveness, however, as a corporation heads toward insolvency. Contractual breaches will be unenforced, or underenforced, because the corporation does not

[46] See *Central Manhattan Properties, Inc. v D. A. Schulte, Inc.*, 91 F2d 728, 730 (2d Cir 1937) (Judge Learned Hand) ("[A] lessor has no conceivable interest in whether the lessee fails to pay in due course, provided a judgment against him be good. No one needs an equitable lien unless his debtor's assets will not go round."). Creditors may see a decline in the market price of their claims against the corporation, but that decline does not give rise to a cause of action. See Thomas R. Hurst and Larry J. McGuinness, *The Corporation, the Bondholder and Fiduciary Duties*, 10 J L & Commerce 187, 196 (1991) ("[T]o state that bondholders have an interest in the market price of their securities does nothing to strengthen the conclusion that the bondholders' interest rises to the level of a legally protected right. It would be anomalous to recognize a right in bondholders in this respect when the courts have long refused to recognize a duty owed by management to shareholders to maintain the market price of its shares or to act in such a manner to maximize the current share price.").

have the assets to pay damages.[47] Moreover, corporate insiders are likely to take risks that they would not have considered when the corporation was solvent.[48] Managers have been chosen by directors, who are in turn chosen by shareholders (who may include the managers themselves). Once shareholders' equity has been eliminated, managers and shareholders face no downside in taking what previously would have been considered unreasonable risks, but they do enjoy the upside potential of avoiding bankruptcy if the risky venture pays off.[49] As a result, managers may undertake post-insolvency projects with negative expected values for the corporation. Frauds against third parties are an example of such high-risk projects.

Under the absolute priority rule, bankruptcy wipes out the interests of shareholders. At the same time, managers face a substantial likelihood of termination,[50] in addition to reputational losses.[51]

[47] Regulatory oversight will be diminished as well, because managers will assume a very short time horizon, trying to keep the corporation afloat for the next few months in the hope that the corporation's fortunes will improve. Regulatory violations can be covered up, at least for a while. The FDIC is granted substantial regulatory oversight by statute, but the events of the 1980s testify to the ineffectiveness of that monitoring. In addition, the FDIC is limited in its ability to turn away customers for its insurance. To a large extent, it is an involuntary creditor. Even commentators critical of the view that the Treasury Department's Office of Thrift Supervision is owed fiduciary duties by everyone involved in the banking industry concede that such duties are appropriate when the bank becomes insolvent. See Lawrence G. Baxter, *Fiduciary Issues in Federal Banking Regulation*, 56 Law & Contemp Probs 7 (1993); Andrew J. Nussbaum, *Like Money in the Bank? An Economic Analysis of Fiduciary Duties to Protect the S&L Deposit Insurance Fund*, 44 Admin L Rev 355, 368-71 (1992) ("Nussbaum, *Economic Analysis of Fiduciary Duties*"). This weakness of the FDIC's monitoring abilities, of course, suggests the need for a uniform federal rule, which the Supreme Court declined to devise in *O'Melveny*. Further exploration of that problem is beyond the scope of this article.

[48] Nussbaum, *Economic Analysis of Fiduciary Duties* at 364 (cited in note 45) ("As the current thrift crisis shows, the decisions just prior to insolvency may well be the most costly to the federal taxpayer.").

[49] While managers may be more risk averse than shareholders while the corporation is solvent, their interests align upon insolvency. At that point, managers' interests will diverge sharply from those of creditors. See Susan Rose-Ackerman, *Risk Taking and Ruin: Bankruptcy and Investment Choice*, 20 J Leg Stud 277, 296 (1991) ("Rose-Ackerman, *Risk Taking*") ("[I]f the liquidation value is a function of the manager's investment choices, the identity of interest fails since creditors prefer small losses to large losses while managers are indifferent to the level of the loss. This conflict of interest will be particularly acute for firms that are already insolvent since the manager is then biased toward high-variance projects. Given two projects with the same mean, the higher-variance project maximizes the chance of survival but will impose heavy costs on creditors if the gamble fails.").

[50] Stuart C. Gilson, *Bankruptcy, Boards, Banks and Blockholders: Evidence on Changes in Corporate Ownership and Control when Firms Default*, 27 J Fin Econ

Managing a corporation into bankruptcy is hardly a marketable credential, while bringing a corporation back from the brink is sure to bring kudos. If creditors learn of the insolvency, they are likely to file an involuntary bankruptcy petition,[52] thus depriving management and shareholders of one more throw of the dice. Moreover, if management has been involved in fraudulent conduct, this will give creditors cause to petition the bankruptcy court to appoint a trustee, rather then allowing management to continue to run the corporation as debtor-in-possession.[53] Managers therefore serve their own interests as well as those of shareholders by disguising signs of insolvency from creditors.[54]

Obviously, this scenario leaves much to be desired from the creditors' perspective. Creditors expect no upside potential from taking such risks, and they face a substantial probability that their losses will be exacerbated by managerial risktaking during insolvency. Frauds such as the one at issue in *O'Melveny,* if uncovered, expand the number of creditors grabbing at the diminished pie of assets. No one will be paid in full, and as the insolvency deepens, creditors can expect a smaller and smaller pro rata share of the corporation's assets. Note that the *Schacht* non-imputation rule protects not only existing creditors, but also potential creditors such as the victims of potential fraud. If these potential creditors became actual credi-

355, 356 (1990) ("On average, only 46% of directors who sit on the board prior to financial distress, and 43% of the CEOs, are still present when their firms emerge from bankruptcy or settle privately with creditors less than two years later.").

[51] See Eugene F. Fama, *Agency Problems and the Theory of the Firm,* 88 J Pol Econ 288, 292-93 (1980) (arguing that the value of managers' human capital depends on success or failure of firm).

[52] 11 USC § 303(b)(1) (1988) (three or more holders of undisputed claims can file involuntary petition).

[53] 11 USC § 1104(a)(1) (1988) (trustee can be appointed "for cause, including fraud, dishonesty, incompetence, or gross mismanagement of the affairs of the debtor by current management, either before or after the commencement of the case").

[54] Thomas H. Jackson and Robert E. Scott, *On the Nature of Bankruptcy: An Essay on Bankruptcy Sharing and the Creditors' Bargain,* 75 Va L Rev 155, 158-59 (1989) (shareholders prefer to delay liquidation of insolvent corporation while secured creditors prefer prompt liquidation).

There is one exception to the managers' general preference for avoiding bankruptcy. Where insolvency is simply the product of a financial reversal, rather than managerial incompetence, wrongdoing, or excessive risktaking, managers who believe that the business is viable may seek the protection of the bankruptcy court. See George G. Triantis, *A Theory of the Regulation of Debtor-in-Possession Financing,* 46 Vand L Rev 901 (1993) (availability of automatic stay and administrative priority for debtor-in-possession financing provides incentives for cash-strapped businesses to file for bankruptcy). If this is the only exception, the group that does not voluntarily file (the incompetent and the fraudulent) is the group from which creditors are most in need of protection.

tors, their claims would further dilute creditors' pro rata shares of the corporation's assets. Thus, creditors want a monitoring device to deter corporate insiders from taking on such risks, and to help maintain the pool of assets available to creditors.

The *Schacht* rule encourages lawyers and accountants to serve as monitors on behalf of creditors when serving corporations that are in financial difficulty. If they come across managerial fraud, their duty of reasonable care would oblige them to inform the board of directors, and withdraw their services if the board failed to take corrective action. Some fraud by the corporation would be deterred, because the threat of malpractice damages would lead professionals to take due care to ensure that managers' statements were accurate. Moreover, managers of corporations in precarious condition would find it more difficult to hire the professionals who are needed to carry out deals like the one that went awry in *O'Melveny.* No lawyers, no accountants, no deal.[55]

A corporation's difficulties in retaining outside professionals may serve an important signalling function for creditors. While the corporation is solvent, the imputation-of-fraud rule applies, so professionals will not face liability for negligent failure to uncover fraud. Professionals are accordingly willing to stick with the corporation, and creditors receive the signal that the corporation can pay its obligations. Upon insolvency, however, with managerial fraud not imputed to the corporation, liability concerns may induce professionals to head for the door. When professionals exit, the resulting signal to creditors is that the time has come to pull the plug on the corporation by filing an involuntary bankruptcy petition. Insofar as the professionals' liability exposure is tied to fraud, the departure of professionals could also signal the need to petition for appointment of a trustee. This signalling device could help side-step managerial reluctance to file a voluntary petition.[56]

[55] As such, the *Schacht* rule provides a form of "gatekeeper" liability. See Reinier H. Kraakman, *Gatekeepers: The Anatomy of a Third-Party Enforcement Strategy,* 2 J L Econ & Org 53 (1986) ("gatekeeper" liability induces private parties to withhold cooperation from wrongdoers). See also George H. Brown, *Financial Institution Lawyers as Quasi-Public Enforcers,* 7 Georgetown J Leg Ethics 637, 692-98 (1994) (applying gatekeeper theory to financial institution lawyers); Howell E. Jackson, *Reflections on Kaye, Scholer: Enlisting Lawyers to Improve the Regulation of Financial Institutions,* 66 So Cal L Rev 1019, 1049-72 (1993) (same).

[56] The FDIC may be especially in need of this signalling device. The 1980s saw a series of banks delay receivership (thereby exacerbating their insolvency) through the purchase of political pressure from amenable Congressmen. See, for example, *Lincoln Sav. & Loan Ass'n v Wall,* 743 F Supp 901 (DDC 1990). Given the susceptibility of the FDIC to political manipulation, especially blatant signals may be necessary to induce the FDIC to perform its liquidation duties. See generally Jonathan

Thus creditors prefer a rule barring imputation for insolvent corporations. Holding accountants and lawyers liable for damages when they have negligently failed to uncover fraud by a corporation's officers will mean that insolvent corporations will undertake fewer risky transactions at the expense of creditors. Moreover, the signalling function that results from professionals exiting when the corporation becomes insolvent will help creditors wind up the corporation's affairs while there are still assets to go round. To be sure, professional monitoring has its limits: under the negligence standard, professionals cannot be held liable if they could not have reasonably uncovered the officers' fraud or the corporation's insolvency. Still, professionals will engage in some monitoring, allowing creditors to charge a lower risk premium when contracting with the corporation. This lower cost of credit in turn makes the corporation more profitable, and increases shareholders' dividends.

These reasons explain non-imputation post-insolvency, but they do not explain why *Cenco* imputes managerial fraud to the solvent corporation. Creditors *always* dislike corporate risktaking, and they would prefer a rule that always induced professionals to monitor for fraud. The formal legal reason that creditors cannot insist upon such monitoring (i.e., they cannot sue fiduciaries for malpractice) is that they are not in privity with the professionals, and without privity, there can be no reliance. Only the corporation is in privity with its outside professionals, and while the corporation is solvent, creditors cannot bring actions on the corporation's behalf. The corporation, through its managers, sets the terms of the professionals' engagement and the professional's duties run to the corporation.

Beyond these legal formalisms lies a more functional rationale. Creditors cannot expect risk to be totally eliminated from the corporation's business, because that would undercut the very purpose of the corporation. Limited liability allows corporate shareholders to take on manageable levels of risk, and thereby profit from that

R. Macey and Geoffrey P. Miller, *Kaye, Scholer, FIRREA, and the Desirability of Early Closure: A View of the Kaye, Scholer Case from the Perspective of Bank Regulatory Policy,* 66 So Cal L Rev 1115, 1132-39 (1993) (discussing the need for early closure of insolvent financial institutions and the FDIC's unwillingness to timely close banks in light of political pressure). Moreover, the business of banking is especially susceptible to insider abuse and suboptimal monitoring. See, for example, *Bates v Dresser,* 251 US 524 (1920) (bookkeeper stole from bank over period of six years). See generally Peter P. Swire, *Bank Insolvency Law Now That It Matters Again,* 42 Duke L J 469 (1992) (banks especially vulnerable to insider abuse); Rose-Ackerman, *Risk Taking* at 307 (cited in note 49) ("The federal insurance agencies, especially FSLIC, apparently accepted risky lending activity by profitable banks that would have been unacceptable to most private creditors. The roots of the savings and loan crisis were laid in the investment choices of solvent banks.").

risktaking, without facing financial ruin should the firm collapse. Thus, in order to allow shareholders to assume risk while the corporation is solvent, creditors are relegated to their contractual remedies. During this time, creditors cannot sue managers, directors, or outside professionals for failure to perform their duties.

This risk-enabling rationale of the corporate form also lies behind the business judgment rule.[57] Shareholders precommit themselves through the business judgment rule to allow managers to take on certain risks on behalf of the corporation. Shareholders presumably want managers to be able to recruit the outside professionals necessary to complete such risky ventures, and the imputation-of-fraud rule makes that possible.

Even when considered in light of the business judgment rule, however, the imputation rule remains something of a puzzle. Risk is desirable, but surely shareholders do not want managers committing *fraud* on the corporation's behalf. Fraud seems to fall on the wrong side of an obvious dividing line between reasonable and unreasonable risks. Shareholders are unlikely to benefit, on average, from fraud committed by managers on the corporation's behalf. The fraud is likely to be uncovered eventually, with serious negative consequences for the corporation's bottom line, and consequently, its share price.

Why, then, does *Cenco* require imputation when the corporation is solvent? Judge Posner suggests a non-imputation rule would undercut shareholder deterrence. But shareholders are not realistically in any position to monitor their managers' conduct toward third parties, and shareholders might well be willing to pay higher fees to accountants and lawyers who help ferret out fraud by the corporation. If those professionals faced liability when they failed to exercise due care in ferreting out fraud, they would be much more likely to serve as fraud monitors. Judge Posner's reasoning that shareholders should not benefit from wrongdoing by their managers simply begs the question. On the model of corporation as contract, if shareholders want outside professionals to serve as "fraud-cops" on their behalf and are willing to pay higher rates for that service, the law should permit it absent negative externalities.[58] And here the externalities from such contracts would be unambiguously positive: fewer frauds on innocent third parties.

Can the *Cenco* rule be justified? The answer to this question draws on the law of fraud as much as the law of corporations. Although judicial rhetoric portrays fraud as a narrow, bright-line doc-

[57] See the text accompanying notes 26-30.

[58] I am indebted to Charles Goetz here.

trine with high standards of proof, allegations of fraud have become much easier to plead and prove than they once were. The federalization of fraud through the securities laws, and the advent of state unfair practices acts, have loosened fraud's boundaries. Most significantly, the category of actionable fraud has expanded from affirmative misstatements to include omissions of material fact.[59] Once fraud incorporates omissions, the line between fraud and non-fraud become murky. Risky decisions, proved wrong ex post, are easily transformed into allegations of fraud by enterprising plaintiffs' attorneys.[60] Inevitably, some fact was not disclosed, and lawyers can always construct a story explaining why that omitted fact would be material to the average investor.[61] In today's litigious society, the merely risky always verges on the actionably fraudulent, at least ex post.[62] If accountants and lawyers think themselves likely to be held accountable for negligent failure to uncover such omissions, they will shy away from providing their services to the most risky enterprises, even when those corporations are clearly solvent.

If the boundaries of fraud have become murkier, then fraud can easily be confused with the merely risky. Under such a regime, shareholders prefer the *Cenco* imputation rule, despite that rule's seeming tendency to excuse professionals who turn a blind eye to "fraud." Putting professionals on the hook for negligently failing to uncover such instances of "fraud" would make it very difficult for speculative—but nonetheless wholly legitimate—enterprises to find the legal and accounting services needed to effect wealth-maximiz-

[59] Compare *Laidlaw v Organ,* 15 US 178 (1817) (Chief Justice Marshall, on circuit) (buyer of tobacco had no duty to disclose that War of 1812 had ended) with *Chiarella v United States,* 445 US 222 (1980) (buyer has duty to disclose non-public information where there is a fiduciary duty to seller) and with *Basic, Inc. v Levinson,* 485 US 224 (1988) (adopting materiality standard of *TSC Industries, Inc. v Northway, Inc.,* 426 US 438 (1976), for fraudulent non-disclosure under Rule 10b-5, and removing traditional reliance requirement of fraud). See also Paul G. Mahoney, *Precaution Costs and the Law of Fraud in Impersonal Markets,* 78 Va L Rev 623 (1992) (fraud on the market theory leads to substantial overdeterrence).

[60] See, for example, *In re Apple Computer Sec. Lit.,* 886 F2d 1109, 1115 (9th Cir 1989) (triable issues of securities fraud raised by unwarranted "optimistic statements" concerning future business prospects).

[61] Neither stock price manipulation nor material omissions are necessary conditions for successful litigation under Rule 10b-5. Rather, significant and unexpected price surprises are the best predictors of private civil litigation under Rule 10b-5. See Steen, *Fraud-On-The-Market* at 23-36 (cited in note 12).

[62] See J. Carter Beese, Jr., *Now It's SEC vs. the Lawyers,* Wall St J A16 (Oct 28, 1994) (discussing SEC proposal to provide safe harbor for forward-looking statements: "Never bashful about exploiting new opportunities, plaintiffs' attorneys have used class-action lawsuits as a means of making companies guarantors of any and all forward-looking statements.").

ing transactions. This would have a serious chilling effect for high-risk ventures. But high-risk ventures are, on average, high-profit ventures, and at least some investors value such risky opportunities, if they can limit their liability to the extent of their investment. Enlisting professionals to ferret out "fraud" in solvent corporations would likely price such risky opportunities out of the market, thus discouraging investment in enterprises that prove most lucrative to investors in the long run. On this theory, shareholders (unlike creditors) prefer the *Cenco* imputation rule because (like the business judgment rule) it precommits shareholders against ex post second-guessing of unlucky deals, in order to make high-risk deals available more generally ex ante.

How to resolve this conflict? The analysis of the corporate form presented in Part II suggests that the tension between the shareholders' and creditors' preferences is appropriately resolved by matching the duties of professionals with the beneficial ownership of the corporation. Shareholders, who own the corporation while it is solvent, seek to take on risk; creditors, who own the corporation while insolvent, seek to avoid risk. The *Cenco/Schacht* rule allows shareholders to take on risks while the corporation remains solvent, but limits the ability of shareholders and managers to exploit creditors by excessive risktaking post-insolvency. Thus, the rule reduces the cost of credit to the corporation without unduly limiting the discretion of the corporation's management and shareholders. Properly applied, the imputation-of-fraud rule can satisfy both constituencies, ameliorating the tension between their tolerances for risk.[63]

V. CONCLUSION

This article analyzes the imputation-of-fraud rule as one element of the broader question of how the corporate form controls—and encourages—risktaking by managers. Fraud is simply another, albeit higher-stakes, form of risktaking by the corporation. Stripped of the moral connotations that "fraud" carries with it, the typical misrepresentation action (under the loose standards of contemporary fraud jurisprudence) may be little more than second guessing by plaintiffs' lawyers of a risky business decision that failed to pan out. But ex ante, shareholders are willing to take on such risks. That is why they chose equity investments.

[63] See Posner, *Rights of Creditors* at 509 (cited in note 31) ("An efficient corporation law is not one that maximizes creditor protection on the one hand or corporate freedom on the other, but one that mediates between these goals in a fashion that minimizes the cost of raising money for investment.").

But risk has its costs. Creditors seek to minimize the corporation's riskiness, and they must be compensated for unavoidable risk. The bargain that creditors strike with shareholders (acting through the corporate intermediary) places few limits on that riskiness while the corporation remains solvent, but when the corporation approaches insolvency, the parties have struck a different balance. Whereas creditors must tolerate shareholders' taste for risk during solvency, shareholders must tolerate creditors' risk aversion upon insolvency. Creditors do not enjoy the upside potential, so they must minimize the downside. Enlisting fiduciary professionals on their behalf as "fraud monitors" when the corporation becomes insolvent minimizes that downside. Shareholders benefit as well, because creditors who face less risk will charge less for the use of their funds.[64]

In sum, the appropriate application of the imputation-of-fraud rule turns on which class of claimants hold beneficial ownership at the time of the fraudulent transaction. When the corporation is solvent, shareholders hold that claim, and their preference for risk mandates an imputation rule. When the corporation is insolvent, creditors hold that claim, and their risk aversion mandates a rule of non-imputation.

[64] See Triantis, *Effects of Insolvency* at 686 (cited in note 39) (firm can reduce costs of financing if it can credibly commit against excessive risktaking); Saul Levmore, *Monitors and Freeriders in Commercial and Corporate Settings*, 92 Yale L J 49, 51 (1982) ("Inasmuch as creditors fear broken promises that in effect lower the interest rate ex post, it is in the debtor's interest to lessen these fears by offering a package of promises that creditors can easily monitor and therefore trust.") (footnotes omitted).